D1369834

SEARCHING FOR THE SPIRIT OF ENTERPRISE

SEARCHING FOR THE SPIRIT OF ENTERPRISE

Dismantling the
Twentieth-Century Corporation—
Lessons from Asian, European, and
American Entrepreneurs

Larry C. Farrell

A DUTTON BOOK

To Julie and Heather and Ben
"a lot has happened since you went crazy"

DUTTON
Published by the Penguin Group
Penguin Books USA Inc., 375 Hudson Street,
New York, New York 10014, U.S.A.
Penguin Books Ltd, 27 Wrights Lane,
London W8 5TZ, England
Penguin Books Australia Ltd, Ringwood,
Victoria, Australia
Penguin Books Canada Ltd, 10 Alcorn Avenue,
Toronto, Ontario, Canada M4V 3B2
Penguin Books (N.Z.) Ltd, 182–190 Wairau Road,
Auckland 10, New Zealand

Penguin Books Ltd, Registered Offices:
Harmondsworth, Middlesex, England

First published by Dutton, an imprint of New American Library,
a division of Penguin Books USA Inc.
Distributed in Canada by McClelland & Stewart Inc.

First Printing, February, 1993
10 9 8 7 6 5 4 3 2 1

REGISTERED TRADEMARK—MARCA REGISTRADA

LIBRARY OF CONGRESS CATALOGING-IN-PUBLICATION DATA
Farrell, Larry C.
Searching for the spirit of enterprise : dismantling the
twentieth-century corporation : lessons from Asian, European,
and American entrepreneurs / Larry C. Farrell.
p.   cm.
ISBN 0-525-93573-8
1. Industrial management—Cross-cultural studies.
2. Entrepreneurship—Cross-cultural studies.   I. Title.
HD31.F27   1993
338'.04—dc20   92-25773
                                                       CIP

Printed in the United States of America
Set in Janson and Renault
Designed by Julian Hamer

CONTENTS

ACKNOWLEDGMENTS

My first debt is to the entrepreneurs around the world whose stories fill these pages. I am especially grateful to those who took the time to share their wisdom in long interviews for this book. Entrepreneurs make great teachers because they're obsessed with common sense—a rare trait in a world full of crazy ideas. From Osaka to Edinburgh to the Shenandoah Valley, these are ordinary people, using ordinary means to accomplish some very extraordinary things. Big business needs to relearn their entrepreneurial spirit of enterprise. Yet, in a larger sense, we are all indebted to them for they are truly the engines of our own prosperity.

Of course, chasing entrepreneurs all over the world for ten years doesn't necessarily mean you get to (or can) write a book about it. In fact it had never even occurred to me until Bob Diforio, then the CEO of NAL/Dutton, suggested I give it a try back in 1987. Bob has since moved on to his own entrepreneurial venture, but he never gave up on the project and I am deeply grateful to him for his early inspiration and ongoing support. Arnold Dolin, a

Senior V.P. at Penguin and the Associate Publisher of NAL/ Dutton, has also been essential to the effort from the beginning. Arnold is a very busy man but graciously performed as my editor —both an honor and an advantage for a first-time writer. And I can't forget the drumbeat of enthusiasm showered on me during the writing by my longtime friend and intrepid lecture agent, Joe Cosby.

I'm also indebted to all my former bosses—my role models before my own entrepreneurial plunge. I've never had a boss I didn't like and couldn't learn from. Maybe I've just been lucky, or possibly it's because they've all ended up as entrepreneurs themselves. It started with the colorful salesman from Harvard with the colorful name of Marcel Xavier Rocca. Marcel gave me my first real job as low man on his totem pole in sunny Saudi Arabia. Then in a wild leap of faith he transferred me to Manhattan, called me Marketing V.P., and convinced me that David Rockefeller was just another sales prospect. Next came Alan Baker from the hard working, commonsense state of Maine. Alan taught me that "following your bliss" isn't just good karma—it's good business. He rapidly rose to vice chairman of giant Macmillan Publishing but chucked it all and went back to Maine and bought a small-town newspaper. It's thriving and so is he. And from Ben Tregoe, Merchant Marine, Harvard Ph.D., and creator of the world famous KT method of decision making, I learned much. Ben's great gift to the world is rational thinking, but his greatest gift to me was passionate thinking—about the business. Read his interview in the book and you'll see what I mean.

And finally there is Ben Tregoe's cousin and my spiritual boss for three great years, Tom Peters. When Peter Drucker called *In Search of Excellence* a "book for juveniles," I knew Peters and Waterman were on to something. Promoting and teaching Tom's message of Excellence in twenty-five countries to thousands of managers convinced me that the closer we get to the simple basics of business, the better. I've tried to do what he said—to find the basics of the purest form of enterprise and test them against the broadest global perspective.

INTRODUCTION

> The conduct of successful business merely consists in
> doing things in a very simple way, doing them regularly
> and never neglecting to do them.
> —WILLIAM HESKETH LEVER,
>   founder, Lever Brothers (Unilever)

At the end of the lecture, the frail Chinese man approached me at the front of the long hall. With eyes moist and in very broken English, he managed to tell me I was the first American he had seen since World War II. He wanted to thank me for coming to China to share my "management wisdom." He said I had to know how much they had missed in forty years. I asked what his job was. "Manager of the rolling steel mill outside of Beijing." Then I asked this small, aging communist how many employees he managed. "Sixty-five thousand!" I gulped and wondered if he had any questions about management. He nodded. He had it ready. On a slip of paper he had written the word *entrepreneur*. "I want this. Can you teach me to be this?"

I'll never forget that question. The question I couldn't answer. That simple-sounding question, from such a simple man, from such a "backward" place completely baffled me. My blue-chip consulting clients never asked that. We certainly never studied it at the Harvard Business School. I've spent the last ten years trying to get the answer. This book is the result of that search.

Searching for the Spirit of Enterprise is a worldwide investigation of entrepreneurs and their high-growth companies—a search for common sense. You're about to take an inside look at the real practices of real builders of business from Asia to Europe to North America. Some of these entrepreneurs are giants: legends in their own time. Many are unknowns: the unsung heroes of enterprise. They all offer a damning indictment of modern management theory—not debates about this technique or that, but attacks on the fundamental premises of twentieth-century management thinking.

The message here is straightforward. Old-fashioned entrepreneurship, not modern, professional management, is the driving force of successful, high-growth companies. Indeed, the twentieth-century promise of the giant, rational corporation as the engine of prosperity comes up myth. The facts show that the real growth in all economies comes from younger, smaller, more entrepreneurial companies. Whether it's shareholder return, product innovation, or job creation, the performance differences can be downright shocking. Against all expert prediction, and the best intentions of managers, the world's great experiment in mass-produced enterprise is not working—anywhere! Something has gone terribly wrong. And tinkering at the edges won't fix it. The time has come to *dismantle* the monstrosities we've built. We need to bury these relics of "scientific management" and *start over* with zero-based enterprise.

As this new reality sinks in, we are brought full cycle in our thinking about what really propels growth and prosperity. Few would disagree that a company's prosperity, like a country's prosperity, has always been fundamentally dependent on its spirit of enterprise. This doesn't change with age or size. It doesn't change with technology. It doesn't even change with culture. But what exactly is the spirit of enterprise? It sounds like a good thing, but what is *it* really—and how do we make *it* happen?

Common sense should tell us that if we really want to get at the basics of enterprise, we have to search out the masters. The lessons of enterprise don't come from the world's "best-managed" bureaucracies. They certainly don't come from business schools and consultants. They come from world-class entrepreneurs: Asian giants like Matsushita, Honda, and Morita; or the builders of great European companies like Lever, Benz, and Forte; and legendary American enterprisers such as Disney, Watson, Perot, and Walton. They also come from a million, not-so-famous entrepreneurs—the silent majority who keep every economy afloat. Regardless of culture or public profile, these are all people who create opportunity and wealth out of thin air. Their mission in life is not to manage, or consult, or teach case studies. They make things and sell them. They create jobs. They build businesses. It's *their* business practices that are the true engines of prosperity. When you think about it, why would you look anywhere else?

Ironically, we've looked everywhere *except* to entrepreneurs for lessons in enterprise. Huge, past-their-prime bureaucracies have always been a favorite place to look. Ever-changing lists of "the biggest and the best" are pored over for nonexistent clues. Remember the forty-three "Excellent" companies? Do you also remember that only two years after *In Search of Excellence* was published, fourteen of these "best-run companies" had fallen on hard times? Even though the authors clearly warned that this might happen, too few listened—focusing more on the individual companies than the underlying message.*

---

* Peters and Waterman don't need me to defend their powerful, tradition-breaking work. But for the record, I believe the underlying message of *In Search of Excellence* was right on the money. It broke a fifty-year march in management thinking that was leading most of us over the cliff. I know something about this as my company had the job of introducing Tom Peters's "excellence" seminars in some twenty countries. My criticism is more a warning against relying on the surface antics of any big company that happens to be on some list for a few years. As Waterman himself warns, "If you're big, you've got the seeds of your own destruction in there." *Oops! Who's Excellent Now? Business Week*, 5 November 1984, 77.

Another favorite source: the likes of Harvard, Stanford, and the London Business School. The academics eagerly oblige by test-firing theory after theory. These theoretical bombs, sort of the management version of a Scud missile attack, rarely hit the target but always leave a hell of a mess. And God only knows where and how the consultants come up with prizes like "learning curve theory" and the "7-S" organizational model. However they do it, you can bet they're hard at it right now, dreaming up answers to questions you haven't even asked.

The bottom line on all this looking in the wrong places is not good. We've been left with an ever-growing stockpile of management fads, revolving people theories, and financial black magic—all of which has virtually nothing to do with growing a business. And while the experts fiddle, Rome keeps right on burning. What has really happened is that the original entrepreneurial basics of most companies have simply been overwhelmed—buried under an avalanche of theories that don't work and a bureaucracy that won't budge.

All the while, millions of real entrepreneurs go on creating growth and prosperity. For anyone who cares to look, there are surely fundamentals to enterprise—simple, basic things, practiced obsessively. It is these bedrock principles of entrepreneurship that have been lost in the management maze of the twentieth century. The goal of *Searching for the Spirit of Enterprise* is to distill these fundamentals and present them as management practice—as the absolute basics of successful enterprise.

When I started jotting down notes and going out of my way to meet entrepreneurs, the last thing in my mind was writing a book. I had just started my own company with offices in Asia, Europe, and the United States. Things were really hectic, and I was often struck by how differently I was spending my time as an entrepreneur than I had as a president or vice president at earlier jobs. I was beginning to feel the extreme differences between enterprising and managing.

Increasingly, I found myself questioning the conventional management wisdom I had learned and practiced before. My priorities seemed totally changed. The more I questioned, the more I became convinced that entrepreneurial behavior and standard, big-company management practice are different to the core. And I noticed something else. All the entrepreneurs I met, whether Asian, European, or American, were fundamentally focused on the same things. There may be different styles in corporate boardrooms, but down at the boiler-room level of enterprise, everyone eats from the same trough.

All this began to really interest me. I collected all manner of economic data on small companies—and compared them to *Fortune* 100–type giants. The astounding differences in performance (growth, return, cost of innovation, overhead ratios, etc.) made me determine to learn as much as I could about entrepreneurial practices—and why they always seem to get lost in the shuffle as the company grows large.

The absence of ready-made sources was of course a blessing in disguise. It forced me to go out and find them. For over a decade I was on the road 250-plus days a year, covering some thirty countries. I logged about a million miles and a thousand hotels. I got caught in a couple of revolutions (Iran and the Philippines), a real hotel bombing, numerous typhoons, and places you don't want to be at night—like Beirut and Belfast. Of course it wasn't all bad. There was Finland in January, Saudi Arabia in August, and lying flat on my back, two miles below ground, watching jackhammers attack the face of the deepest gold mine in Africa. And during this time I listened to, observed, and worked with hundreds of company founders around the world. It's a rare privilege to learn from living legends like Lord Charles Forte in London, or Dr. Edward Penhoet in San Francisco, or Po Chung in Hong Kong. And for old-fashioned inspiration, nobody beats the likes of Brian Wolfson at Wembley Stadium, Takeshi Okawara in Tokyo, or the redoubtable Buel Messer in the Shenandoah Valley. Occasionally, even first-hand accounts by the employees of a departed enterprise can stir the emotions. Such was the session at Panasonic, where the room was filled with the power of the philosopher-businessman Konosuke Matsushita. There are, of course, some examples and data for which I had to rely on company archives or published information. In these cases, I tried to use the most authoritative sources available. And to better define certain practices of entrepreneurs, I've included numerous real-life counterexamples. These are never intended to discredit, only to sharpen the image of entrepreneurial behavior. The effort has been to demystify entrepreneurs and what they do for a living. The ideas put forth in the book are their ideas. The business practices are their practices. These are the masters. If you want to learn the fundamentals of enterprise, you need look no further.

Perhaps the best evidence are the thousands of managers around the world who have attended my lectures and seminars on entrepreneurship during the past years. Their embrace of the enterprise message has convinced me that the premise is right—and the time is right. Indeed it's hard to find any managers or workers anywhere who still believe that the buttoned-down, giant corporation is the end-all and be-all in the pursuit of prosperity. I hope my book shows that learning the strategy of doing simple, basic things and never neglecting to do them may be the most important business lesson of all. I think this is the answer. The answer I didn't have for my friend in Beijing.

January 1992

CHAPTER ONE

BIG TROUBLE AT BIG BUSINESS

Big business is drowning in theories that simply don't work. Look at the track record. Of the hundred largest U.S. companies in 1900, only sixteen are still in business. More help like this from Harvard and McKinsey, and we'll all be working out of a garage.

A joke? Hardly. The last thing big business needs is more management "know-how." The junk heap of management science is overflowing with failed theories and techniques. But hope springs eternal in the hearts of the consultants, business schools, and corporate bureaucrats who dream up such theories. You can be sure the worldwide army of "management experts" is hard at work today creating more new ways to help you manage.

Here's the rub, really. Famous business schools and expensive management consultants make easy targets—but it's big companies that buy their product. The reality is, all of us bought in, lock, stock, and barrel, to the uniquely twentieth-century notion that enterprise can be and should be mass-produced. We could bottle it, label it, and seal it tight with a cork. And if the enterprise got bigger, we'd simply get a bigger bottle.

It's this belief that has driven big business for the past hundred years. Professional managers were created to streamline what entrepreneurs started. Consultants were created to help them. We had enough success along the way to keep at it and to keep improving the methods and stay one step ahead of the growing bureaucracy.

Larger and larger companies were offered up as answers to the world's ills, from economic prosperity to world peace and understanding. Never mind that most of the promises never came true. Any shortcoming could be overcome with the next round of management and organization theory. If there was failure, it was a failure of methods, not the underlying assumption that anything, anywhere, and any size could be "managed."

Simply put, the facts are at great variance with this fundamental assumption. America invented (and exported) the science of management to cope with size and success. In spite of all the promises and the often heroic efforts of managers, getting bigger looks more and more like a competitive disadvantage. Big companies are in big trouble and need to learn some different lessons, fast. What kind of trouble? The kind that knocked off 84 percent of America's biggest companies this century.

The combined growth, less inflation, of the world's giant companies is limping along at a paltry 1 or 2 percent. Hardly a performance to justify million-dollar salaries and corporate jets. The larger the company, the worse it gets. Scrutiny of the top hundred companies on the first *Fortune* 500 list in 1955 shows that a whopping seventy-one of the top hundred have dropped off—a 71 percent drop-out rate over just thirty-seven years. A few have merged or been acquired (most of these were in decline) while the bulk have simply disappeared. That's a depressing legacy for the shareholders, workers, and suppliers of once powerful economic giants.

And over time, it's getting worse, not better. The most depressing performance era of the fabled *Fortune* 500 is now. Bear in mind, through the decade of the 1980s, the total U.S. economy achieved the longest consecutive expansion in history and created nearly 20 million new jobs, an all-time high. Viewed against this backdrop, *Fortune* magazine's own report on the 1980s makes chilling reading: "As decades go, this one was no day at the beach. While the economy's expansion set a new peacetime record, companies on the 500 strained harder than ever just to hold their ground. Measured in constant dollars, total sales were up only 7.1% higher in 1989 than in 1979. Real profits ended up 3.6% *lower*. All in all, not much to show for ten years of back-breaking effort. . . . By decade's end, restructuring had pared 3.7 million workers from the payroll. The 21% decline in 500 employment since 1980 was considerably steeper than the drop in total U.S. manufacturing jobs."

Dig a bit deeper and you'll see that these lumbering bureaucracies have been gaining downward velocity for several decades. Their average annual sales and profit growth by decade has been

1960s	1970s	1980s
9.2 percent	5.5 percent	0.7 percent
7.5 percent	5.1 percent	(0.4 percent)

The 500s' incredible decline in jobs to 12.5 million has led them to their lowest number of workers in twenty-five years. This could be touted as a heroic productivity gain, but that sounds a little like claiming the *Titanic* was a marvelous drill in life-raft etiquette. There are no kudos for making productivity gains while driving the company to the poorhouse.

Lest we delude ourselves that this is just another example of America's industrial decline while the rest of the world's big companies are humming along, feast your eyes on these sorry figures. So far, in the 1990s, the annual growth figures for the five hundred largest companies in the *world* are about 5 percent for sales with a 20 percent decline in profits. That's 5-percent sales growth *before* inflation. Recalculate it in constant dollars and what have you got? Nothing—no growth at all! Even Japan's supposedly unstoppable machine of giant companies posted an anemic (pre-inflation) 1.7-percent total sales increase. Of course numbers can mislead, and no one has decades-old growth statistics on the world's biggest companies as a group. But no matter how you fudge it, the decade of the nineties isn't shaping up as a bed of roses for big business anywhere.

Such sluggish financial performance shouldn't surprise anyone. There are lots of big, intractable troubles at big business. In the mid 1980s, Arthur Young & Company reported the results of a major study on innovation in big companies. The sad conclusion: the cost of innovation is twenty-four times greater at large companies than at small companies. One can only marvel at how such finite conclusions are reached, but even if the report was only half right, the big company disadvantage is enormous. If you're the CEO of IBM or Sony or ICI, this could keep you awake nights. It costs your company twenty-four (or maybe only twelve) times what it costs your smaller, fast-moving competitor to bring new technologies and products to market.

This is no idle threat. With 2 million growth-driven, entrepreneurial companies pouring into the fray each year, nobody's safe. Business as usual, never a good idea, has become a recipe for sudden death. Innovation and the action-taking that underpins it are prime examples of where economies of scale don't work. It's a reasonable bet that the lack of innovative action, fostered by complacency, is the number one cause of the high death rate of large, bureaucratic companies.

Another trouble that clearly increases with size is diminished employee satisfaction. The Hay Group, which is supposed to know about these things, throws very cold water on the notion that all the programmed hoopla of big company life beats the chaos of working for entrepreneurs. Hay teamed up with *Inc.* magazine (which covers small business) to compare employee satisfaction in the *Inc.* 500 versus the *Fortune* 500. This unusual peek at the Davids and Goliaths of business produced some real surprises.

The bottom line of the report: "What we found everywhere

were employees who were more satisfied with their jobs, and had more respect for their companies, than the employees of Corporate America. If I were a *Fortune* 500 CEO, I'd be worried. The positive attitudes of their employees give small companies a great competitive advantage." Not too surprising? Keep reading. "In terms of pay and benefits, they lag well behind the employees of large publicly held corporations. To get similar results, large companies have to pay cash—higher wages and benefits—and that makes their cost structures just that much less competitive." There you have it— conventional wisdom stood on its ear. At small companies employees are happier—and they're paid less!

The report highlights those company attributes that produce the greatest contrasts in employee satisfaction: being concerned with quality, listening to customers' ideas, focusing on long-term profits, and yes, recognizing good job performance. These are very basic business practices, and the small companies scored significantly higher on all of them.

Is there a serious lesson here for big business? Could it be, as the president of a jet engine manufacturer quipped, "Great! Does this mean if I cut everyone's salary they'll be happier?" Not likely. It may point out, however, the futility of trying to buy employee commitment and pride. It may even mean the obvious—human beings just don't like working in groups of two hundred thousand as much as they like working in groups of twenty.

Measured by employee satisfaction, economy of scale just doesn't work. And that same old belief that we can manage anything and everything, even human commitment, keeps bloated personnel departments looking for answers that don't exist. The "how to manage people" industry, riddled with psychologists and assorted gurus who never met a payroll, isn't even asking the right questions. A Japanese manager said it best: "Lifetime employment only works if the company lives longer than the workers. The most important personnel policy is to make sure that happens."

From a national perspective, the most important "personnel policy" for governments may be to wake up and look at where growth in jobs really comes from. Betting on big business (or big labor for that matter) to spur jobs and prosperity is a dead end. The bulk of new employment in every economy in the industrial world is coming from young, smaller companies. The United States, still the world's most prodigious creator of jobs, leads the pack in this category. Over the past decade, America's largest companies actually lost jobs in absolute numbers—not exactly a big contribution to national prosperity. Meanwhile, the total American economy created close to 20 million new jobs. This breathtaking achievement all came from small and medium-sized firms.

Obviously, something has gone *very* wrong. The twentieth-century myth of the giant, rational corporation as the engine of prosperity has been shattered. Controlled by professional managers and drowning in bureaucracy, big business as we know it—from Tokyo to New York to Frankfurt—is beginning to look like a relic of another age.

To hasten its decline, the international political and social climate has never been more favorable to entrepreneurs, the very people who love nothing more than stealing markets from complacent competitors who are too big to notice. It's increasingly clear that big business is no match for the 2 million fast-moving entrepreneurial competitors pouring into the world economy every year. Even for die-hard economy-of-scale fanatics, it's hard to find much good news for big business.

Maybe the only good news in all this: the typical CEO is nobody's fool. More than anyone in the company, he is frustrated with slow growth, a bureaucracy that won't budge, and an endless array of theories that don't work. The best of the CEOs already know that more and more management of a bigger and bigger bureaucracy can't be the solution. They suspect it's the central problem.

The message for the CEO: The time has come to *dismantle* your giant corporation and start over. You can't "manage" the company out of managerial gridlock. If you've inherited (or created!) a deep, dark hole to work in, the first rule is—stop digging! "Growing big by staying small" may not sound rational, but it surely beats growing small by staying big.

The Life Cycle of All Organizations— from Riches to Rags

So how did big business get in this mess? Good question. Here's the historian's answer. Companies, like everything else in our world, live in a cycle. There's creation followed by growth. Growth peaks and decline sets in, leading ultimately to death. And of course there's always the possibility of *untimely death* along the way. Beating this cycle is tough indeed.

All companies begin with an abundance of the entrepreneurial spirit, inspiring workers as well as owners. Basic entrepreneurial practices fuel the start-up and drive the company well into a phase of high growth. During the start-up and high-growth eras, everyone is fixated on a few fundamental notions such as getting customers because it's the only way to get paid.

The resultant high growth gets you size. And the passage of time gets you new leaders, who are almost always professional managers. These subtle shifts in size and leadership produce a new set of objectives. Presto! Planning, streamlining, and controlling the enterprise become the new order. Managing this and that becomes more important than making this and selling that. The highest-paid jobs become managing other managers. Meetings, reports, and bureaucracy erupt on every front.

To handle the emerging bureaucracy, more planning and streamlining are called in. To make sure things are done "right," controls are locked in place. And slowly but surely, lost in the shuffle are the simple, basic entrepreneurial thrusts that got you going in the first place. Too much managing against too little entrepreneuring sets in motion the painful cycle of decline. Heavy-duty consultants are called in to tell you what's wrong. It takes three years to get the consultant's re-organization idea in place. It doesn't help and the decline picks up momentum. You're heading into a survival phase—and, if unchecked, ultimate demise.

Arrogance and Ignorance

It's not every day one sits across the sofa from a living legend. Lord Charles Forte, still going strong at eighty, had just asked me to help him get the "entrepreneurial message" across to his operating board, which manages the eight hundred-plus hotels of Trusthouse Forte—built stone by stone by Charles Forte.

Forte explained that he had tried to keep his global empire, spread across five continents, focused on the basics. He wanted to keep a spirit of entrepreneurship alive. He had turned over the running of the company to his son, Rocco Forte, who I soon discovered to be exceptionally bright and incredibly conscientious toward his father. In his new role of "elder statesman," Lord Forte was on the lookout for ways he could be helpful without interfering. Encouraging the entire management team to maintain and foster the company's "enterprise culture" fit right in. Bureaucracy and other forms of inefficiency seemed to be especially high on his list of things to avoid. He hoped that an outsider could help deliver the message he so strongly believed in.

Only in a couple of offhand remarks did he even hint at the frustration he obviously felt with the evolving nature of the company. In something of a backhanded compliment, he let me know that using me was sort of a last resort. My impression was that his message of enterprise was falling on increasing numbers of deaf ears. He quipped almost to himself that dealing with really important issues (presumably the enterprise culture) was increasingly difficult because the whole company seemed to be in management meetings most of the time.

In any event, and with Rocco's seeming enthusiastic support, the special board session was scheduled for two weeks later. Interestingly, a "pre-meeting meeting" was requested by the heads of planning and personnel. The purpose seemed to be to make sure I understood the recently written "Organization Mission Statement"—and in some detail, the big, new planning system. The clever young planning manager (since departed) was a London Business School MBA and a recent refugee from McKinsey.

At the session Forte was his usual effervescent self, asking lots of questions and raising action points. He seemed pleased. The board members participated and nodded approvingly. After the session, the planning man buttonholed me. I expected him to comment on, even take exception to, some things I had to say. But, no. To my surprise, he only wanted to again describe his planning system. This was obviously a man who loved planning!

A week later I bumped into him and asked what had happened since the board discussion on entrepreneurship. With a touch of irritation and dismay, he answered, "You got the chairman all excited. Now he's poking all around the company—asking questions—looking for entrepreneurs. We're all in damage control until it blows over." This flip response speaks volumes about entrepreneurs and managers, and their respective roles in the life cycle of organizations.

On the one hand we have MBA-style *arrogance*—the writing off of practical experience. Never mind that Forte, the poor Italian immigrant who built a global empire from a single Oxford Street sweetshop, hardly needs a lesson in business from anyone, let alone an MBA planning guru. On the other hand, and much more importantly, we have enterprise *ignorance*. The highly educated planner never got Forte's point. The basics of enterprise may just be too simple to sink in.

Both of these traits—arrogance toward and ignorance of old-fashioned enterprise—are living proof of the alien worlds all com panies cycle through. No one would claim that entrepreneurs need no help as their enterprise grows big and complicated. Some planning, some procedures, some controls are not only helpful, they're necessary. But this isn't the issue.

The issue is much more basic: What business lessons can we depend on to inspire and propel significant growth? This is the central question. The answers require some understanding of what really causes high growth—20, 30, even 100 percent—in the life cycle of organizations. My answer of course is *entrepreneurship*. It is entrepreneurship that builds companies. And there are methods to its madness and fundamentals to be practiced. The managerial phase of the cycle has to be about perfecting these fundamentals —but it isn't. Professional management is focused on and often superb at planning, codifying, systematizing, reporting, controlling, and the like. As useful as these may be, they don't make you grow! When they become what management is really up to, you're headed down the wrong road.

All this raises some very interesting questions. The evidence says all companies could do with a lot less management science and a lot more devotion to the spirit of enterprise. But what is it exactly that gives entrepreneurial companies such competitive advantage and rapid growth? And is it simply law of nature that as a company grows larger it must slow down, become uncompetitive, and ultimately die? Indeed, can large companies do anything to strike a balance between entrepreneurial and managerial approaches to the business?

On our way to the answers, just to make sure, let's take one quick peek at what we're trying to do a lot less of, that "opium of the managers," the seductive world of management science.

From Those Wonderful Folks at Harvard and McKinsey

In everyone's climb up the corporate ladder, there comes that de-fining moment when the last set of heavy oak doors swing open—and you know you've entered the inner sanctum. My moment came in the closing hours of the seventies. I had just been named president of the company. The chairman, the chief financial officer, and I were scheduled for a closed-door session with Towers, Perrin, Fos-ter and Crosby (TPF&C), the bluest of the blue-chip consultants. TPF&C is the worldwide authority on management compensation, and no subject gets management's attention like management com-pensation. The purpose of the annual get-together: to set our pay packages for the following year.

The TPF&C consultant addressed us from the head of the boardroom table. Smooth as silk, he laid out the scenario. As his charts and graphs demonstrated, executive compensation was rising across the board, even faster than TPF&C had forecast. Next year it was certain to go still higher. The range for our industry and our jobs would therefore be "X." To remain competitive, we'd have to go with substantial raises. Stock options were becoming standard practice, and we'd also have to take a serious look at this. We all nodded. The articulate consultant sat down and that was that. In the ensuing shuffling of papers, it slowly dawned on me that we had just awarded ourselves fat increases for the year. Of course the details would have to be approved by the board's compensation committee, but that was just a formality. TPF&C had shown us what we had to do to keep up with everyone else—to remain competitive, as they called it. This truly was the inner sanctum. The three highest-paid people in the company, egged on by the consultant, got to set their own salaries. No wonder most of the *Fortune* 1000 use TPF&C. What a great system!

So great, in fact, it has propelled executive pay in America into the stratosphere. In his born-again confessional *In Search of Excess*, Graef Crystal, TPF&C's former top guru, describes exactly how CEO pay in America has leapt from 34 times the average worker's pay to the current obscene ratio of 150 (the ratio in Japan and Germany, by the way, is only 15 to 20). Admits Crystal: "I helped create the phenomenon we see today: huge and surging pay for good performance, and huge and surging pay for bad performance too. . . . I acted in full realization that if I didn't please a client, I wouldn't have that client for long." So there you have it: An ever-spiraling system where CEOs pay good money to hear what they want to hear, where the consultant's job is to sanctify the spiral and keep everyone on top. It's worth noting that Crystal has only come clean now that he has retired from TPF&C into the relative security of the University of California, Berkeley. While Graef Crystal is no hero in all this, his kiss-and-tell account of the consultant as highly paid co-conspirator in the surreal world of executive pay brings us to the broader issue.

That issue is the rapidly growing sideshow of "experts" who influence professional managers and live very handsomely off the carcass of big business. From consulting firms to investment bankers to business schools, just about everyone has their hand in the corporate till. How and why big business has spawned such an industry of helpers is a puzzle. No one really knows how much these experts suck out of big business each year, but it's in the tens of billions. One consulting house alone, the venerable McKinsey & Company, is approaching a billion dollars in annual billings. This pervasive industry of corporate helpers has its roots in America's fascination with the profession of management. But the lure of high-priced help is apparently so powerful that big business around the world is now lining up to get helped. This is nothing short of amazing given the utter lack of evidence that all these helping hands have ever helped their American clients actually make better products and sell to more customers.

The variety of expensive helpers over the years is wide. At one extreme, we have the crusaders of office automation with their sophisticated gadgets and systems. Big companies have been loaded up with electronic tools for decades—from underused computers to conversation-stopping recorded messages in place of real customer service. There is mounting suspicion today over whether any of this stuff has ever produced office efficiency, let alone business growth. Take the simplest and most pervasive of such tools, the photocopier. Copiers have destroyed the carbon paper business, but what have they really done for office efficiency? Before 1946 (the invention of the copier), interoffice memos were usually typed with one carbon copy for the file. Today, memos with copies to twenty managers are common—sort of a shotgun "FYI" method of communicating. Say five or ten of those managers feel the need to reply—and they recopy the original twenty. One insignificant message can create a blizzard, blowing around the office for weeks. Why do we do this? Because we need all this paper to run the business? No, because everyone has a photocopier. One of those electronic gadgets the "OA" experts sold us to improve office efficiency!

The list goes on. The 1950s saw the rise of the planning gurus, who converted a simple three-step process called MBO into five-pound planning books that take months to fill out. By the 1960s, any company worth its salt had to have several behavioral psychologists advising the personnel department. These essentially antibusiness do-gooders brought sensitivity training and group therapy to corporations—and in the process brought many good companies to their knees. The cast of corporate helpers just goes on and on, right up through the eighties when Wall Street wizards dominated the scene and junk bonds became the currency of go-go companies everywhere.

This has always been a sideshow dedicated to the quick fix and working the periphery. Getting back to basics is a concept that seems to be both below the dignity and above the competence of most of these performers. Of all the acts in this long-running circus of business advisors, none have had more impact than business schools and general management consultants. The Harvards and McKinseys of the world deserve special attention, if for no other reason than their staying power—a remarkable feat given the fact that they've produced so little of value for enterprise.

Business Schools

At thirty-eight, I entered Harvard's "school for presidents," their expensive and much ballyhooed Advanced Management Program. Over a period of two years, my classmates and I observed one of the great ironies of American education. Business schools are overflowing with condescension and disdain for real business and real businesspeople. Their heros are not great enterprisers, but great professors. Producing great products is not nearly as important as producing great theories. And since management education is essentially an American export, the same holier-than-thou attitude exists in the faculties of most overseas schools. Certainly studying the grungy, dirty business of entrepreneurship, the backbone of every economy, has been virtually nonexistent at prestigious schools. The top professors much prefer finance, big-company strategy, and organization theory. Of course there's very little outside consulting work at the corner grocery store.

It's very difficult to show that studying business at any university has any value whatsoever. America's obsession with business schools and MBAs defies logic. Japan and Germany have been beating the socks off U.S. companies for the past twenty years without business schools or MBAs. On the other hand, it's easy to spot major flaws in this uniquely American idea. The most obvious is the original, dubious concept that training general managers is what business really needs. Steve Jobs said it best in his waning days at Apple. All the experts had him convinced he needed professional managers. His frustrated comment: ". . . we hired a bunch of professional managers—sure, they knew how to manage—but they couldn't *do* anything."

A more specific flaw has to do with curriculum. Simply stated there's too much attention on how to "count" the money versus how to "make" the money. Finance has become the dominant subject at almost every business school. Wickam Skinner has been for many years the guru of production strategy at the Harvard Business School. He must also be a very lonely man. Few MBAs today have much interest in learning how to make things or getting their fingernails dirty in a factory. Skinner is a brilliant teacher and something of an anomaly at Harvard. He actually had a real job, as head of manufacturing at Honeywell, before he joined the faculty. But the lectures on finance are overflowing, while Skinner's classes on making products are sparsely attended.

Finally, and most seriously, business schools have taken on a life of their own, dreaming up and propagating all manner of exotic theories and untested fads. This is downright dangerous. Most professors exhibit utter disregard for "doing things in a very simple way, doing them regularly and never neglecting to do them." These words of William Lever, Great Britain's nineteenth-century master of enterprise, need to be taken to heart by twentieth-century management theorists. If we must have business schools, let's at least learn the basics from the masters. Understanding the simple practices of William Lever and Walt Disney and Konosuke Matsushita has got to be at least as valuable as mastering the latest hot theory from Harvard and Stanford and the London Business School.

At the end of the day, we still have to answer the central question. Does America (or anyone else) really need 650 business schools producing seventy-five thousand MBAs a year—more each year than were graduated in the entire decade of the sixties? What is the point when two-thirds of these young MBAs become bankers and consultants? What's happening to the spirit of enterprise while we're producing legions of bright, young general managers who know how to manage but can't do anything? We're left to wonder.

Management Consultants

Consultants think like professors, but they wear three-piece suits and make a lot more money. They're experts at packaged solutions, and once inside the door, they're off on a billable witch-hunt to find some problems—problems you usually don't even know you have! Make no mistake about it, consulting is a great job. It's a giant ego trip and the pay is outrageous. This is why it's the career of choice for MBAs everywhere. Most consultants work incredibly hard and they love what they do. That is, they love to advise companies. The trouble comes with what they're able to advise about. None of them has much, if any, real experience in real jobs. Fewer still have the foggiest idea of what it takes to create a Honda or a Wal-Mart and build it from scratch. Mostly young MBAs, armed with all manner of charts and theories; it's fair to say they contribute little to growth and the spirit of enterprise in their clients.

In a now classic article published several years ago, *Business Week* traced the history of business fads and the consultants behind them. The conclusion: "Consultants have always had a role in launching fads . . . but they have been working overtime since the 1970s. The result is a mad, almost aimless scramble for instant solutions. The search has fueled an industry of instant management gurus, new-idea consultants, and an endless stream of books promising the latest quick fix."*

Nothing has changed. From Frederick Taylor's time and motion studies to the corporate psychiatrist's sensitivity training to today's corporate ethics gurus, the search for magic solutions to basic busi-

* "Business Fads: What's in—and out," *Business Week*, 20 January 1986.

ness problems marches on. Anyone who crawled around on his hands and knees in the dark in a sixties T-Group session has earned the right to be skeptical of all consultants. As one American executive lamented: "If we got as excited about our products and customers as we do about the latest nonsense from our consultants, we might actually be able to grow this business."

Out of this bubbling pot come two troubling questions. The first has to do with the consultants themselves, and the second is directed at the companies that hire them. First, where do the consultants come from and where do they get their ideas? Take strategy consulting, for example. The rage of the consulting business used to be the Boston Consulting Group. The technique they used was actually inspired by the straightforward planning process used at General Electric Company. Not content with GE's plodding emphasis on cost and market share, BCG gave it a fancy name— learning curve theory—and a memorable matrix with stars, cash cows, and dogs. It was a master stroke of form over substance. In its heyday, business was so good at BCG they were desperate to hire as many bright-eyed MBAs as they could get their hands on. They (and others) employed the infamous "negative offer" at Harvard and other leading business schools to secure their share of young stars and starlets. When they saw someone they liked, they made an immediate offer, say forty-five thousand dollars, and the offer dropped a thousand a day until the student accepted. Well, the heyday is over. Today BCG is in shambles. The strategy matrix they sold has been widely discredited. Clients all along the way became disenchanted with the BCG approach for good reason—it rarely delivered the growth the clients wanted. Now here's the catch. The typical strategy assignment at a big company ran several million dollars. And if the consultants could get into every division, the tab could run as high as $20 million. Question: How can it be that a simple idea, converted into a catchy matrix, ends up costing $20 million a pop when delivered by a band of young, overpaid MBAs? It boggles the mind—but that's the old consulting racket.

This leads to the second question: Doesn't it also boggle the mind that CEOs making $2 million a year and division managers scraping by on $1 million need to hire anyone to tell them how to do their job? Especially when it comes to fundamentals like organization structure and strategy—the two biggest "products" of blue-chip management consultants. If the high-priced management can't do these basics, what are we paying them for? Can it possibly be true that one senior consultant and his team of billable footsoldiers know more about your business than the top management team? If the answer is yes, what does that tell you? The moral of the story: For 2 million bucks, the shareholders deserve to get someone who knows at least as much about the business as a band of twenty-seven-year-old MBAs with graphs.

It's hard to say what the 1990s will offer up to help you manage better. But if you're looking for old-fashioned growth, you'll probably have to turn to your own common sense. Strategy matrixes, another reorganization, and more management courses won't get you a penny of growth. To get growth you've got to have: *high purpose, absolute focus on customer and product, a lot of action, and self-inspired people*—the four fundamental practices of the world's great entrepreneurs. If you're really searching for the spirit of enterprise, this is where you start!

CHAPTER TWO

SENSE OF MISSION

Creating High Purpose
and High Standards

The beliefs that mold great organizations frequently grow out of the character, the experiences, and the convictions of a single person. More than most companies, IBM is the reflection of one individual—my father, T. J. Watson.

—THOMAS J. WATSON, JR.,
past chairman, IBM

In the beginning, all organizations reflect the beliefs, philosophy, and sense of mission of their founders. In practical terms, founders believe they are doing something important. They see genuine value in their work—value for their customers, their employees, and certainly themselves. They are convinced that their products produce needed benefits. And without exception, they know the only way to stay alive is to produce products and services that someone, somewhere will pay for. None of this is surprising.

What can be surprising is the high degree to which their start-up employees also share this sense of mission. In the young, entrepreneurial company, spirit or mission comes with the territory. It's a gift of enormous competitive value. Keeping it alive beyond the founder and the original team is the trick. Most companies don't even try. It's the complete absence of any sense of mission that so often characterizes large, corporate bureaucracies. The CEO doesn't have it, and certainly the rank-and-file workers don't have it.

Who could disagree that trying to re-create purpose, challenge, and inspiration is a worthy pursuit? But doesn't this have a certain fuzzy ring to it? Does it mean we need a company fight song, or a dozen consultants, or a thousand wall plaques with our latest "mission statement"? You're in good company with these questions. Much of what is preached today on corporate mission or philosophy sounds more like "getting religion" than running a business.

Indeed, most organization theorists are strangely silent on the most obvious element of any company's mission—picking the right products and markets, an old-fashioned version of business strategy and still the sine qua non of avoiding the trash heap. And they hopelessly confuse the real purpose of Mr. Watson's beliefs—namely, to insure that the organization culture is connected to that business strategy.

Creating an enterprising sense of mission is not about pop motivation theories or sophisticated planning systems. Sense of mission *is* about picking the right customer/product strategy—and creating a culture that inspires expert performance and extraordinary commitment to that strategy. Setting strategy and creating culture is the work of CEOs and division presidents. It has never been and will never be the work of planning departments and organization behavior gurus. If you want to see it in action, it's best to look through the eyes of people with their backs to the wall—a common position of entrepreneurs.

Buel Messer

It's 1980. A snowy Friday in the Shenandoah Valley of Virginia. The kind of day fathers knock off work early to be home with the family. Buel Messer was already home with the family. Knocking

off early was not an option. He didn't have work. There weren't
a lot of career possibilities for a convicted felon, a cattle rustler.
Bored and frustrated, he grabbed his two young sons and a shovel.
"Let's go shovel some snow." He needed the boys to be his "eyes."
Buel Messer is also blind.

Hardly the stuff of a great story of enterprise? Think again.
It's just a little more earthy than anything you'll find in the *Harvard
Business Review*. From shoveling snow and mowing lawns, always
with his boys, Messer has created a multi-million-dollar landscaping
empire. Today, Messer Landscape has thriving retail operations, a
booming wholesale business moving thousands of plantings, and
$250,000 commercial projects are taken in stride. Not bad for a
business that grossed $5,400 ten years ago.

Buel Messer's story has a lot of lessons. The one we're interested
in here is all about building a business—in this case to feed your
family and regain your name—without resources, without theories,
with absolutely nothing but a driving sense of mission.

Messer was born dirt poor in the impoverished hills of eastern
Kentucky. He was also born with optic atrophy, leaving him with
a sliver of sight, about 5 percent, in one eye. He struggled through
grammar school and was finally admitted to a state-supported high
school for the blind in Ohio. School didn't interest him a whole
lot, but athletics did.

On a sports scholarship, he went on to college. To see if he
could do it, he made the dean's list his first and last semesters in
college. In between he was an intercollegiate wrestling champion
and set the state record for the mile in Ohio. In a moment of glory,
he ran in Madison Square Garden on national TV, against the
world record holder, Jim Ryan. Ryan blew the field off with one
of the first "under four minute" miles on an indoor track. Still, not
a bad day's work for a poor, blind kid from Kentucky.

Because of his boundless energy and courage in overcoming his
own disability, Messer was a natural as a role model for handicapped
students. He threw himself into his first job at the School for the
Visually Handicapped in Wisconsin. There he became interested

in helping the multiply handicapped and started graduate study at night. In Wisconsin, he met and married his wife of twenty-five years, also a sightless person. From there, Messer transferred to the Virginia School for the Deaf and Blind. He completed his master's degree at the University of Virginia and enrolled in the doctoral program.

Being an academic, in the challenging but specialized world of teaching the handicapped, wasn't the only thing Messer thought he could do. Along the way he dabbled in other things that he knew, like farming. He started a small cattle and hog operation. For several years he taught by day and worked the farm at night. Being a farmer entrepreneur became more and more his passion. He expanded the business. In the early days, financing was relatively easy to come by. His reputation was excellent. He expanded again, and again. But he was getting in deeper and deeper financially. With the first hint of trouble the lenders cut off his credit. Everything was at risk. He didn't know where to turn—until one black night when he signed on with a group of desperadoes to make a few "easy" bucks. In one fell swoop, one act of desperate dishonesty, Buel Messer's hard-earned accomplishments and his family's modest but honorable way of life came crashing down.

Despite the novelty (how *does* a blind man rustle cattle? "Not very well, that's why I got caught"), judges and peers weren't amused. In rural Virginia, stealing livestock is as much a sin as a crime. Not only do first offenders do hard time in prison, they can do hard time forever back in their community. This was the outlook on that snowy Friday in 1980. The family was wiped out financially. Messer was persona non grata in the academic world. And decent jobs didn't go to ex-cons. An eventual full pardon by the governor restored his voting rights, but not his dignity.

Never one to feel sorry for himself or blame others, Messer says of that period: "I didn't hold it against anybody. I was the one who created it, and I recognized that. I think the fact that I had, through my own bad judgment, committed the criminal acts way back there early forced me to do things honestly. To be forthright and honest at what I do: It's a challenge and a driving force for me. . . ."

Let's take Buel Messer at his word. The overarching mission of his life became the redemption of his honor. He had few options but to reach for it through his own enterprise. How has he done it? What are the business beliefs arising from the *character, experiences*, and *convictions* of Buel Messer? What exactly is his sense of mission?

To understand Messer's approach to business, you have to relearn plain, blunt English. You'll find no "corporate-ese" here. *Backward integration* becomes "we had to have our own trees to sell," and *market segmentation* gets translated as "little old lady types versus fussy lawyer and doctor types." Once you get the language down, you begin to understand that Messer speaks with a passion and focus rare in business. He knows his markets, he knows his products, and he knows exactly what it takes to beat his competitors. This is the "no-frills" version of *mission*. This is *strategy* and *culture*, entrepreneurial style.

Starting with the snow shovel back in 1980, Buel's description of the start-up is pure passion: "I had to completely liquidate . . . while I was in prison, which was real depressing and demoralizing. . . . It really was rock bottom for me. I'm thinking all the time that there's got to be some way back to something. . . . So my two young sons, who were about nine and eleven years at that point, and I went around neighborhoods shoveling snow for people. That gave me an idea. Snow shoveling was lucrative, and it was a public-service-oriented type thing. So that week I stuck an ad in the paper, hoping to get something for the two kids and I that we could do together while I'm being house daddy. We ran an ad: 'Wanted, in the Northend, Lawns to Mow for the Season.' This was in the first week of March now. So we get about twenty-five or thirty responses to an ad that ran two or three weeks. And so we selected about fifteen lawns in our neighborhood that we could ride a small riding lawn mower to and pull a small cart behind since I didn't drive and the boys weren't old enough. So that's the way

Messer Landscape began. And that was ten years ago this past season.

"I thought it'd be just a little something to really keep the boys occupied and out of trouble. I got tired of cooking and cleaning house pretty quickly. I didn't know there were so many related things to doing those lawns that summer. And I had more time now to think about things, to really let some creative imagination take place.

"At any rate, we did some sidelines. A lot of them were retired people or little old ladies. Those were the types we thought would be best, rather than doctors and lawyers and people who had lots of money. We felt they'd be too fussy, and we didn't know what we were doing anyway. We thought that little old ladies would put up with what we had. I should really say, I thought that because the boys didn't have any input at that point. It was hard enough keeping them working at it. And they were my eyesight, of course, even early on then, since I didn't see well enough to do what we were doing. So there was the thing of 'Would you prune my shrubbery?' And I said sure, we'll try it. We'd never pruned a bush of our own before but got to doing it and got to reading articles and things about how to do it. It just seemed pretty natural, after that. That first year we had a gross income of fifty-four hundred dollars.

"I guess the next kind of major step was a realtor/builder–type person that I knew had two spec houses that he'd built. . . . He wanted to know if we'd be interested in taking some rakes and trying to rake that rough ground out and put in some grass for him. That was our second year. We'd expanded to the point where we had this one part-time guy with his own truck. Think he might have had his own wheelbarrow. Anyway, that's how we got back and forth to the job to do those houses. We did rake those out and put in seven or eight shrubs in front of them, mulched them, and miraculously the grass grew and everything did well. So right away, we're landscapers! My mind starts going kind of wild at that point."

Enterprise doesn't get any more basic. And what's behind it?

Doing something worthwhile. Pursuing an honorable mission. This is what enables people to do the impossible. Value-driven missions are personal. They don't come out of the mouths of consultants. Yours must be yours. Buel Messer's meant overcoming incredible odds to redeem his dignity: "It gave me an opportunity to prove that I was not altogether dishonest. Probably I've bent over backward trying to prove my honesty all along the line. I was trying to prove that despite this terrible reputation that I had developed, I still could be a success and a viable entity in the business world and this community. Which I feel like I have."

Strategy and Culture
as Common Sense

Messer's description of his company's strategy and culture is unadulterated common sense. It has none of the management consultant's conceptual elegance. It's not "big picture" stuff. It's a bunch of snapshots about where he's headed and how he's going to get there.

Messer's strategy comes straight from the marketplace. Where he's headed with customers and products underscores his knowledge of and respect for the market. He turns almost reverential when talking about it: ". . . it's not me . . . it's the need in the marketplace! I've been able to see areas where there's a strong need, or will be in the future, that I can capitalize on." His sense of gratitude toward customers borders on the Japanese: "I just feel really fortunate that we were able to convince the public that we would give them their money's worth and if something went wrong we'd make it right."

The culture is a direct reflection of Buel Messer's eternally optimistic view of human potential. He sees employees as great contributors to a great cause: "I love taking people that have not maybe had a good opportunity or something of that sort and motivating them, seeing them grow. And through their growth, the business is going to grow. I've always had the theory that you don't necessarily need all the highly trained personnel that some people might see a need for. I feel like I'm a good teacher. I thrive on being able to develop people to help them to be better than they were. . . . You've got to make people feel strong about themselves and be motivated. I would say being able to manage people might be the secret to everything."

Messer Landscape's spirit of enterprise hasn't come from sophisticated strategic planning—which they don't do. Nor has it come from intellectualizing their culture—which they don't do. Their sense of mission and astonishing growth have truly come from "the character, the experiences, and the convictions of a single person." And like Mr. Watson at IBM, Messer's mission has been sewn into the daily fabric of the business. Will it last? Probably as long as Buel Messer is around. Will it stick after he's gone? It could, but nobody knows. But if you want to see it in action, Messer Landscape is a living example of a business built and operated on a powerful sense of mission.

There's a lot of Buel Messer in all of us. The trick is to let it out, at least some of it, on the factory floor, throughout the sales force, and even in the corporate offices. Is this really so difficult? Why can't General Motors, with all its million-dollar executives, figure out how to instill in its workers a little sense of mission, a little bit of the spirit that seems to come so naturally to a blind landscaper in Virginia?

Walt Disney, a pretty fair entrepreneur himself, gave us some of the answer in his simple reply to why he worked so long and hard to create perfect cartoons: "By doing that, I please and satisfy myself." Satisfying ourselves through doing *that* might be the key. But what exactly is *that*? How do we convert *that* into a self-satisfying mission? What does sense of mission really mean, in the practical world of everyday business?

What Are We Doing?
How Are We Doing It?

In pursuit of their mission, builders of companies devote enormous energy to *what* they are doing—let's call it corporate strategy—and to *how* they go about it, which we'll call corporate culture. Knowing the *what* and *how* would seem to be the fundamental requirements of any successful mission. It doesn't get any more basic than this.

Of course, organizations can be good or bad at what they're doing and how they're doing it. It's even possible to be good at one and not so good at the other. Having a great culture won't, by itself, prevent a stupid strategy. Or, even if a company is a lousy place to work, its strategic choices on products and markets can be smart. And, of course, the corporate graveyard is full of companies that were bad at both. The goal is to be smart at what you do and great at how you do it! This is what you're after. A winning sense of mission. Your MBA won't help here. The primary ingredients are sweat and adrenaline. This is entrepreneurial turf, where everyone eats, breathes, and sleeps what and how they're doing!

Corporate Strategy,
the Old-fashioned Way

Old-fashioned strategy takes old-fashioned focus on the *what* of the enterprise. And to entrepreneurs, the *what* of the enterprise can only mean: *what customers* and *what products* will I pursue? After all, customers and products are not functions of the business, they *are* the business. Being wrong on these questions is certain bankruptcy. In this environment, corporate strategy is all about being right on specific products and markets. And being close to customers and products is not an occasional activity designed to wave the flag or impress workers. Rather, it's the most valuable weapon the strategist has in making the most critical decisions in business.

A Humble Man with a Hundred Yen

Talk about focusing on customers and products! The no-frills strategy of a young salesman in Osaka would be hard to beat. In 1918, Konosuke Matsushita invested his life savings of one hundred yen (about fifty dollars) in imported electric sockets. His mission: resell them all. He didn't do so well. In fact so many people didn't want his sockets, he went bankrupt. By his own account, he was unsuccessful because he was thinking too much about selling and not enough about what customers really wanted. He was disillusioned but determined to learn from his troubles.

He went back to all the people who wouldn't buy and, for the first time, asked them how the sockets could be improved. He took their suggestions, tinkered with his sockets, and made a few of his own from scratch. He went back to the market and tried again—and again, and again. He spent years designing, selling, redesigning, and reselling electric sockets. It was this process of back-and-forth customer/product strategizing that produced Konosuke Matsushita's marvelous invention: the world's first two-way electric socket. With it he began winning customers. But the process continued. Every new customer was a new opportunity to learn what to improve and find new applications.

His simple invention at least doubled the possibilities. Every two-way socket could connect to two appliances. From electric fans to radios to cookers, his mission became the building of a business around the new, mysterious technology of electricity. His strategic process never changed: a constant search for the right customers and the right products. It opened a new world of product and market possibilities. And as we know today, this strategy gave birth to the world's largest producer of electric and electronic products.

For Matsushita, strategy and purpose weren't things to be hammered out in a morning, or even a year. In 1932, some fourteen years after start-up, Konosuke Matsushita started thinking about and putting on paper the principles of enterprise as he had lived them. It took him five years to get them all down, and the result was a twenty-three-page booklet titled *Matsushita Management Philosophy*. This very thin booklet contains as much wisdom about enterprise as some entire business school libraries. It provides a strategic framework for the company, which not surprisingly boils down to customers and products. Product and market criteria are clearly laid out. These criteria read like a synopsis of the strategy of Japan Inc: "Broadest possible consumer markets, highest possible product quality, lowest possible product cost, etc."

Ever since, the *what* of the business at Matsushita has been dominated by knowing *what* customers want *what* products. Picking products and markets gets a lot easier when you know a lot more about customers and products than anyone else. This has been the driving competitive advantage of Matsushita Electric for seventy-five years. Konosuke Matsushita raised customer/product strategy from black magic to near certainty, and it all comes from those unsold electric sockets back in 1918.

This was hard-nosed enterprise from Japan's greatest entrepreneur. And unlike most big companies, Matsushita does not re-create its strategic framework every year. Konosuke Matsushita's original principles are still very much alive today. Of course he only died in 1989, and his son was chairman until 1991. The test of time and new management is just starting. At least up to now, however, Matsushita Electric, led by its Panasonic products worldwide, is Japan's most successful company of the twentieth century. It is currently number two in profits, behind giant automaker Toyota, three times bigger than archrival Sony, and number one in the world in electrical appliances. This is in no small part due to Mr. Matsushita's masterstroke of laying out his old-fashioned but apparently timeless approach to setting corporate strategy.

Setting Strategy and the Spirit of Enterprise

Right down to his tennis shoes, everything about Larry Hillblom says, "I'm in a hurry." Hillblom, the guiding spirit and the "H" of DHL,* had a special approach to strategy. He opened a new market every time he found someone crazy enough to do what he was doing: spending his life on airplanes and at each stop racing to get the bag of documents delivered. Apparently he found a lot of crazy people, in every corner of the globe. He found them in taxis, on street corners, and in bars. How could Hillblom get away with this madness? Simple. His customer and product strategy was crystal clear. He had to connect his product to every market in the world. The trick was to get it done in a hurry. He didn't have time to plan the moves. He was too busy making the moves. Not very scientific, but it got DHL into its first one hundred countries in less than a decade. They're up to 190 today, and UPS and Federal Express are still trying to catch up.

Here's the point. Larry Hillblom devised and executed one of the most ambitious and successful company strategies you'll ever come across. But asking entrepreneurs like Hillblom to describe their strategic process usually gets you a blank stare. Even when they answer, it can sound downright vague.

The fact is, entrepreneurs don't do a lot of strategy *setting* period. Choosing products and markets is not an intellectual exercise

---

* The other original founders, Dalsey and Lynn, dropped out early on, but the DHL name stuck. Hillblom remains as the spiritual leader with his designated CEO, Pat Lupo, running the worldwide business.

that happens every October. It's not filling out reams of planning forms. It's certainly not taking a week in Hawaii going through some consultant's long-range planning process. Choosing products and markets goes on all the time. If it's a process, it's a *doing* process as much as a *setting* process. Setting strategy happens when ideas and opportunities happen. And most of the great market ideas don't come in October, and no great product has ever been invented at a meeting in Hawaii.

However inelegant the "process," the enterpriser's focus is still on markets and products. Matsushita created his breakthrough product by asking potential users, face to face, what they really wanted. Karl Benz only produced new models after he had made significant improvements on the old model—sometimes in six months, sometimes two years. George Cadbury, devout Quaker and great chocolate entrepreneur, was passionate about the needs of his market and the purity of his product. He produced drinking chocolate as an alternative to the demon ale, for Britain's working class. His insistence on using pure, unadulterated cocoa, made "eating chocolate" available to the masses and revolutionized the British chocolate business. Watson's IBM used to say that the ideas for 95 percent of their successful products came from customers, not from the IBM research and planning departments. And Soichiro Honda created an empire by connecting very simple needs to very simple products in the chaos of postwar Japan. On and on it goes, reading less and less like strategic planning a la the Harvard Business School.

Of course all this flies in the face of conventional management wisdom. While entrepreneurs focus on customers and products or they go out of business, big company strategy is often focused on creating financial projections to please the board and excite Wall Street. The notion seems to be that some customers and some products will magically appear to make the projections come true. Apparently, the entrepreneur does his strategic thinking in reverse! Big companies just seem to like strategic planning. Tom Peters called it, "Ready, aim, aim, aim, aim, aim." Where the aiming is more important than the firing. When *setting* the strategy becomes a bigger deal than *doing* the strategy. And where is the focus when senior management, the people who absolutely, positively must be focused, get swept up in a thousand shifting priorities and start delegating strategic planning to the planners? The focus becomes whatever the planners are focused on. Of course, if you own a high-priced strategic planning department, it makes perfect sense to expect them to do something. Unfortunately, the more they do, the less you do, and you're well on your way to delegating the future of the enterprise.

Whether it's Matsushita, Cadbury Chocolates, or even Messer Landscape, the lesson is clear. Whatever your approach to corporate strategy—formal or informal, six months out or ten years, discounted cash flows or numbers on a napkin—the part you have to get right is *what customers* and *what products*.

The Entrepreneur as Strategist

Picture the last blue-chip, strategic-planning session you attended. See if this rings a bell. You're in an exclusive resort or the even more exclusive corporate boardroom. All-powerful executives sit as judge and jury, while scores of underlings parade to the front making the projections everyone wants to hear. Projections become facts as they're burned into the corporate memory by the most perfect pie charts known to man. The usual assortment of pinstriped consultants come and go, pitching their own matrixed vision of your future. And of course there are the reams of research and planning books, piled high on the table, that nobody ever reads. Somehow out of this surreal, big business ritual comes one big black book called *Strategic Plan*, and everyone goes back to work for another twelve months. If it doesn't ring a bell, be thankful. Because this is no way to pick products and markets.

For better or worse, the entrepreneurial approach to setting strategy is really a pretty down-to-earth business. It's still that old-fashioned business of picking the right products and markets. Here's how entrepreneurs approach it.

▪ It's a Matter of Survival

The goal is survival, not an affirmative nod from the board. If we fail, we don't get to try it again next year. We're history!

▪ Don't Make It a Big, Complicated Project

Doing the plan is not the objective. Growing the business is. Strategic planning is not a week at a resort or a career option or an excuse for consultants to get rich. So keep it simple and do it fast.

▪ Stay Focused on Customers

The best partners in business are customers. They know more and cost less than market researchers and consultants. Design your strategy *with* them, not *at* them.

▪ Stay Focused on Products

Of course it's true that entrepreneurs "love their product." But what keeps them in business is making sure their customers love their product. The best product consultants turn out to be users and competitors.

▪ Know the Criteria That Count

Choosing products and markets is the name of the game. The information entrepreneurs want most is intimate knowledge about *market need* and every possible way they can raise their *competitive position*. These are the two criteria that always count most!

So now you've got the picture! Your vision of markets and products is clear. The only thing standing between you and them is knowing *how* to get there. This is where corporate culture is supposed to get plugged into the business.

Corporate Culture, the Old-fashioned Way

The *how* dimension can be loosely translated as corporate culture: "How are we going to go about our business?" In society and in business, cultures are defined by the values or beliefs of the people. Entrepreneurs, by definition, set the values of their companies and reinforce them through their daily behavior. Their actions determine what's important to do and not to do. How employees should behave, how quality is treated, and the level of respect given customers are all determined by the personal example of the founder. The entrepreneurial culture is based on two no-nonsense criteria: What behavior will give us competitive advantage and what behavior am I personally committed to—without compromise? The answers to these questions reveal the values that set the culture of the enterprise. To the entrepreneur, the culture must directly and powerfully support the customer/product strategy. To be guided by values that are unconnected to the business strategy simply wouldn't occur to an entrepreneur. It certainly never occurred to Konosuke Matsushita.

A Humble Man—Again

In his *Matsushita Management Philosophy*, the great teacher left no stone unturned. Not only did Matsushita frame the company's strategy, he also described the culture he believed necessary to get there. The *how* of the business got plugged into the *what*. Under what he calls "The Seven Objectives," the guiding values of the culture are laid out for all employees to learn. And just so no one will forget them, they are repeated in unison (or discussed in groups, whatever the local culture dictates) every morning by 195,000 Matsushita employees in 130 countries. After seventy-five years, the company seems pleased with the results. Says Masaharu Matsushita, the founder's son and recently retired chairman, "The original statement of purpose now provides a high ideal for each employee. It will remain a living symbol as long as Matsushita exists."

I got my first glimpse, in an unlikely place, of just how serious Matsushita is today about keeping alive this "living symbol." One Panasonic Way, in the re-claimed marshlands of Secaucus, New Jersey, is the U.S. headquarters of Panasonic, Matsushita's major international trading division. The top management team, including the president, all Japanese save one, was gathered for a very specific reason—in their words, to do an even better job in the future on the "inculcation and implementation of Matsushita's Basic Business Principles in MECA" (Matsushita Electric Company of America). My job was to tell them everything I knew about corporate culture, American style. In what initially appeared to be cultural overkill, a company "expert" on "The Seven Objectives," from Osaka, was in attendance. Hiroshi Asano, I later learned, was part of an elite corps who spend their life helping divisions understand the company philosophy. Extraordinarily Japanese perhaps, but also an extraordinary company commitment to maintaining their original sense of mission.

About thirty seconds into the meeting, it became clear that we were discussing bedrock issues of the business, not the usual touchy-feely stuff that always seems to hang up culture implementation. Asano connected "The Seven Objectives" one after another to bottom-line success. Improving quality to exceed customer expectations was discussed more as moral truth than good business practice. Inculcating every employee with the noble cause of efficiency produced heated side conversations in Japanese. The group discussed every point of the "The Seven Objectives" in relation to customers, products, capabilities, and financial growth. They asked me how they could do a better job of communicating and instilling the objectives into the minds and hearts of the American employees. While I talked they all furiously took notes. Then there were a thousand questions, and a lot more discussion in Japanese. At the end of the day I was exhausted. They were still fully charged. I left determined to learn more about Konosuke Matsushita.

By the time of his death in 1989, Matsushita had become a revered philosopher in Japan. His later writings are read not for their business wisdom but as a twentieth-century philosophy of life—an unusually lofty position for an entrepreneur in any society. As you might expect, *Matsushita Management Philosophy* makes for an unusual read. It's sort of a blend of Mahatma Gandhi and Sam Walton. Only after the second or third read-through does the subtlety of the message begin to hit you. "The Seven Objectives," indeed the entire philosophy, are based on the notion that industrialists take resources from the earth and are honor-bound to do something useful with them before they are returned. Particularly they must work with these resources for the betterment of society. This is the high calling of Matsushita Electric.

The paragraph on profit sets the tone: "Yet the ultimate purpose of a business enterprise should be not to gain profit but to contribute to and to promote the welfare of the public. This is equally true for all professions. The worth and lasting significance of each depends on how well it serves the public. If Matsushita Electric renders such service it is rewarded in the form of a profit, which should be in direct proportion to the contribution. This is Matsushita's interpretation of profit."

Having established the broad purpose of the enterprise, Matsushita proceeds to tell his people how to behave in doing this. "The Seven Objectives" really boil down to four—since three of them are devoted to the treatment of employees. First, the obligation to community and nation is put forward, with a re-emphasis on profit: ". . . remembering that our purpose is not solely to gain wealth and industrial strength." Next, fairness to employees, harmony among employees, and the company's responsibility in the "struggle for betterment" of employees are described. These three objectives are capped off with the flat-out declaration "The accomplishment of this challenge will lead to happiness, peace, and prosperity in society." Then we come to a real Matsushita strength: "We shall be flexible in an ever-changing world, thereby assuring continued progress." This objective, labeled "Adjustment & Assimilation," fuels Matsushita's legendary ability to innovate on the run. And finally, the culture is brought full circle with the company's and employees' obligation to give thanks. This one sort of keeps things in perspective. Simply called "Gratitude," it seems to say that a bit of humility in industry will carry people a long way: "We shall be ever grateful to our nation, our community and our associates (customer, suppliers, each other) for their kindness. This feeling of gratitude will give us peace, joy and unlimited strength to overcome all difficulties." There you have core values, Matsushita style.

Early on, Matsushita was worried about maintaining the mission. He was convinced that size and good fortune could be the culprit: "There is a danger in an expanding company that its workers, through overconfidence, will lose their original devotion and skill, and will forget their duty to the community. Enthusiasm will be replaced by indifference. But no matter how large or successful our business, we should never lose sight of our essential debt to the community. We should at all times apply ourselves diligently to the work at hand."

Is this all philosophic overkill? Some of the "we're different" Japanese thing? More mumbo jumbo from the public relations department? Well, judge for yourself. The least we can say is that Matsushita is still trying not to forget the values that drove its original spirit of enterprise. Something the bureaucracy in Armonk, IBM's world headquarters, seems intent on doing.

Creating Culture and the Spirit of Enterprise

Before Armonk, there was another IBM. Let's go back for a moment to the company that Thomas J. Watson, Sr., founded in 1914—to the original IBM culture that was driven by Watson's now famous set of beliefs: customer service, respect for people, and striving for perfection. The same culture that pushed his people to create the most profitable company in the history of the world. Were these just motherhood slogans? On a piece of paper they may look that way. But back in the real world of Watson's IBM they were anything but. The part that rarely gets quoted is the other half of Mr. Watson's message: ". . . we will not settle for anything less than a superior effort in everything we do." A superior effort in customer service. A superior effort in managing people. A superior effort in doing the job right, every day. As every employee knew, these were rules that absolutely couldn't be broken, and Watson enforced them with a passion.

This *was* a corporate culture designed to inspire employees and to beat the competition. IBM was the one large company where every employee knew what the values were and what they meant on the job and that violating them was the one sure way to get fired. Not until 1963 did anyone even bother to write them down. So much for banners and wall plaques. They were deeply ingrained by Watson's legendary personal commitment and example.

IBM today is a perfect example of the dilemma that faces all great companies. How do you know if you still have it or if the culture that inspired you to great heights has slipped away? After reaching a staggering record profit of $6 billion back in 1990 (no other company has ever come close), IBM has clearly come to a crossroads.

When you're at a crossroads, like IBM, it can be hard to tell if you still have it. But in other situations, it can be painfully easy. One of the biggest and oldest U.S. banks has been searching for inspiration for decades. Let's just affectionately call it "the bank." In the mid-eighties in Hong Kong, I found myself facing fifteen rather unenthusiastic senior bank managers. Going in I knew this bank was one of the least popular places to work in Hong Kong, and had never been a star performer. Anyway, I broached the subject of company mission. I asked about purpose and shared values, using all the descriptions and phrases I could think of. I received blank stares. I asked pointedly if the managers had any sense of mission at all about their work. As eyes were beginning to glaze over, I gave it a last shot and asked if anyone had ever heard of the bank's "Statement of Vision." I had never seen it, but I knew the chairman had at one time spelled out the four or five things he believed the bank stood for. No one had ever heard of it. Thankfully, we took a coffee break, during which several phone calls to various departments turned up nothing. Finally, the young Chinese administrator who had set up the conference room came running up with a copy of the chairman's Vision. It seems this young man filed everything from New York, including memos from the big boss.

Returning to the meeting, we all looked at the Vision and discussed it for a minute or two. But it was futile. The Vision had no meaning for them; it was just a lot of words about "being the best in an uncertain world" and a listing of five "core values." These managers hadn't lived this vision of the bank at all. They didn't believe in it. They didn't know what it meant exactly. No one had ever talked about it. And they couldn't really think of any shared values within the bank. So we moved on to more earthbound issues in their business.

Later, in a closer inspection of the Vision, I noticed it was in fact quite new. And the language was a real tip-off. This was clearly the handiwork of some culture gurus. It read more like a wish list from the Moonies than a statement of the business mission. The core value of "Teamwork" got this line of jargon: "To achieve the highest level of synergy, teamwork will underscore and drive our efforts, and be a core value in our culture." Presto, there you have it, folks! Another great line on the wall plaque.

The story of the Bank is instructive—not for rendering judgments on the managers involved, but for helping top management learn how to create and maintain a sense of mission. Even with the best of intentions, newly-announced and elegantly-crafted Vision statements just don't have the same ring as old Tom Watson's insistence on three simple behaviors. Once again we learn that our behavior is more eloquent than our words. Or as Mr. Watson showed, if you do it for fifty years, you don't have to write it down.

In the culture-creating business, it's always the day-in and day-out behaviors that count. Certainly Charles Forte's sixty-five years of near obsessive attention to the basics in his eight hundred hotels will be remembered long after the big, new planning system bites the dust. And Sam Walton's habit of driving his run-down Chevy pickup to work garnered more enthusiasm and respect from Wal-Mart employees than the astounding fact that a retailer from Bentonville, Arkansas, became the wealthiest man in America. And the four humbling years that a young Akio Morita spent selling his transistor radios store to store in the United States says everything about Sony's intent to understand foreign markets.

The fact that it's the simple things that really count may explain why so many companies are going around in circles, trying to change their culture. Coming up with "core value statements" and all manner of "corporate renewal" programs looks a lot easier than actually changing the behavior of the leadership. Most of these cosmetic versions of corporate culture violate the two cardinal rules of how Forte, Walton, and Morita et al. went about doing it. For starters, they rarely evolve out of the business strategy and seem unrelated to the competitive wars taking place in the real world. And secondly, nobody at the top seems all that committed to the new raindance. *Saying* we're going to stop producing junk or *announcing* we're the most innovative company won't make it happen.

In fact, proclaiming values that the whole world knows aren't true is probably the worst thing to do.

In the midst of such misguided efforts, however, there is reason to cheer. Dramatic changes in an organization's culture can and do occur. The effect on customers, employees, and shareholders can be extraordinary. Take Jaguar Ltd., a classic example of Margaret Thatcher's "enterprise culture" revolution that worked. Britain's once proud producer of high-quality automobiles had fallen on hard times. By 1980, it was interred in the growing British graveyard of nationalized companies. Its customers, employees, and government owners were ashamed and demoralized. In just five years, new CEO John Egan tripled the number of customers, quadrupled the company's market value, raised employment by 40 percent, and got it privatized, where it always belonged. The lasting image of Egan in those years is sleeves rolled up, out on the factory floor, personally making the Jaguar a great product again. The London *Sunday Times* had it right when it reported: "He devoted virtually all his time to improving quality and reliability. . . . When he's faced with a major issue, he almost has tunnel vision, focusing on that alone, virtually to the exclusion of all others." This is how cultural revolutions come about. You just go out and do it, and do it, and do it again. It doesn't have the cachet of floating a new set of "corporate values" down through twenty layers of management—but it has one redeeming value. It changes the culture.

The Entrepreneur as Creator of Culture

Just as with corporate strategy, it's not a good idea to ask entrepreneurs how they create their corporate culture. Most of them don't feel comfortable with such jargon. Some of them just won't know what the hell you're talking about. It's best to watch and listen over a period of time, to see and hear what they really do, day in and day out. They set their corporate culture by living it, period. If you look long and hard enough, you'll see it does depend on a few basic ingredients. The *how* of the business has to provide some competitive advantage and requires the personal commitment of management, and then the workers. These are the only musts on the list. The overarching reason for fostering a particular corporate culture is to support your strategy—to improve your competitive position. And the culture will never take hold without the binding personal commitment of senior management. To find and create the culture that maximizes your competitive prowess, consider the following:

▪ Competitive Advantage

What values, behaviors, or practices in the daily operation of the business will raise your competitive position? Product quality? Innovation? Employee relations? Customer Service? Cost efficiency? Fast action? There are no universal selections. Whatever those few items are for your business, they must be the cornerstones of your culture.

▪ Personal Commitment

Becoming the very best in the world at those few practices most critical to your competitiveness requires the full and active commitment of top management. Ultimately, it will require the personal commitment of at least a critical mass of the entire workforce. For management, there can be no exceptions. The rule has to be severe. Buy in or get out. Even so, managers as well as employees do have to see a connection between what's good for the company and what's good for them. Increasing shareholder return as an isolated value, for instance, is not going to generate raves of commitment on the production line.

▪Behavior, Not Words, at the Top

Your behavior is more eloquent than your words. Believe this if you believe nothing else in this book. The moral for top management: Don't announce the "new culture" until and unless you are the best example.

▪It's Not a Big, New Project

As with setting strategy, the entrepreneurial approach to creating culture does not include setting up a "culture staff," hiring consultants, or packing the executives off to Bermuda to create new wall plaques. This is truly an "on-the-job" task.

▪Few and Simple

How many things can you be best at? Try for three and maybe you can hit one or two. There's another reason to keep it simple. The culture of the company has to be carried around in the minds and hearts of people. It can't be buried in a thousand-page manual.

▪Never Compromise

Unfortunately, compromises are more powerful than principles. One well-placed compromise can reverse years of principled effort. So, never means never.

The Entrepreneur as Maintainer of Culture

Creating an enterprise culture is half the battle. Maintaining it for generations can be even harder. And keeping it going when the going gets really tough is more than most can do. No company I know has withstood more pressure and challenges than the San

Miguel Corporation—the proud Philippine company that has lived a hundred years under the motto "Profit with Honor." With operations extending westward to Spain and east to California, San Miguel is the food and beverage leader of Southeast Asia. It has withstood Spanish rule, American control, and the ravages of a particularly brutal Japanese occupation. It has learned to live with perpetual political instability and communist insurrections. It has survived (barely) the enmity of President Marcos and his cronies, who wrested control away from the founders. And San Miguel has been doomed from the start to operate out of one of the world's truly desperate economies. Yet the company has retained its profit and its honor. Why hasn't it just collapsed? What gives this company such great staying power?

It's not San Miguel's business strategy that saved the day. It's always been their culture. Since the turn of the century, three generations of Sorianos have made San Miguel Corporation much more than the Philippines' greatest company. In a world of unpleasant surprises, they've created a company that is a refuge for employees and their families. In a thousand ways, the company supports its extended family in a country with no other survival net. Small things happen like Christmas presents for employee children, delivered by the founder in a Santa Claus suit—in the blazing heat of Manila! And big things happen such as financing employee businesses, where family members make factory uniforms, with San Miguel the only customer. For a very long time, San Miguel has taken care of its people. And the people have taken care of their company through thick and thin. To this day, to work at San Miguel is considered an honor. It's the IBM, the Honda, and the Daimler-Benz of the Philippines, all wrapped into one. Andres Soriano was reinstated as CEO after the Marcos era. As with his father and grandfather before him, San Miguel's competitive advantage remains its culture—a culture that produces extraordinary commitment and performance from the workers. So now it's back to business as usual—making "profit with honor" and waiting for the next disaster to strike.

Even if you've been hanging on by your fingertips lately, you may not need a *new* culture nearly as much as you need to revive and maintain your *old* culture, your original spirit of enterprise. Old or new, the question remains: How do you keep it alive? Here are three things that will help:

▪ Daily Behavior of Top Management

Senior management is "on stage" every minute of every day. Your most insignificant behavior is of intense interest to employees, customers, suppliers, shareholders, you name it. It seems that these days you can't fool any of the people any of the time. The only way around this is to surprise everyone and actually behave, all the time, as the best example of the company values. It's not a fair world, but it's a price you've got to pay.

▪ Organization Rituals and Practices

Everyone knows the policy book is not what the culture is all about. The culture reveals itself in the mundane rituals and practices that go on every day. How do supervisors actually treat workers on the line? How much service is really given after the sale? Do executives get bonuses even in bad years? Is extra care taken to make the product perfect? What's the reaction to losing a customer: Does everyone shrug their shoulders or do they go all out to regain the business? It's at this level that the culture lives or dies.

▪ Reward and Penalty Systems

How do you get to be president around here? And what does it take to get fired? The culture ultimately depends on what employee behavior gets rewarded and what behavior gets penalized. If you hope to maintain an enterprising culture, entrepreneurial behavior must be rewarded and lackadaisical, bureaucratic behavior must be penalized. This is the blunt reality that so many big companies around the world refuse to face. Some still depend entirely on punishment to control employees. Many, striving to be "progressive," have gone berserk with rewards and positive feedback for everything. And the great majority, raging bureaucracies all, do nothing. No positives, no negatives. Here the message is clear: It really doesn't matter how you behave. To keep a spirited and competitive culture alive, *it really does matter*. From million-dollar CEOs to lowly paid clerks, it matters very much.

A Long, Hard Look in the Mirror

Whatever your situation, whether you're growing 50 percent a year or in a free-fall to disaster, it's important to remember that a "great culture" can't overcome a "stupid strategy." But if you've got a strategy with a fighting chance, then creating a well-connected and inspiring culture will make all the difference in the world. And when the Company mission is on your shoulders, there's no room for a lot of other hands on mission control. It's time to start leading by example. All entrepreneurs feel the mission *themselves*. But the lesson of the truly great ones, the Watsons and Matsushitas of the world, is that they also inspired others to feel it.

Inspiration from a
Radar Station in North Carolina

If inspiring others is one of the marks of great entrepreneurs, Ben Tregoe should be proud. Beyond his own employees, he's inspired somewhere around 5 million managers and workers, spread across three dozen countries: a Guinness-league record unmatched by any other entrepreneur or corporate chieftain around. Kepner-Tregoe, Inc., was founded in 1958 by Charles H. Kepner, a Ph.D. from Michigan, and Benjamin B. Tregoe, a Ph.D. from Harvard. Kepner left midway through KT's odyssey to pursue archeological treasures and generally follow his bliss. Tregoe, always the driving force of the company's growth, is still chairman and chief missionary. With operations in some twenty-five countries, backed up by thirty-five years of growth, KT stands alone in an industry littered with fads and fly-by-night operators. Based on his and Kepner's earlier research, Tregoe built the business on the unusual idea of teaching managers and workers how to think better at work. In sheer numbers, KT's famous problem-solving and decision-making process has been learned by more people than all the business schools in the world will graduate this century! And on a "usefulness" scale, five days of learning how to think has got to be a better bargain than two years of learning MBA theories.

On top of all this, and especially interesting for us, around 1970 Ben Tregoe turned his steel-trap mind to the subject of strategic decision making. And again, he turned his research into a thriving business: the Kepner-Tregoe Strategy Group. But you can be sure that Tregoe has never succumbed to the big fallacy of management consulting. He doesn't tell his clients what they should do. He shows them how to figure it out for themselves. KT is and always has been focused on the *process* of decision making. So Tregoe's comments become doubly relevant to the notion of creating a *sense of mission*. First, he is an entrepreneur in his own right. Second, his business is articulating the commonsense basics of strategy formulation that apply to all companies.

For the millions of businesspeople around the world who have learned the "KT process" but don't know where it really came from, now it can be told! According to the man who was there, it all started in a radar station somewhere in North Carolina in 1958: "Chuck Kepner and I were with the Rand Corporation [the famous think tank] working on various types of research projects there. We got really intrigued with the whole subject of decision making because of the differences that we saw in U.S. Air Force officers' decisions in response to simulated information. One of the things that was going on at that time was the whole notion of computerizing the U.S. air defense system. What portions could be computerized, and also what could we do with noncomputerized radar stations to improve performance? What we were supposed to be doing was tracking, looking at, the performance of the crews, with particular focus on how they went about processing information when they first recognized that there was trouble of some kind or an unusual situation. The objective was to improve the performance of the radar crews—not the officers.

"But particularly in this project we did in a radar station in North Carolina, where we had all of these simulated air threats played through the radar scopes, we saw what decisions the commanding officers were making and we saw some real differences. The commanding officers were all more or less the same age, and they were all West Point or ROTC graduates, but because we controlled the simulation, we could see that some officers' decisions were good and some were really bad. That really got us intrigued with why some people are better at sizing up situations and recognizing problems and making decisions than others. We were interested in following up on that. Rand at that time was totally funded by the air force, and the focus was really on moving toward a rather major change in the air defense system. There wasn't a lot of interest in messing around with the individual officer's decision-making ability. The reaction was sort of: 'These fellows are all West Point graduates, don't worry about them!' That was the thing that really led us to leave: the desire to pursue that and do some research on it.

"We left Rand at the end of May 1958 to set up our own business. I don't think either one of us had any notions that we were going to make this into some big business. We set up an office at the back end of my garage in Pacific Palisades, California. One day we were sitting there and one of us said: 'Do you think this could ever develop into a million-dollar business?' We both thought: 'No way! Now that's just being unrealistic.' I think our motivation was much more that we saw the possible need. We saw some real interesting differences in decision making in this research which nobody seemed to care about. We thought how the same thing must be true in organizations and businesses generally. There must be a way that you can improve the performance of individuals in terms of their problem solving and decision making.

"Well, there wasn't much progress on the commercial side. Nobody cared. It was a case of our seeing a need and our having a concept of how to improve the skill of people in this area. So we felt, now here is an obvious need, but nobody else recognized the need. Nobody gave a damn. If we had done what they say you should do to start the business, go out and do market research, we never would have started the business.

"It was a matter of just going around and seeing a lot of people, and people started to get interested. Then the seminars themselves, our product in those days, sort of got people caught up in it all. The ideas and the way we taught them through simulations were very, very powerful. They would say, 'My God, maybe I *have* got something to learn about this.' So this is how the thing got started. And the ideas by the way were just things that we saw the more successful people doing. We saw certain patterns of ideas and certain sequences of things. It wasn't something we just dreamed up. Maybe this is being too self-serving; however, thirty-five years ago nobody even talked about this subject. I think it was our work over those many years that really brought about a clear recognition of the need to improve the problem-solving and decision-making skills among the work force."

Self-serving or not, 5 million people is still a lot of people! And for all those Japan bashers in Europe and America, take heart. Since 1973 KT has done a mountain of business there. In fact, Japan is KT's second-largest revenue producer, next to the United States.

And what about the strategy business? "I became interested in doing something in strategy when working with the top managements of some of our clients back around the late sixties, early seventies. The decision-making process that we were using wasn't all that helpful in addressing strategic kinds of decisions. As you know, the decision-making model is easier when you can set some objectives or decision criteria relatively easily, usually in an operating situation. But when you are talking about what kind of *products* and *markets* should we be looking at, ten years down the road, it was very hard just to sit down and set out the criteria.

"So it seemed obvious that we needed some other way of helping the company think through what they wanted to be like down the road in terms of *products, markets, resources*, and so on. That was what led us to this research that we did in the early seventies—which led into the strategy decision-making ideas. So this also stems out of seeing a need—in terms of the work that we were doing with clients. It was obvious that the need was there, but the long-range planning that was being done wasn't filling the need that existed. Actually, the same problem re-occurred. The executives would say, 'Well, we do that.' Even when strategy got to be more popular, sort of a fad word, everyone kept doing their long-range planning but said it was strategic planning. It was still basically a projective planning exercise, which is, obviously, not the way to go about setting the company strategy. The way we do strategy was sort of swimming against the tide. It's a heavy involvement of top management. Saying planning isn't strategy, and you've got to have another way of doing it, was very unusual. The companies were resisting that. Now, things have changed—the tide has sort of turned and is much more in line with what we are doing."

I asked Tregoe what advice he'd give someone starting their own business. Any baseline lessons for setting strategy? "Well, let me see how would I answer that. I would have to be somewhat hesitant as to how I answer the question in terms of recognizing a need in the marketplace. I guess the issue is, to what extent is the need recognized in the marketplace, or to what extent does the potential entrepreneur see a need which may emerge that isn't quite recognized? So I would be a little leery about putting all of the emphasis on market research, which may tell you the need's not there. So, I guess one piece of advice would be to persist and have some patience and to develop the need, and not drop the whole thing just because you go around and talk to some people and they say, 'Hell, there's no need for that.' If I hadn't been persistent, we never would have had a business. See, the kind of field that we're in—and it's not different for others—if you are just picking up on the needs that are articulated by the managers in the business, you're always behind the curve. So that would be one point.

"Another, maybe the final one on strategy, would be to really think strategically right from the beginning. By this, I don't mean developing big projections and plans that you can take into the bank. I swear that is what most of the business schools are teaching. You know, you go and develop this long-range plan, you take it into the bank, and you show them this and that. Fine. But much more important than that is to really have a strategy so that—and this is where the notion of 'driving force' is so important—you know where you are going to get your focus. I think this is where so many companies run into trouble. They get their entrepreneurial focus initially from a product or technology and a particular market need. This gives them their focus, but then they get to a certain stage of their growth and they feel, wait, this isn't going to be enough to necessarily carry us and keep us growing. So they start to lose their focus in terms of moving into different markets or moving into different products and services. Then they run into real problems. You see this over and over again. So a company has to think pretty carefully, right from the beginning, about such questions as product and market priorities, and where they are going and what they are going to focus on.

"I think a tremendous factor in our success was that we stayed very, very focused. The natural temptation when you have two guys who start a company is to start doing a lot of different things that people are willing to pay you for. We did that only once. Early on we took a contract to work on a system to prevent the wheels coming off of navy aircraft landing on aircraft carriers. Then we thought, what the hell are we doing this for? All this is doing is diverting us. We would be better off to keep eating peanut butter sandwiches another year and staying focused on what we want to do, rather than screwing around with this kind of thing. We kept that focus as the company developed over the years. We said we can be the best in the world in this thing, but we can't be the best if we start trying to be all things to all people.

"Of course, the trick is at what point do you need to diversify—and how do you diversify and still maintain focus? For example, should you diversify into new markets where there is a need for your products and services? Or should you focus on the market where you've established a strong position and diversify into new products and services to serve a broader range of needs in that market? One thing is clear: Diversifying is where a sense of focus and priority is essential.

"Companies should not worry so much about planning and projections because most of that doesn't mean a damn thing. You may need it to get money from the bank, but recognize that is why you're doing it. What's really important is to think more strategically about where you are going to get your focus. The loss of focus is the death of any company, whether it's a small entrepreneurial company, or a giant corporation, if they start to lose their focus, they've had it!"

It's clear that Benjamin Tregoe is fairly focused on focusing on products and markets. He and every other successful entrepreneur you'll ever meet all sound alike when it comes to the *what* of the business.

Let's switch over to the *how* of the business. Tregoe includes as a critical part of strategy the role of company culture (my words), which he refers to as purpose or values or basic beliefs (his words). Whatever it's called, he obviously thinks it's damned important: "One thing we haven't talked about which I see as really significant is the importance of a person's sense of purpose and values that transcend the business. Certainly, tremendously important to me was the feeling that we were doing something that had significance far beyond building a company or making money. I was convinced that we were doing something that had tremendous importance and that could really help improve rationality all over the world. As you know, this company has always had this sort of strong missionary zeal. That's the reason for our international expansion. If we had been looking at it strictly from the standpoint of business strategy, I'd have never gone to London in 1965 to open an office, and then to Germany in 1966.

"It may have appeared sort of stupid from a straight business standpoint, but we said this is something that is really important in the whole world. That is the same reason we went to Japan in 1973. Now it wasn't totally ridiculous in that we thought Japan was going to be a major power in the world. But still, the fundamental thing was the feeling that we had something that was really important, that could help in terms of better understanding."

Tregoe was warming to the subject of a higher calling, what I'd call the Matsushita effect: "The point is, it's tremendously important to have a sense of purpose or mission that goes beyond this thing of 'I want to develop a business and make a fortune.' I don't think that is adequate. I think a person has got to have a sense of mission and purpose. To have a sense of purpose that is going to give some meaning to this enterprise when it is young, and continue to give it meaning as it matures. These values, this sense of purpose, should not only have strategic significance, but they also must have day-in and day-out operational significance. They are going to say something about the kind of business you pursue and will pursue over a period of time, which is very strategic. They also say something of how you are going to operate together as a business over a period of time."

Ben Tregoe was saving his best for last. A final, take-no-prisoners attack on the business schools of the world: "MBAs don't learn this because the business schools have been teaching the wrong things. There is no question in my mind that we would be in a much better position competitively in the United States in the world market right now, if we hadn't had all of these damn business schools. They've done more harm than good. I mean they are focusing on the wrong things. The whole sense of mission idea, purpose, and values that we're talking about right now. The whole question of leadership and the utilization of human resources, participation in problem solving and decision making by people down through the organization: all of that they are not getting out of the business schools. Because they have been focusing on the wrong things. They are only right now starting to make some adjustments—way behind the curve. Up to now they have done more harm than good. I'll tell you, I don't know whether this ought to be said or not—but one thing that I thought was really interesting: Ian McMillan, who heads up the new entrepreneurial section of the Wharton School [University of Pennsylvania's business school], told me that regular undergraduates of the university are twice as likely to start their own businesses as the MBAs! So there!"

The Mission of the Victorian Liberals

Just in case you are beginning to wonder, be sure that Sense of Mission isn't an American—or Asian monopoly. The Europeans know how to play this game too. For true believers in pursuing their mission, it's hard to beat the great entrepreneurs of Victorian Liberalism. Between 1850 and 1900 these worshippers of enlightened capitalism transformed Britain into the greatest commercial power the world had ever known. They were all followers of the great Liberal party leader W. E. Gladstone, whose mid-century vision created Britain's free market economy in which they all flourished.

Stern advocates of Protestant values and social progress, this group of exceptional enterprisers reads like a Who's Who of British industry. It includes Barclay, Lloyd, Cadbury, Rowntree, Beecham, Morley, and that great teetotalling Yorkshireman Sir Titus Salt. Most of them were card-carrying members of the "Nonconformists" (non-Anglicans), and a high percentage came from just two denominations: the Quakers and the Congregationalists. Their business strategy was very aggressive, some even called it imperial, yet their corporate culture, particularly their concern for workers, was a hundred years ahead of the times. No one embodied these two characteristics more than the most famous of them all: William Hesketh Lever.

Today Unilever is the sixteenth largest corporation in the world, with annual sales of $25 billion, and far and away the largest consumer goods company. It is world-renowed for setting smart strategies and maintaining a great culture for its employees. How did it get this way? Well, it didn't happen yesterday. Back in 1925, the year of William Lever's death, Lever Brothers* was already the most far-flung commercial empire in the world. Made up of 282 operating companies spread across five continents, it employed an amazing sixty thousand people. Most spectacular for the times, however, was the fact that eighteen thousand of these employees were already members of the company's unique Co-Partnership Trust. Lever had initiated Britain's earliest employee profit-sharing program, a truly revolutionary concept, in 1909. It was among his proudest achievements. It was this double-barreled mission—aggressive and expansive business growth, along with the liberal belief that workers get their fair share of the pie—that drove William Lever and in a large measure drives Unilever today.

When it comes to business, Lever was a very tough competitor indeed. He traumatized the gentlemanly world of London commerce with massive and outlandish American-style advertising. He literally invented brand recognition by plastering Britain with posters of his first big product, Sunlight Soap. He introduced prizes and gifts for customers who turned in large numbers of soap wrappers, though his competitors cried foul and called it unethical. In 1885 he was the first manufacturer to cut soap to bar size and wrap it in paper. The paper simply provided another opportunity for promoting the name and furthering brand recognition. He quickly followed up with Lifebuoy, sold as a germicide, and Lux, the first flaked soap for washing clothes. In the twinkling of an eye, William

---

* Unilever was formed in 1929 through the merger of Lever Brothers and several smaller Dutch companies. The company operates today as a Dutch/UK group, with headquarters in both countries.

Lever also invented the notion of market niches and producing brands to compete against each other. By 1888 he was dominating the British market for soaps, and he turned his guns overseas. Not wasting any time, in quick succession he entered the United States, Canada, Australia, and central Europe, building his first foreign plant in Switzerland. By 1910 Lever Brothers was making soap in such far-flung places as Durban, Shanghai, and Tori-Shindon, Japan. Always one to think big, Lever was also buying up his own sources of raw material. In one gigantic purchase in 1911, the company acquired 6 million acres of coconut and palm oil estates in the Belgian Congo. As they say, the rest is history.

While Victorian Liberalism and the Protestant work ethic produced great entrepreneurs, it concurrently demanded great philanthropy and respect for the common man. It also put William Lever ahead of his time as a creator of corporate culture. No doubt about it, he set a teetotalling, Bible-reading model of behavior, perhaps a bit dated in our "enlightened" times. But beneath the obvious, we find caring words and deeds that are painfully absent to this day in many a large company. If nothing else, William Lever put his money where his mouth was in urging workers to cast their lot with the company.

The most famous example is of course Port Sunlight, the model community Lever Brothers built for its employees seven miles outside of Liverpool. Work on this mammoth project began in 1889. Lever believed the company had an obligation to do more than pay salaries; it should also be in the business of raising the total quality of life of workers and their families. Working-class Britain at that time generally endured living conditions equivalent to the worst modern-day slum. Port Sunlight eventually housed thirty-five hundred people and became a model of company-sponsored living unequaled to this day. Each house was separate, with its own garden, an unheard-of luxury for the working class. Health facilities, schools, swimming pools, concerts, and art exhibits were all available. And of course the church. But the religious ceremony was interdenominational. And in what must have been a real stretch of personal values, Lever permitted alcohol to be served as long as it wasn't on Sunday. You can visit the town today—a living testament to a company taking care of its people.

A less famous example, but in some ways more telling, was Lever's battle with the trade unions over the length of the work day. No, management wasn't pushing for more and the union less. Quite the opposite. For some time Lever had been urging the British government to reduce the standard work day to six hours and somehow provide two hours of "self-improvement" classes for workers. Lever thought this was in everyone's best interest. His fellow industrialists thought he had lost his mind and the proposal got nowhere. So he decided to do it experimentally in his own company. At company expense he undertook to set up an evening staff college. Surprise of surprises, the union leadership opposed the idea of "compulsory education" and that was that. Talk about being ahead of your time!

Lever recovered from the "compulsory education" impasse and went on to pioneer many new concepts in employee relations that set the company apart from nineteenth-century thinking. The Co-Partnership Trust in one fell swoop, made owners out of vast numbers of workers. Sick pay, annual paid holidays, and pension plans were all early, innovative Lever programs. The result of all this has trickled down through the decades. It is no secret that Unilever has consistently enjoyed a loyal, highly committed work force. While many of Britain's (and Holland's) big companies have been brought to their knees by years of labor strife—Unilever marches on. The Congregationalist from Lancashire would be proud.

Perhaps the capstone of Lever's efforts to honor the dignity of the common man came late in his life while he was serving in the House of Commons. In 1907 he was the author of Britain's very first legislation to provide old-age pensions for its working-class citizens. Not exactly the act we'd expect from a soap tycoon. So what are we to make of this super-entrepreneur and his Victorian Liberal buddies? Were they capitalists with heart? Socialists with a nose for business? Whatever else they accomplished, they should make us stop and think about the mission we're on, about the value of our purpose, about what we're doing—the strategy, if you will—and about the standards we employ to get there, the culture we're prepared to live with. If you're going to spend your life at it, it's worth thinking about.

God Help You If You're Not Proud of It

Sense of mission is important because it produces more success for the company. It's hard to imagine a growing, profitable company that doesn't know where it's headed and doesn't know how to get there. But think about this: There's another reason besides company success why organizations should pursue high purpose and high standards; it relates to you and me and it's pretty basic.

If you're like most of us, you have to work. And if you have to work, it means you're going to spend over half your life at a job. You'll spend more time at work than with your family. You'll spend more time at work than with your friends. You'll spend more time at work than on any hobby you will ever have. You'll spend more time at work than on any single activity of your life—and God help you if you're not proud of it!

This may be the most important reason for creating and holding dear a sense of mission at work. This is not to say that work per se is or should be the goal of your life. But who in their right mind would choose to spend over half their life doing something they're not proud of, that achieves nothing worth talking about? No one I know would make such a choice.

Let's face it, everyone wants and needs to feel some pride in how they spend their life. Everyone wants to have something to tell their grandchildren. "This is what I did. This is what I achieved.

This is why the forty-five years I worked was not a waste of time."
It's too big a slice of our total existence on this earth to toss away
to boredom, frustration, and apathy. So at the end of the day, it's
important to have a sense of mission about work because it's really
your life we're talking about.

Not coincidentally, it will help your company. It certainly helps
entrepreneurs and their people do some amazing things, often with
meager resources. For the large, mature company, re-instilling purpose and challenge can turn night into day. Stodgy and stale companies, some struggling to survive, can and do just take off. Such
a reawakening of the spirit of enterprise is always driven by a
renewed sense of mission—a focused strategy around customer and
product, supported by a culture that inspires. So do yourself *and*
your company a big favor. Give it a try. You won't need any
management theory—just a lot of energy and focus on *what* you're
doing and *how* you're doing it.

CHAPTER THREE

CUSTOMER/
PRODUCT VISION

My Customer, My Product,
My Self-respect

> . . . the computer is the most remarkable tool we've ever
> built. The most important thing is to get them in the
> hands of as many people as possible.
> —STEVE JOBS, founder, Apple Computer;
> founder, NeXT, Inc.

Vision?

Every book ever written about entrepreneurs says they have *vision*. But vision of what? Think about it. Imagine you're starting your own small business tomorrow morning. What will you be thinking about? What do you absolutely, positively have to be racking your brain over? If you're going to get to day two of the enterprise, you'd better be thinking "What can I make or do that someone will pay me hard money for?" In the mundane world of day-to-day entrepreneurship, the vague notion of vision can mean only one thing: a clear picture of a specific set of customers who need and will pay for a specific set of products and services. Nothing could be more basic to the entrepreneur. This is the sine qua non of enterprise. The vision is precise. It is intense. All else revolves around it. Entrepreneurs are blessed and obsessed with this integrated vision of customers and products. It's not really so surprising when you think about it. Business can take many forms, but there's never been a business, or at least a business that survived, without a product or service of some sort and a customer somewhere willing to pay for it.

Now here's the point that's gotten lost in the shuffle. Great entrepreneurs are not product inventors alone. Nor are they just great promoters. Is Steven Jobs a scientist or a salesman? A "product person" or a "customer person"? Well, Jobs had a vision—a vision of "the most remarkable tool we've ever built." He was a computer junkie from the word go. Sounds like a product guy doesn't he? But then he says, "The most important thing" is to get them used in every office, in every home, and by every child in every class-room. Like no other computer maker, Jobs understood the needs of naive users. That's why Apple made computers inexpensive, easy to learn, and fun to use. Now he sounds like a customer guy. What's going on here? The obvious answer—he's a product guy *and* a customer guy all wrapped up in one, an expert on both, the classic customer/product vision of an entrepreneur.

The Customer/Product Vision of Disney

How about Walter Elias Disney? Ever have a management school course on Walt Disney?* Of course not. Why would anyone want

---

* It's not quite a management course, but through diligent research I located the Disney case study we read at the Harvard Business School. It covered long-range financing for Walt Disney World. The point holds. Of all the rich lessons to be learned from Disney the entrepreneur, financing strategy is hardly the place to start. For any dedicated Disney aficionados, try "Management, Disney Style" and "Service, Disney Style," two fun seminars offered at Walt Disney World.

to study the business practices of a cartoonist. It sounds too silly for such a serious subject as management. Of course, Uncle Walt did create the second-most-recognized product in the history of the world. The people who study such things tell us that Coca-Cola is number one and a mouse named Mickey is number two. I can believe it. I'll never forget sitting in the cavernous dining hall of the Friendship Hotel in Beijing—in the waning days of China's "cultural revolution." On the only TV set for miles around, staff and customers alike watched intermittent segments of the "Gang of Four" trial and Mickey Mouse cartoons. And with the Chinese staff, the Mandarin-speaking Mickey was clearly winning the evening ratings. I took this as corroborative evidence that Madame Jang's revolution was over!

The point for now is—anyone who can create the second-most-recognized product in the history of the world must have done something right! Maybe we *should* study the business practices of this cartoonist/entrepreneur.

Disney Product Focus

Some observers say Uncle Walt was a lot more than just a cartoonist. They're right. The fact is, he's the greatest product creator in the history of the entertainment business. His list of product achievements is long. He produced the first "talking" cartoon, a 1928 black-and-white about Steamboat Willie (later renamed Mickey). He also produced the first technicolor cartoon, *Flowers and Trees*, in 1932. Through the use of multiplaned cameras, Disney introduced the earliest version of 3D movies in 1937. Disney later perfected true three-dimensional animation through his audio-animatronics electronics system. Nineteen thirty-seven also marked one of his greatest product achievements and the beginning of a new era in filmmaking. In the face of great Hollywood skepticism, Disney Studios released *Snow White and the Seven Dwarfs*, the first feature-length animated cartoon. Fifty-five years later, *Snow White* still makes millions for the company every time it's re-released. *Fantasia* in 1940 was the world's first stereographic movie, and in 1955 Disney unveiled the world's first 360° projection at Disneyland. Moving into television, Disney simply created the longest-running (1954–83) prime-time television series ever. *True-Life Adventure's* remarkable twenty-nine-year run will probably never be matched, and it single-handedly revolutionized the TV documentary. Along the way, in addition to Mickey Mouse, Disney was busy creating an entire family of world-famous characters such as Donald Duck and Goofy. From these lovable characters, licensing rights and products like the Mickey Mouse watch continue to fill the coffers of the Walt Disney Company. The amazing fact is, most of Walt Disney's original products continue to produce profit. The vaults at Disney Studios contain reel after reel of pure platinum. Film classics like *Snow White*, *Pinocchio*, *Cinderella*, *Peter Pan*, *Sleeping Beauty*, and *Alice in Wonderland* add up to a perpetual profit stream unparalleled in business.

But the capstone of Disney's product vision came in 1955, with the opening of Disneyland in California. His "dreams come true" theme parks are far and away the top entertainment product in history. The combined parks are pushing a hundred million "guests" a year. The money just pours in from Anaheim, Orlando, Tokyo, and EuroDisney near Paris.

The number one lesson from the instant and incredible success at Disneyland was that it was way too small. Disney determined to insulate future theme parks from the tacky development of motels and fast-food joints that rapidly engulfed Disneyland. Before he died in 1966, Disney had laid the groundwork for Walt Disney World in Florida. With 27,500 acres, it would be 150 times bigger than the California property. Disney had trouble convincing the financial community that the company could digest such a massive undertaking. But he wouldn't budge, and Walt Disney World became the largest private construction project in the United States. Under the careful eye of Roy Disney (Walt's brother), it opened on October 1, 1971. Only ten thousand people showed up for opening day. A ripple of doubt went through the company. But by Thanksgiving Day, the cars were backed up for miles, and the biggest theme park in the world has never looked back. That first year it drew an unprecedented 11 million customers, making it overnight the biggest tourist attraction in the world. Today, these forty-three-square miles of land built on a Florida swamp draws close to 30 million visitors a year, which dwarfs the number of tourists visiting entire countries like Germany and Great Britain. Not bad for a cartoonist!

EPCOT Center, not opened until 1982, was Uncle Walt's final great product creation. Back in 1964, Disney described his vision of the future: "EPCOT will take its cue from the new ideas and new technologies that are now emerging from the creative centers of tomorrow that will never be completed, but will always be introducing and testing and demonstrating new materials and systems. And EPCOT will be a showcase to the world for the ingenuity and imagination of American free enterprise." No, a bit more than "just a cartoonist." His record of product creation, development, and high quality is unparalleled. Surely, then, Walt Disney is a great product person—a creative "scientist" par excellence.

Disney Customer Focus

Other Disney watchers, however, call him the greatest promoter in the history of entertainment—perhaps the greatest in all business. His genius was marketing—a customer person through and through. They make a good case. What really is his record on the customer side of business?

The cartoons and films show Disney's magic touch in pleasing customers. But it's the theme parks that most dramatically illustrate Disney's extraordinary care for and understanding of what customers want. The opening of Disneyland in California was the culmination of a twenty-year dream for Disney. In his own words, the idea came straight from a customer—himself: "The idea came along when I was taking my daughters around to those kiddy parks. While they were on the merry-go-round, riding forty times or something, I'd be sitting there trying to figure out what I could do."* From such simple thoughts of a slightly unsatisfied parent-customer eventually came the idea for great outdoor entertainment centers for the whole family. Not amusement parks. Rather, he was interested in performances or themes in which the customers (he called them guests) are not spectators but participants in the show. Disney had no customer strategy other than creating something fun for everyone. The development process went on and on: "It took many years. I started with many ideas, threw them away, and started all over again."†

There must have been a lot of parent-customers just like Disney, wishing for something different. Enough at least to instantly make Disneyland America's favorite place to go. It was here in Disneyland that Disney's real magic revealed itself. Disney loved his *products* for sure, but the one thing he loved even more was seeing the faces of his *customers* using his products. One of those first-year guests at Disneyland was a fourteen-year-old girl named Julie. While she was waiting her turn to ride a teacup at the Mad Hatter's Tea Party, who should appear but Uncle Walt himself. As if it happened yesterday, Julie vividly describes the scene from thirty-seven years ago: "I'll never forget it. He was just leaning against the fence, watching the children whirl around in the teacups—with a big smile on his face. He was enjoying it all as much as the children were!" Hardly scientific, but the source is *impeccable*—my wife of twenty-seven years!

Disney's magic of course works its way to the bottom line. Like millions of other early customers, we've now taken our own children, numerous times, to Disneyland and Disney World. And

* Walt Disney World brochure, The Walt Disney Co., 1986, p. 6.
† Ibid.

when the time comes, they'll undoubtedly treat theirs to the thrill of the teacups, Pirates of the Caribbean, and 20,000 Leagues Under the Sea. The fact is, tens of millions of fourth-generation guests are now pouring into the theme parks for one simple reason: They do exactly what Walt Disney said they should. They make people happy!

Disney, the customer fanatic, had some pretty straightforward ideas about how to treat the people who paid his salary. Underpinning them all is the concept of "themeing" the entire production and making the audience participants, not spectators. Themeing is creating a perfect illusion for customers. When you walk down Mainstreet, you're swept back a hundred years. Your stroll down the street is part of the show. When you enter Fantasyland, you're actually in a land of fantasy. Creating these themes or illusions requires perfect products *and* perfect service. The service theme at Walt Disney World tody is pure Uncle Walt: "We Create Happiness by Providing the Finest in Family Entertainment." The theme is supported by clear-cut priorities on exactly how to do this. The priorities that all cast members are expected to follow are safety, courtesy, show (the setting of any area), and efficiency (for guests, not the company).

The relationship of employees and customers is crucial to the concept. Employees, from janitors to Snow White, aren't "service providers"—they're performers, members of the cast. When they work, they're "on stage." They relax and eat lunch "backstage." There are no customers—only guests. A cast member's sole reason for being is to make the guests happy. They must treat guests with the same courtesy as they would guests in their own home. Guests with questions are never avoided, they're sought out. In this very special relationship between cast members and guests, little is left to chance. Cast members are expected to be proactive toward guests, but they're not sent out into the park unprepared. Disney training is explicit on how to make guests happy.

From Walt Disney World's seminar on "Service, Disney Style": "Walt Disney drilled the message into all of his employees. . . .

'You are DISNEYLAND'. . . . His belief was that EVERYBODY in the Walt Disney Company was in a service role and that the final benefactors of that service had to be the people who visited the park—or in Disney terms, 'our guests.' To be consistently effective in delivering quality service, an organization should develop a service strategy as well as a product strategy. Most of us know what products we sell or service we provide, but have we clearly defined *how* we want that product or service delivered? This becomes our *Service Strategy* or *Theme*."

Creating the best customer service in the world was Disney's goal. An extremely high standard is set and expected of all employees. Disney may have been the first person in the service industry to really understand that service is everyone's responsibility—and that it has to permeate every aspect of the business. His attention to detail is legendary. Every inch of the park has to be picture-perfect, and not just the streets and the attractions, but right down to the details of every cast member's appearance.

Disney said it best himself: "Give the people everything you can give them. Keep the place as clean as you can keep it. Keep it friendly, you know. Make it a real fun place to be." Was Uncle Walt a great customer person? A great marketeer? A great "salesman"? You better believe it!

Disney People—Connecting Products to Customers

At Disney, as at most service companies, people are the indispensable link between products and customers. Disney has no peer in making this work. In an extraordinarily frank employee pamphlet, *The Disney Look*, appearance and grooming for cast members are covered in excruciating detail. The opening message to employees makes absolutely clear that the customer comes first: "Each guest who makes up our audience is our 'boss.' He or she makes our show possible and pays our wages. If we displease our guests, they might not return, and without an audience, there is no show. For this reason, anything that could be considered offensive, distracting or not in the best interest of our Disney show such as a conspicuous tattoo, will not be permitted."

The Disney Look has separate sections for hosts and hostesses and instructs on everything from costumes and hair styling to deodorants, sunglasses, and fingernails. The section on deodorants for hosts sets the tone and drives home the customer point: "Due to close contact with guests and fellow cast members, the use of a deodorant or anti-perspirant is required. The use of heavy colognes is discouraged. A light after-shave or cologne is acceptable." *The Disney Look* for hostess's fingernails seems to cover everything that could ever possibly happen to one's nails: "Fingernails should be kept clean, and if polish is used, it should be clear or in flesh tones in cream enamels. Polishes that are dark red, frosted, gold or silver toned are not considered part of the 'Disney Look.' Fingernails should not exceed one-fourth of an inch beyond the fingertip." Following these guidelines is a condition of employment for ticket takers and street sweepers as well as Captain Hook and Sleeping Beauty.

At first glance, some of Disney's rules and expectations of its people may appear harsh, even unrealistic. It's true that many large companies couldn't get away with the extraordinary levels of product perfection and customer care that Disney has always maintained. But it's like comparing the "Rivetheads" at General Motors to the hand craftsmen at Rolls-Royce. If the leaders have permitted junk to go out the door for fifty years, they end up with Rivetheads who make junk. If the leaders absolutely will not tolerate junk, they end up with craftsmen making a Rolls. Disney was a product and service fanatic. He'd never allow anything to get in the way of making his customers happy. So the magical voyage continues. The Walt Disney Company sails into the future with a long history of taking pride in being the best in the world at making people happy.

The Real Magic

The real magic of Disney was simple. He was a product expert and a customer expert at the same time—a scientist and a salesman, an unbeatable combination—the perfect entrepreneur. It's the beautiful balance between these two basics of business that make the world of Disney what it is. Focus on both is the answer. How could it be otherwise? Well, unfortunately, it can, and often is *otherwise*. There are at least three other possibilities. You'll recognize them all: the Scientist, the Salesman, and the Bureaucrat.

▪The Scientist

Ever come across people or even whole companies who are so into their technology or product that they forget they're creating it for someone else to use? This is the *scientist only* syndrome. In the world of Disney it could be the filmmaker who loves to make films—but doesn't much care if anyone watches them. In the world of Jobs, it's the computer scientist who builds a machine so elaborate it takes four Einsteins to figure out how to use it. This is more common than it at first appears. It ranges from user "unfriendly" products, to simply unusable products, to the adding of so many bells and whistles to a product that no one can afford it. The scientist often has a peculiar disdain for the need to sell and satisfy customers. He tends to look down a bit on his own salespeople and even his customers. Of course there's nothing wrong with being a scientist for science's sake—if everyone agrees that's the mission. The trouble occurs when you end up with employees who love the product but hate the customer. That's not quite the focus for growing the business.

▪ The Salesman

Is it possible to love the customer but hate the product? You bet it is. Most of us run into the *salesman only* syndrome every day. This is the "I can sell anything" type—the professional salesman who loves to sell but doesn't give a damn what he's selling. Cars last year, computers this year, and Mexican real estate the next. It probably never has worked and it certainly doesn't work today. Most salespeople know how to sell. They're trained *ad nauseum* on sales methods. But that's the problem. They know ten times more about selling techniques than they do about their product. Substituting courtesy for competence is another variety of the salesman syndrome. On the phone it's the ever courteous voice that never solves your billing problem. Or the smiling baggage clerk at Kennedy who announces that your luggage just went to Karachi. The bottom line is that customers don't want or need more selling and smiling. They want real product and service experts—the ones who really care about the product and really know how to make it work! This is what loving the customer really means.

▪ The Bureaucrat

Then there's the unfortunate case of employees and companies that seem to hate their products *and* their customers. At the end of a bad day of "customering," some of us might get the idea that this is the driving force of most of the places we deal with. If you're one of those poor souls who has no interest in products or customers, don't despair. This won't put you on the dole. You'll make a perfect bureaucrat! You'd fit in nicely at some of the world's giant corporations, and there's always the government. Complete lack of concern for both customers and products is the one surefire characteristic that qualifies any organization for world-class bureaucracy. But don't count anymore on lifetime employment—today, such spiritless competitors have become easy prey for entrepreneurially driven companies.

The Entrepreneur—Disney Magic

How about loving the customer and loving the product? The entrepreneurial mind is locked on an inseparable vision of customer and product. Entrepreneurs are close to their products. They're intensely interested in the design, manufacture, and usage of their product/service. They take it personally. They're ashamed when the quality is bad, and they're proud when they get it right. They're thrilled when customers love their product. They are clearly product experts. Entrepreneurs are also very close to their customers. They have to be. Their paycheck depends on it. They never forget that they need the customers a lot more than the customers need them. They push the organization to its limits to meet special requests of customers. They listen carefully to customers, not because someone told them to, but to pick up any new ideas to improve their product or service. If a customer is unhappy, it's a major crisis. Entrepreneurs are clearly customer experts.

Of all the characteristics of entrepreneurial behavior, this dual focus on customer and product best illuminates the difference between entrepreneurs and professional managers. Like the craftsman of old, entrepreneurs are intimately involved in both making *and* selling. This produces expertise, and respect for both customers and products. It also produces great competitive advantage against the bureaucracy of giant competitors.

Of course great entrepreneurs don't always come to the task naturally. Creating a strong customer/product vision is usually the result of absolute necessity. It comes with the territory in any start-up business. Thomas Watson, for example, was a salesman for NCR before founding IBM. But he developed an unparalleled standard of excellence for product development and manufacturing. The same is true of traveling salesman Konosuke Matsushita. Akio Morita, on the other hand, was an engineer by training and inclination but he had to sell. It was his four early years of store-to-store selling in America that put Sony on the map. Jesse Boots grew up as a medical herbalist in Victorian England. He became the Sam Walton of British drugstores (or was Walton America's Jesse Boots?) through brilliant advertising, superb service, and massive discounting. In all these cases, the early focus was by necessity a constant interweaving of product possibilities and customer desires, daily shifting between the scientist and the salesman. Unfortunately there's nowhere to learn all this—certainly not at a business school, where the very first question your MBA advisor asks goes something like, "Well, what's your major? Do you want manufacturing or marketing or finance?"

Harvard Scientist/Master Salesman

Ben Tregoe never had to answer that question at Harvard, where he got his Ph.D. in sociology. Sociology is hardly the typical training track for great salespeople, and Tregoe has probably never been comfortable with being called a salesman, but you do what you have to do. This Harvard trained scientist grit his teeth and became his company's most powerful salesman. No one has sold more big corporate clients around the world than Ben Tregoe. For thirty-five years he has led by example, remaining both scientist and salesman of last resort for Kepner-Tregoe.

Combining your scientist/salesman instincts up front may be the most important lesson of all in creating successful products. In the process of doing research, Tregoe learned why people needed his product, and even more importantly, he learned why they didn't think they needed it: "We were still doing a lot of field research. We would go out and see companies and interview managers and

CEOs—anybody we could get to talk to. We would sit in on meetings and watch what they were doing. We tried to reconstruct their decisions, whether they were good or bad, and tried to get some feeling as to why some people were better decision makers than others. We found that nobody could really articulate how they were doing what they did. When we would ask them how or why they made a decision a certain way, they would say, 'Well, I just sort of felt it.' Everybody had difficulty articulating how they were doing their decision making. It seemed to be something that people learned sort of by osmosis. That's the reason nobody paid any attention to it. So we felt that the obvious thing that we could do was to improve people's decision making by making them more aware of the decision process."

It's not a one-two step. Tregoe didn't change from scientist to professional salesman after the product was created. If the salesman is important to the scientist in creating the product, the scientist is equally important to the salesman in selling it: ". . . we just started going out and seeing as many people as we could and tried to interest them in what we were doing. Neither one of us was a businessman. We were both from academic backgrounds, but it didn't take a rocket scientist to see if you sold a big company, you had the potential of doing a lot more work than if you sold a little company. So we pursued these bigger companies, most of whom were in the Midwest and on the East Coast. There is no doubt that both Kepner and I were excited about the product. The concept. The technology. And the potential benefit of what the customers could do with it. I'm not sure about the notion of all the different steps of selling and all of that. I'm not sure I would be a great expert on that. I think the thing that carried me on the selling was that I was very enthusiastic about what we were doing. I could certainly talk about it with some authority. This may be a self-serving comment, but I have a feeling that when I'm selling things, people tend to trust me. So when I go in, they think, 'Maybe that's something that we ought to pay attention to.' It obviously took calling a lot of people, trying to set up appointments. A lot of hard work. I never read any books about selling or anything like that, but maybe it would have been smart to do that. I don't know."

Well, we know. You're not going to learn enthusiasm for your product from a sales book or seminar. Sales training won't shower you with "authority" or create "trust" in the product you're selling. This all comes from the scientist in you. And creating usable products that customers really need doesn't come from the engineering manual. It's the salesman's instinct that gives you such insight. Contrary to the scientific notion of product and customer specialization, the salesman turns out to be crucial to the development of products—and the scientist turns out to be crucial to the selling of products!

The Scientist Father and the Salesman Son

Everyone can be both salesman and scientist to a large degree. Millions of entrepreneurs do it every day. And every once in a while a super-salesman and a super-scientist come together to combine their skills in one dynamic enterprise. Miki Pulley, Japan's ultra-high-quality leader in power transmission products, has made it look easy with a father-and-son team. This combination of scientist and salesman has produced a $200 million company, with joint ventures in the United States and Germany, and sales offices throughout Europe and Southeast Asia. Here is one of the entrepreneurial Japanese companies you rarely hear about. It doesn't make cars or VCRs and it's not part of a big Japanese group. Miki Pulley is an independent, world-class producer of products like pulleys, coupling devices, and clutches. Its science is backed up by the father's two hundred product patents. Company growth has been spearheaded by breaking tradition with the domestic supplier role of small and medium-sized Japanese firms. The company goes around the giant trading groups by directly exporting and importing anywhere in the world. Its selling is backed up by the son, who made his first sales call in the United States at the age of twenty and has never stopped.

In the late thirties, Yoshiharu Miki was a twenty-six-year-old engineering graduate in Kawasaki, Japan. He wanted the independence to design and engineer his own products, so he started his own small machine shop. The Pacific war changed all that. Instead of inventing, his shop was ordered to produce precision parts for Zero fighters. By the end of the war his shop had been totally destroyed in a B-29 raid, and he was a prisoner of war in Siberia, where the Russians were in no hurry to release skilled engineers. Ironically, it was here that he invented the product that would later propel Miki Pulley's first commercial success.

Son and present-day CEO, Harukazu Miki, tells the story: "In 1943, he [Yoshiharu, his father] was sent to Manchuria by the Japanese military, not as a soldier but as an engineer. At the end of the war the Russians came into Manchuria and took all the skilled people and college graduates and drove them to Siberia. My father worked as a prisoner in Siberia for a couple of years after the war. His camp was producing locomotives for Russia. He was very unlucky. If he had been captured by the Americans here he would have had a better life then. But he had nothing, not enough to eat over there, and it was very cold in Siberia. Since he was an engineer and he had a lot of time, he invented many things there, from eyeglasses to locks and so forth. The lock is interesting. In Siberia they had a problem opening locks with keys. They were always frozen. The keys would break so the locks wouldn't work. So he invented a deep lock: You push the key in once, and then push it in again. This would break the ice, and then you could turn it—a simple invention that nobody before had ever thought of.

"Anyway, when he came back from Siberia to Japan, in late 1947, he saw opportunity in making better locks here. You know, many soldiers came back to Japan with nothing to do, no work, no jobs. So we had a lot of robbers and crime at that time. Security became important. So my father invented a double secure lock that was impossible for robbers to pick. Once he started making this, it sold quite a lot. He was always looking for something to make. For example another big problem in postwar Japan was the shortage of electricity. So he invented a rechargeable light that used a kind of a car battery. While the electricity was on, you would recharge the battery for use when the lights went off. I was very little then, but I remember the shop was next to our house and it was my playground. I remember my mother helping to assemble those batteries.

"By 1954, my father was making those small things, like the locks and rechargeable battery-type lamps. Gradually, Japanese industry came back, so we also started to supply some precise parts to the big companies. It was in 1954 that my father finally invented the Japanese variable speed pulley. The variable speed pulley became quite important to Japanese industry as they tried to increase speed and quality of production. The old power transmission equipment just didn't meet the new demands. The pulley was really the start of our business as we see it today. Of course my father loved to invent things, and he continued inventing. He has a couple of hundred patents now."

So how does a single dedicated scientist build his inventions into a $200 million company in the land of Mitsubishi, Matsushita, and Toyota? Well, it really helps if you have a dedicated salesman for a son. Harukazu Miki, who used his father's first small factory for a playground, says he didn't want to be an engineer—he wanted to be a businessman. Whatever we call him, his history says he's a damn good salesman. In 1960, when he was only twenty, he went to Kansas City to do two things: get an American education and find American customers for Miki Pulley: "Japan was a very poor country, and it was very difficult to go abroad. At that time the government would only allow businessmen who had at least one hundred thousand dollars in trade to go abroad. Or you could go as an exchange student. So I went as a student to Kansas City. I was lucky. Very lucky! Going to America had great meaning— not only for myself and my father, but also for the Miki Pulley

Company as we know it today. When I was at the university, over thirty years ago, no small companies in Japan looked outside of Japan for their business. But when my father came to see me, we went to many manufacturing companies together. My father showed the products and I translated. And some of those first companies that my father and I visited together are still very good friends and business partners. These U.S. companies introduced us to several companies in Europe that were in the same field. So again we developed good friends and business partners there."

From these early relationships, Harukazu created both export markets for Miki products and a thriving import business for precision instruments from his German and American partners. Just seeking out good products to import to Japan was very rare for small Japanese companies: "As I told you, at that time no one except the big companies, the big trading companies, were interested in touring other countries or markets for their business. Small companies never thought about how to make business with American or European companies. But I saw I could expand our business with new foreign products by getting the license to import and sell. We had our own variable speed pulley, but from one of these companies, Zero-Max in Minneapolis, we got a new type that was very unique and no one had the same kind of product at that time. So we could get into the Japanese market quickly. I was sort of a pioneer in this. No competitors there for me and I was quite welcome to sell their products because the Japanese market was so small for the big U.S. and European companies. Also, at that time, Japan made nothing to sell to these big foreign companies, and our new relationships helped us learn to make products for export."

Harukazu maintains a close relationship with his customers and his partners. This has produced about five thousand dependable customers and thirty-seven years of sales increases in the company's forty-year history. It has also produced an extraordinary level of respect from Miki's overseas distributors, suppliers, and four joint venture partners. The Zero-Max story is illustrative: "We started to import their product in Japan and it was quite successful. But this was an independent, family-owned company. About ten years ago the owner decided to sell to a big U.S. company. Then this company was bought by a bigger company and the new owner decided to sell Zero-Max because it was not their line. So the management and the employees asked me to buy the company because they did not want yet another owner and they even feared the company would be shut down or moved to another state and they would all lose their jobs. So they asked us to buy it and we did.

"After we bought Zero-Max, the owner of an even smaller, independent company came to me and said, 'Okay, I've been in this business for many years, it's profitable, but I'm ready to retire. Why don't you also buy my company? Make your investment in Minneapolis a bit bigger.' So we said yes, but only if he agreed to stay on as president. He agreed and we bought his company too. But these purchases were not dangerous adventures for us because we had been doing business with them for twenty years. We knew their products well, and we knew their management and their employees." This is the way Harukazu Miki likes to expand his business—with people with whom there has been an ongoing relationship of mutual trust. Just the kind of relationship all salesmen dream about!

There's an old Japanese saying that you can pick your friends, but not your relatives. Well, apparently the Mikis got lucky. Could Harukazu have done it alone? No, he needed a scientist. Could Yoshiharu have done it alone? Of course not, he needed a salesman. The point: Entrepreneurial vision depends on both.

The Functional Organization— Death Knell of the Craftsman

That business requires customer/product vision is a simple, obvious truth. If you care about both, you're at least on the road to the two absolutely irreplaceable requirements of the spirit of enterprise. But this bedrock truth about enterprise has the drawback of most simple truths. Its so basic that it begins to seem too simple to be important. That's exactly what happened to the craftsmen of the world. Enter the modern answer to growing bigger and more efficient forever—the functional organization.

The entrepreneur's integrated vision of customer and product has been organized out of existence for most employees in today's highly functionalized business. Pursuing the holy grail of organizational efficiency has created unnatural barriers and strange bedfellows in large companies everywhere. Some employees— salespeople, service personnel, market researchers—by the nature of their jobs are more or less focused on customers. Others—scientists, assembly line workers, product designers—are more or less focused on products. And rather amazingly, huge numbers of workers don't seem to be focused on either. These are the people who cut the payroll, write the leases, handle personnel—all the administrative functions. So today's large, rationally designed organization ends up with, more or less, three super-functions. In the process, employees have been transformed from business people to "product people," or "customer people," or "administrative people." The craftsman, the original make-and-sell businessman, focusing on both his customer and his product, has simply been wiped off the organization chart. The hierarchical, functional organization has given us instead a very large, very rigid, and nearly *dys-functional* form of enterprise.

Maintaining power and control was the driving force of functionalizing business. The three super-functions were designed to be tied together at the top of the pyramid. This executive command-and-control tower was somehow to make sure the entire organization worked together, all moving toward a common goal. Inherent to the notion of functions is the need to specialize. Specialization was driven home by hiring, training, and reward systems all designed to keep employees stuck in their niche in the growing company. The functional organization also looked more efficient. It fit like a velvet glove—the almighty pursuit of economies of scale. Early results, in particular areas like assembly line production, seemed to work wonders. The price of Henry Ford's cookie-cutter Model-Ts, for example, declined for several years running. Functionalizing also produced the first telltale signs of bureaucracy. Communicating up and down longer and longer chains of command was taking more and more memos and meetings.

But overall the functional organization seemed to meet a lot of objectives. Control by a few at the top could be maintained. Specializing would produce high levels of expertise. Economies of scale were possible. And a professional bureaucracy could handle any rough edges. Such a rationally designed organization, it was claimed, could grow bigger and bigger with ever increasing efficiency. Thus was born the pipe dream of infinite economies of scale and mass-produced enterprise. What happened?

A lot—some of it helpful—like driving down the cost of making Model-Ts. But much of it was very bad. Whatever benefits there may be to functionalizing people in enterprise, one of them isn't keeping them focused on the company's customer/product vision. The super functions, like giant glaciers, begin to drift farther and farther apart. The command-and-control executives, instead of knitting it all together for the common good, understandably become much more concerned with the fortunes of their personal piece of the pyramid. So at the end of the day, the number one casualty is the entrepreneur's number one strength—the old-fashioned passion of the craftsman for both customer and product.

The perfectly functionalized company finds itself in the absurd situation of having lifelong product people who wouldn't recognize a customer if they tripped over one. Why? No one ever told the factory workers it was part of their job to be close to the customer. At the same time, the company ends up with dedicated and diligent customer people who have no idea what goes on in the factory. Again, blame shouldn't go to the sales people; in most big companies, they aren't even allowed to visit factories. The sales VP's airtight logic: "There aren't any prospects in there!" And for the administrative people, alienation from both customer and product is extreme. They spend their time passing papers around and going to meetings. The fact is, a shockingly low percentage of employees in large companies have any meaningful involvement with *both* customers and products. Nothing could be further from the entrepreneurial vision of customer/product.

Breaking up real business units into functions and controlling it all from the top still looks terribly efficient on paper. It just hasn't worked out in a world where speed, quality, and cost are all crucial. All the pillars of the modern functional organization have had unintended and unfortunate side effects. Too much control at the top produces inertia at the bottom. An all-out push for economies of scale destroys the personal touch that produces high quality. And professional bureaucracy, the lubricant to keep the gears moving, has become the biggest frozen gear in the place. But nothing has been more devastating than the artificial separation of product and customer. The functional organization has become a proven prescription for creating boredom, building bureaucracy, and killing the spirit of enterprise—in even the best of companies.

Putting Humpty Dumpty Together Again

Today, highly functionalized companies everywhere are trying to put their Humpty Dumpty organizations back together again. The thrust of these efforts is to organize around the real business, not artificial functions: to get product people and customer people back in touch with each other; to re-create customer-driven business units, pursuing a common vision.

The twentieth-century organization model is under attack from all sides. Control at the top has given way to delegation, autonomous units, and a cry to break it up and start over. It's just not possible, from an office in downtown Detroit, to control a General Motors, with $100 billion in sales and close to 800,000 employees. Why would anyone even want to try?

Similarly, the all-out push for economies of scale was an idea that quickly began to dig its own grave. It never worked the way it was supposed to because it was based on a false premise. Giant manufacturing plants are not the most productive because size is not the principal factor. Quality, innovation, and speed turn out to be more critical than scale in attaining overall productivity in manufacturing. To their everlasting chagrin, companies all around the world have found out that "bigger is better" just isn't true. Economy of scale made Model-Ts cheaper for a while—but what does it do for innovation? For employee commitment? For product quality? These are factors the "bigger is better" zealots brushed under the factory floor.

And what has happened to the notion that the professional bureaucracy was going to streamline the whole operation and connect the disparate parts to keep everyone aiming at the same target? You know the answer. Bureaucracy is the biggest nightmare facing the biggest companies. Smart CEOs everywhere are fed up and are making heroic efforts to undo the damage of rampaging bureaucracy.

Yes, there are lots of problems. But none has caused more anguish than trying to figure out how to get the artificial functions back together. How to get the customer people and the product people and even the administrative people to focus on the central issue: "If we don't start making more products that more customers will buy, we're all going to be history." Of course it's not a new problem. Back in the seventies, the idea was to work around the trouble. This resulted in one of business's true fiascos—the matrix organization. Instead of dismantling the functions, the idea was to wire everyone to everyone else. The solution of multiple bosses—functional, geographic, hierarchical, sideways—brought many a big company to a grinding halt.

The change today is that almost nobody is trying to save the functional method of organizing. Even the diehards are ready to throw in the towel. New organization charts are popping up, with all manner of lines and arrows that follow the actual processes of work, from R&D to customer service. This return to the real world forces the reconnecting of the old walled-off functions. It's a giant step in the right direction. Of course there are also some nutty moves being made to keep up with the times like upside-down charts to show how much more important customers are than executives. The big company efforts to regroup range from commonsense, customer-driven strategies all the way down to warmed over pap from the PR department. As always, it's a good idea to separate the serious from the silly. Let's look at a few of the more interesting cases.

▪ ICI

The Australian manager of the ICI explosives business in Taiwan was ecstatic. He said he at last felt that he was in a business with worldwide focus. He was explaining how the giant British chemical company has regrouped around real product/market businesses. If you're a chemist making explosives or a salesman selling them, you're at least both in the same organization: a business that makes and sells explosives around the world. If you're in paints, whether in São Paulo or Sydney, your job fits in somewhere along an organizational line of researching, making, shipping, selling, and servicing paints. You're part of a worldwide paint business. This represents a big change from ICI's previous geographic/functional organization chart—nothing radical perhaps, but a commonsense step in the right direction.

▪ Caterpillar

Caterpillar is attempting to take an even greater turn toward customer/product units. In the nineties the $11 billion company will totally reorganize into thirteen businesses—each based in a Caterpillar factory. Believe it or not, design engineers, manufacturing workers, and marketing people will all be working under one roof. Implicit in this revolutionary shift is Caterpillar's objective of equalizing the status of its factory-production people with its jet-setting marketing types. Given the well-publicized labor strife they've faced, this could turn out to be the biggest benefit of all. It's no secret that the functional organization virtually ensured that the people who made the product, the factory workers, would become second-class citizens. Caterpillar's efforts to put customer and product functions on the same level and in the same building represent a dramatic return to entrepreneurial logic.

▪ General Electric

There's an example a week of companies trying to undo the nightmare of isolating their R&D people, the so-called "lab in the woods" mania that enthralled big business after World War II. The problem hasn't been getting R&D back in touch with the marketplace: These companies are scrambling just to get R&D back in touch with the company.

The *Wall Street Journal* headline trumpets, GE'S LATEST INVENTION: A WAY TO MOVE IDEAS FROM LAB TO MARKET. The thrust seems to be that GE *scientists* have also become GE *salesmen*. They're not selling to real customers, but at least they're selling to the GE people, who have to sell their inventions to the market. The *Journal* story details the new role of a GE researcher, who ". . . sits in a chaotic office surrounded by books on computational logic and esoteric journals, but says, 'I also have to be entrepreneurial.' " The *Journal* optimistically concludes: "GE is turning around the equation of U.S. business. Instead of pushing marketers to come up with ideas and then asking scientists to make them work, the company increasingly gives researchers wide berth to imagine and invent—and then shop the invention around GE's divisions. The result: GE and it's scientist-salesmen regularly manage to transfer technology from the laboratory to the market, a transition that frequently baffles American business." Presumably up to now it had also baffled GE's one thousand eight hundred scientists at their six-hundred-acre "lab in the woods" in upstate New York.

Surely this is a step in the right direction, at a company where any step is worth watching. After all, this is the company that took everything that management science had to offer, including widespread functionalizing, and made it work probably better than any other big company in the world. But when current chairman Jack Welch saw nothing left to take, he simply decided to change course. The story headlined by the *Journal* is only the tip of the iceberg of what Welch is really up to. As *Fortune* reports: "Welch admits that it will take a decade before GE's new culture becomes as hard to change as the one it is supplanting. By then, Welch says, GE's hierarchies could actually wither away: 'Even in a horizontal structure you'll still have product managers, still need accountability,' he says, 'but the lines will blur. The functions will go away, if you will . . . teams will move together from left to right, from product idea to product delivery. . . .' " Amen.

▪ Xerox

Perhaps the most famous case in all business of the disastrous effect of functionalizing and separating product people and customer people is Xerox. Its Palo Alto Research Center (PARC), founded in 1970, virtually paved the golden road to the modern computer industry. The only trouble was, very little of the gold ended up in Xerox hands. Everyone knows that in the seventies PARC invented the Alto, the world's first personal computer, and never marketed it. But the complete list of technologies created by PARC that made others rich is truly astonishing. The following examples are enough to make any Xerox shareholder cry:

A SAMPLING OF TECHNOLOGIES
CONCEIVED AT XEROX PARC*

TECHNOLOGY	LATER DEVELOPED BY
Modern chip-making technology	VLSI Technology
Silicon compilers for chip design	Silicon Compilers
Portable computing	Grid Systems
Bit-mapped screen displays	I.B.M., Apple Computer
Mouse and icon-based computing	Apple
Laser printers	Hewlett-Packard, Apple
Drawing tables	Koala
Ethemet office network	3Com
Graphics computing and computer animation	Pixar
Database retrieval systems	Metaphor Computer
"What you see is what you get" word processing	Microsoft
Smalltalk language, object-oriented programming for computers	Park Place Systems, Digitalk
Postscript language used in high-end printers, especially for desktop publishing and typesetting	Adobe Systems

How did this happen? Here's a hint. When PARC developed the Alto, Xerox marketing executives, sitting three thousand miles away at the Stamford, Connecticut, HQ, simply refused to market it. The customer folks refused to sell what the product folks had been working on for years. If R&D and marketing couldn't get together on the hottest electronic product since TV, the rest of the list is easy to understand. The one thing everyone can now agree on is that "Xerox's management never fully grasped the implications of personal computing and the company was quickly relegated to the sidelines when the International Business Machines Corporation introduced its PC in 1981."*

* *The New York Times* (sec. 3), 6 October 1991, 6.

Tens of billions of lost sales later, what is Xerox doing about it? Under new CEO Paul Allaire, Xerox is trying to recoup its losses and get everyone marching to a new drumbeat. Or should we say the old drumbeat? The entrepreneurial rhythm that inspired Chester Carlson back in 1946 when he made and sold the world's first photocopier—and that produced the customer/product vision Xerox has been living off ever since. Allaire says he's the man to do it: "We changed a lot in the 1980s, but in the next five years we'll have to change so much it will make the last ten look like a practice run." Aiming for the jugular of the functionalizing that has caused so much trouble in the past, Allaire promises "to take a hammer to the bureaucratic walls that keep R&D, marketing, and manufacturing from capitalizing on each other's innovations. After all, why shouldn't Xerox exploit its own ideas as successfully as outsiders did?" He seems to really believe that everyone in Xerox has an ultimate duty to satisfy customers. Some call it a cliché, but Paul Allaire sees it as the way to get everyone on the same wavelength: "You can't get people to focus on only the bottom line. You have to give them an objective like 'satisfy the customer' that everyone can relate to. It's the only way to break down those barriers and get people from different functions working together." Amen again.

Paul Allaire, like CEOs Henderson at ICI, Fites of Caterpillar, and Welch at GE, is one of those coming-of-age CEOs who is not part of the problem. Allaire didn't invent the functional organization nor did he build the Xerox lab in the woods in Palo Alto. He isn't saddled with pride of authorship in the system. But he did have to grow up in the system and work around the structure to get things done. So like his counterparts, he's ready, willing, and finally able to change it.

Well, at least ready and willing. Able may be a bit tougher. Xerox is not alone in this challenge, but it illustrates the point painfully well. Solving old problems like connecting PARC to marketing (and some say the real world) is going to take more than hoisting "spirit of enterprise" flags in Stamford and Palo Alto. True enough, Xerox has put a few marketing people in the research center. And Xerox's mainline copier business is rapidly moving up the hi-tech chain where PARC's contribution could be useful. But beneath the PR stories and the sincere pronouncements at the top, big troubles remain deep in the organization. This may be a case where dismantling, right down to the foundation, is called for.

For starters, PARC is still in laid-back Palo Alto, and the marketing chiefs are still in pin-striped Stamford, three thousand miles away. Palo Alto may be too close to Big Sur and Stamford may be too close to the New York Stock Exchange—but the real question is how close is either one of them to the customer? Marketing questions and critics abound. For nearly fifty years, the Xerox sales force has been selling straightforward office equipment like photocopiers and typewriters. This is the same sales force that had America's first fax machine, the Telecopier, way back in the sixties and couldn't sell it. I remember using it at American Express in the late sixties. We thought it was a great product but gave up trying to use it because apparently no one else in the world had bought one so we could only fax ourselves. Has anything changed? That's a big question, as the *New York Times* points out: "William Lowe, who led I.B.M.'s personal computer business before becoming head of product development at Xerox in 1989, says it is still unclear whether Xerox can market its digital innovations. Earlier this year, Mr. Lowe left Xerox to become president of the Gulfstream Corporation, a maker of business jets. 'An integration has taken place that will allow Xerox to get PARC's technology into products,' he said. 'The real issue is from a marketing and sales perspective. How do you sell systems to customers instead of copiers?' "

And one last but definitely not least question hangs in the air: What in the world are they really doing out there in sunny Palo Alto for the Xerox bottom line? In spite of Paul Allaire's straight talk, the news from PARC is more than a little fuzzy. It comes courtesy of that great chronicler of fuzzy business ideas, the *Harvard*

Business Review. In a long "research knows best" article, the world got an inside glimpse into the "new PARC" from its director, John Seely Brown. He states his case in the opening paragraph of "Research That Reinvents the Corporation": "The most important invention that will come out of the corporate research lab in the future will be the corporation itself. As companies try to keep pace with rapid changes in technology and cope with increasingly unstable business environments, the research department has to do more than simply innovate new products. It must design the new technological and organizational 'architectures' that make possible a continuously innovating company. Put another way, corporate research must reinvent innovation." Who could blame Xerox shareholders, presumably of average intelligence, if they confess to not having the foggiest idea of what Brown is talking about? We learn that PARC is now hiring anthropologists, sociologists, linguists, and psychologists, to join in its mission of analyzing and reinventing Xerox. After eight pages of research-ese, Brown throws a crumb to the customer: "The logical end point of all the activities I have described is for corporate research to move outside the company and work with customers." Predictably, an avalanche of "Letters to the Editor" showed up in the next *HBR* issue—not from businessmen, of course, but from professors, consultants, and other researchers. Even this group of R&D gurus found the article to be, shall we say, controversial. The critique that hit the enterprise nail on the head: "Better yet, if I were the CEO of Xerox and wanted to harness Brown's ideas to *really* reinvent the corporation, I would get him out of Xerox PARC pronto and give him a division to run." Paul Allaire, are you listening?

The bets are he is. The real hope for the future is that it was Allaire who identified the "customer/product vision" problem at Xerox. This is the best reason to think PARC's enormous brainpower and Xerox's mighty sales and service force will start living in the same universe. If anyone can, Paul Allaire will get the Xerox Humpty Dumpty back together again.

▪Toyota

The irony of it all is that it never had to come to this. There are some very large companies that never fell sway to the "functionalize everything" craze. Or if they did functionalize, nobody was ever allowed to forget they were all serving the same master—the customer. Take a look at Toyota, which never fell off the wall.* This agility has paid off handsomely. Judged against any standard in the industry, Toyota is simply the best car maker in the world. Their operating margins are the highest. They can assemble a car in thirteen hours versus about twenty for Honda, Nissan, and Ford (GM is farther behind). They regularly match or beat Mercedes quality using one-sixth the labor of their luxury-class competitor. And a completely built-to-order car can be in the hands of the customer in an amazing week to ten days. Nobody else even comes close.

What's the secret of their success? It can all be laid to the customer/product vision of Eiji Toyoda. He started making cars in 1933 and assumed that the car business, like any other enterprise, had to be built around customers. From design to after-sale service, the customer called the shots. To its eternal credit, postwar Toyota didn't look at U.S. automakers for organizational guidance—it looked at U.S. supermarkets. What founder Toyoda and his legendary production boss, Taiichi Ohno, saw was that American supermarkets were operating in a lightning-fast turnover environment where customers literally pulled products through the company. This was the system they wanted. They called it *kanban*, or just-in-time production.

Much has been made of Toyota's total dedication to *kanban*. As with quality-control circles before it, big companies everywhere rushed to install this latest Japanese management technique. And just as imitation QC circles missed the forest and crashed into trees,

---

* Toyota makes an excellent, positive example. That's why I used them. However, this isn't another Japanese "cultural" advantage. There is ample evidence today that most Japanese managers, finally confronted with truly giant companies, don't have any more of a clue than Americans or Europeans on how to keep these behemoths entrepreneurial.

so has *kanban*. Somehow it got translated as an inventory control system between suppliers and plants. Part of the answer may be that Ohno's classic book on *kanban* wasn't even translated into English until 1990. *Kanban* is not a technique. It's a mind-set that customers truly drive every aspect of the business. You get organized at every step of the car-making and -selling process to jump when your customer speaks. The process becomes a series of suppliers/customers, reaching at the end the car buyer kicking the tires at the dealer's showroom. It's something like pulling a gallon of fresh milk out of the dairy counter that starts a chain reaction all the way back to the cow. Whether it's cows making milk or people making cars, *kanban* produces just what the customer wants, at just the right time.

This mind-set makes it a little difficult to get too excited about functional prerogatives. And it makes it impossible for design people to disregard production people, and for production people to disregard marketing people, and so on. Obviously Toyota is organized. Individuals and groups have specific tasks to perform. But the *kanban* culture, constantly tracking the customer, overrides the entire organization. Toyota's famous *chief engineer system*, for example, specifies that all new models have a chief with enormous authority from design to production through marketing of the new model. The system is a technique, but it's a technique created and driven by the mind-set that says we're all ready to jump together when our customer speaks. This is what keeps Toyota's Humpty Dumpty up on the wall.

The Customer/Product Mind-Set— from Londonderry to Tokyo to Orlando

Before you rip up your organization chart, bring in *kanban* consultants, or appoint any chief engineers, be sure, as Eiji Toyoda was, that you know what you're trying to accomplish. In the interests of cultural diversity, and to prove a point, let's take a quick tour of the entrepreneurial mind-set around the world, beginning in the unlikely town of Londonderry in troubled Northern Ireland.

▪ In Londonderry

The most fun being with Denis Desmond in Northern Ireland comes at the end of the day. That's when his executives and managers and everyone else forget their problems and crank up their songs. And the most amazing thing is that every single person at Desmond & Sons in Londonderry has a great voice! Fortunately, singing isn't the only thing they're great at. Denis Desmond's company also makes great products—garments for the world's greatest retailer, Marks & Spencer. Desmond is one of those famous sole suppliers to M&S. The same M&S that was using *kanban* and *keiretsu* long before Eiji Toyoda saw his first supermarket. Desmond's story is about being a smashing success with the most demanding customer you'll ever know—and against the most ferocious competitors, all those other famous M&S suppliers.

As he is every week, Denis Desmond was in London seeing M&S. Over the best French meal I'd ever had, the articulate but modest man from Londonderry told his story: "I think that probably one thing that is quite unique about our business is that we only have one customer. That, in a sense, makes it much easier for me to actually find out what my customer requires and what he needs. I say that because, if you are running a business even of our size, and you've got hundreds of customers, it's a very different situation than the one I'm in, where I carry very accurate information of what's selling and what's not selling, what my customer is looking for and even what he thinks he is looking for. One states the obvious in saying, any business ultimately succeeds if it provides high-quality customer service. But sometimes actually identifying who your customer is and speaking to him and getting feedback from him can be quite difficult. Very often you only find out when something goes wrong. For us, in that sense, it's much easier.

"But overall, having one customer doesn't make the job easy. The fact is you may be in a situation where the one customer says, well, jump through that hoop, and you aren't left with very much of a choice are you? You might actually want to do something else. Obviously, I'm simplifying the situation a bit. I think the Japanese system [*keiretsu*, a company's network of sole suppliers] is probably the obvious parallel. Marks & Spencer has been practicing that for several generations now. In the past, sometimes people might have felt the relationship between M&S and their suppliers, say ourselves, was somewhat maternalistic or protective. I think that it's not in reality like that at all. It's hard work. But nevertheless, it gives you a very definite objective."

Fair enough, but how does the system actually work? Are you guaranteed business? And what about those competitors? "Well, clearly it's an extremely competitive environment. We have competitors we could lose the business to every season. Every season we produce a range of new styles—new ideas, which reflect what we believe, are what M&S should be selling. Our own suppliers are invited to do the same thing. Of course in that situation, inevitably, you don't always come up with what is conceived to be the best garment. However, I don't think the amount of business we do with M&S purely depends on that. If it did, we would be in a potential situation where in one season you could win all, and the next season you might win nothing. The relationship is much more complex. It's based not just on the product that you design, but on the fact that you are linked into a very fast and sophisticated system of manufacturing with distribution going directly to individual stores. So the design, the quality of the product, the speed and output, the direct distribution and the price you choose are all very important. It is the combination of all of these things.

"I don't know how the Japanese do it, but we certainly don't have any contract saying all right, next year we guarantee we will take so much from you. But there is a very strong element of trust. A lot of it is based on relationships which have been built between individuals, between companies, over a long period of time. We really do see ourselves in partnership. There is no financial ownership in our company by M&S. There is no guarantee that they will fill our factories. But nevertheless, we have a high degree of confidence in our ability to give them what they are looking for on a long-term basis."

Marks & Spencer does have a reputation of being a very tough customer in terms of quality and price. I asked Denis if he thought that put a special strain on suppliers like Desmond & Sons: "First of all, M&S is certainly a very demanding customer, but they are also an extremely fair customer. To me they are the best customer in the world. First, they must reflect the demands of their customers who come into their stores, and we must not forget that M&S has a tremendous reputation with their customers. They are regarded as offering exceptional value in terms of price and quality. And remember, if the customer has a complaint and brings a garment back to the store, they take back all merchandise with no questions asked. So M&S has this tremendous reputation that we must be completely geared to. So M&S is very fair *and* they are very demanding, but that isn't in any way a negative thing. I think it's a very positive thing. They are demanding in that they're looking for a very high product quality consistency. They are looking for us to make it right, make it on time, and deliver it on time. So those are the things we have to constantly strive for. There is no room for complacency. Of that I can assure you!"

I knew Desmond & Sons was quite old, and I asked about their pre-M&S history. The answer was surprising. Desmond described a person who must have been one of the earliest female entrepreneurs in Great Britain: "My grandmother started the business in 1885. It was obviously a very small operation at that time and indeed for quite a few years. She used to go in her pony and trap once a week into Londonderry, which was about eight miles from the village of Claudy, where she lived. She collected cut shirts from one of the many shirt factories and distributed them around cottages to have girls make them up in their homes. After a number of years doing this, my grandmother decided to get the girls to come and work in her home and save her going up all those bumpy country lanes. In those days the girls provided their own sewing machines! But anyway, that's how it all started.

"Also, my grandmother had twelve children. That in itself was a full-time job, so I think she must have been quite dynamic. My grandmother died when she was only forty-six or forty-seven, in 1913. The business essentially was then run by my father, the second eldest in the family, and my uncle, his youngest brother. I joined the business in 1963, so I'm now the third generation. I probably came into the business for all of the wrong reasons. I was about eighteen and very keen to go to the university. In fact I was about to sit an entrance exam for Oxford to study history when my father became quite ill. Well, I didn't go to Oxford and I came into the business with no business training.

"So we have been established for a very long time, but I think the real growth has taken place in the last twenty to twenty-five years. When I joined the company in 1963, we had between three hundred and four hundred employees on one site at Claudy. We only made pajamas. Today we employ something like twenty-seven hundred staff and we have nine factories in Northern Ireland. In addition we source about 20 percent of our production in the Far East. We have our own office in Hong Kong and we are dealing with suppliers in Korea, Thailand, Indonesia, and Taiwan. Today menswear is still our core business, but we have a childrenswear division and we recently went into womenswear. Last year we did £10.5 million turnover in womenswear, and two years ago we did nothing. I was talking to one of our accountants Tuesday. He was saying when he joined the company fourteen years ago, our total turnover was £4 million. Last year it was over £90 million!

"Desmond's was already a seventy-five-year-old company when it decided to go 100 percent with M&S. It was my father and uncle who made the decision by 1960 to close something like one hundred customer accounts and put all of their eggs into one basket. At that time Marks & Spencer were one of the big names, but certainly they weren't the dominant force in retailing that they are today.

My father used to say that there was a time, in the forties or even before the war, when various factories would close the door on M&S and refuse to supply them. They would say who are these upstarts? You see M&S really pioneered in the forties and fifties the whole idea of buying to a specification. Up to that time, retailers like M&S bought what was available. But M&S said, this is what we require. This is our specification. This is the quality of fabric we need and these are the interlinings. Everything. It was a very new concept at the time and not every manufacturer was prepared to undertake it."

Such an undertaking must have given brand-new meaning to the adage "the customer comes first." I asked Desmond how he managed the company in such an environment and what he did in a typical week: "Well, I suppose that I spend a relatively small percent of time at board meetings or formal meetings and such things. That represents at the very outside, half a day a week. I sometimes convince myself that my powers of concentration for long meetings are somewhat limited—as a way for them not to happen. I do believe in two things. I think it is important for me to have a high profile with my customer. So I spend a lot of time visiting their offices on Baker Street. I talk to the management, talk to their buyers, finding out what is going on. I would say that works out on an average of between one and two days a week.

"The rest of the time is taken up by practicing what you might call MBWA [managing by wandering around], which is having a profile with the employees of the company. We have nine plants and I try to get around to all of them at least once every two or three weeks. I really think it's important that I'm visible to my employees. I think it is also important that when I go to the plants I talk to people and supervisors on the shop floor. I suppose in a way it's a PR-type job in terms of, you know, patting on the back. But I also take a great interest in the products that they are making and the product standards, which are so important to us. I take a look at the garments on the floor. I take them into the office. I check them. Just like M&S buyers would when they come to the factory, you know, with a tape line and all. All of that is very important."

If my math is right, Desmond's typical week works out to maybe 40 percent of the time with the customer, 50 percent with his people making the products, and 10 percent in traditional managing. That's what a strong customer/product mind-set will do for you: keep you focused on customers and products and the people who make them.

Desmond & Sons has grown rapidly over the past couple of decades. They've taken large, new chunks of market share within Marks & Spencer. How have they done it? You can probably guess: "Well, I think we have set our sights to provide them with a very high quality of product and service, in some cases better than our competitors. I think that because we come from a fairly small and I think still very entrepreneurial type of company, we react more quickly to what they can sell. I suppose that one of the dangers of getting much bigger is that one becomes less responsive to the customer and, in that sense, less entrepreneurial. With other companies coming up aiming at the same thing, we have to be very conscious about that. I think, almost by definition, that as organizations get bigger they get less efficient.

"We are in a situation that is constantly changing and we have to be prepared to act very, very quickly. If we produce a garment which doesn't sell, we have to deal with that situation today. If General Motors produces a car which doesn't sell, well, it probably takes them months to actually find out that it isn't selling. We don't have that problem. We know very, very quickly and we have to start doing something about it immediately."

That's how it works in Londonderry. We can question over and over whether working for one customer is more or less demanding than working for many. But if that one customer is Marks & Spencer—by far the most demanding retailer in the world—one thing has to be clear. Their most successful suppliers, like Desmond & Sons, come to the table with a ton of what bureaucracies desperately need—an all-consuming customer/product mind-set.

▪ In Tokyo

"Nola & Dola" in Japanese translates as the needs of ladies and the desires of ladies. It's also the company slogan of Uni-Charm Corporation, one of Japan's fastest-growing, independent companies. Founder and CEO Keiichiro Takahara has created an amazing record of producing products that meet the needs and desires of Japanese women. Like Eiji Toyoda before him, he too was fascinated by American supermarkets. But he didn't see a better way to produce cars. What he saw in 1963 was a coming revolution in the buying habits of Japanese women. He put his paper business on the back burner and hit on an old entrepreneurial strategy to become the Unilever and Procter & Gamble of Japan.

Takahara is a handsome and exquisitely attired CEO. He's also absolutely clear on his customer/product vision. He should be. He says he spends 365 days a year thinking about what product the ladies will need and desire next. This laser-sharp focus on products and customers is what gives him a commanding market share with every major product he introduces. He makes it sound so simple: "What does the customer need? What does the customer want? Our entire company thinks about this always. Customer needs or market wants change so quickly, every day, day by day. If we do not know these changes, the company will have the wrong strategy."

But figuring out what the ladies need is only half the battle. Making it better than anyone else is the clincher: "Take disposable diapers, for example. Procter & Gamble was always number one here with Pampers. They introduced the idea of disposable diapers to Japan. They shipped them in from the United States. Now I have tremendous respect for P&G, but I knew if we worked hard enough, we could make a better disposable diaper. We introduced our brand, Moony, in 1981, and it immediately became number one in Japan, which it still is today."

This sounded too easy so I had to find out exactly what he meant by "work hard enough." His assistant, Koji Shima, explained: "At that time, the market in Japan was not too big really.

So P&G shipped their product from the States. It was really made for the American market. But we knew our market was changing rapidly from cotton diapers to paper. So our researchers studied Pampers very, very carefully. And we surveyed Japanese mothers on how the Pamper could be improved. From this we did two things: We added polymer, which absorbed water better than the paper and pulp in the Pamper, and we made it just a bit smaller. You know a Japanese baby is smaller than an American and the Pamper didn't fit very well. That's all we did. But this is the strength of our company. We didn't make an entirely new product or market, but our researchers studied our competitor's products very, very carefully and we made a better product for the customer than our competitor. This is our marketing strategy. We are always looking for small markets with big potential, like disposable diapers."

Is there a message here for the folks in Detroit who are still trying to export left-hand-drive cars to Tokyo? The centuries-old technique of giving your customers something better than your competitor is alive and well in Japan, at least in Uni-Charm markets. One by one, Uni-Charm offerings such as diapers and feminine hygiene products have taken the number one market share in Japan. But this isn't another Japanese-is-always-best story. If Takahara can't come up with a better product, he happily imports the best. Example: In an extension of Nola & Dola, Takahara thought canned or packaged dog food would be a great convenience for housewives and a winning new product. He determined he couldn't make a better product than the existing Japanese competitors, so he recently signed a deal to import Alpo from America. Sales are growing quickly, and Alpo already has the second largest share of the market.

This extreme focus on really giving the customer the best has pushed Uni-Charm revenues near the $1 billion mark. And most of their markets are rapidly expanding with the changing life-styles of Japanese women. At the end of my visit, the dapper Mr. Takahara also "confessed" to another American "product" that has contributed to his business growth. I couldn't help but notice in the office a Uni-Charm poster ad featuring Brooke Shields. Smiling, Takahara said, "Oh yes, she also helps." Shima, the ever-present elaborator, couldn't help adding, "It's just more Nola & Dola. Japanese women also want to be beautiful!"

Uni-Charm's success doesn't come from luck. It comes from the founder thinking about customers and products every day of the year. So who in your company should be thinking about customers and products? The answer—everyone. From CEOs to clerks, everyone has a product or service to provide to a customer. Some deal directly with real, external customers. Others provide services for another employee or department—an internal customer or user. So everyone has a mini-business to run that ties into the corporation's overall customer/product vision. Management's job is to keep this vision alive—to create the mind-set that everyone in the company has a product to offer and a customer to satisfy.

▪In Orlando

Even a small movement in this direction can have enormous impact. There is one step any company can take, anytime, which is practically guaranteed to produce that all-important initial change in attitude: start treating employees as businesspeople, not salesmen or scientists or clerks. It's straight talk, designed to get managers and workers out of their functional pigeonholes and back to the business of enterprise.

Disney lays it out simply for employees in Orlando: "While a department may not deal directly with the public, it is imperative that each department within an organization view its customer or 'public' as the person/people who actually benefit from the service of that department. For example, at the Walt Disney World Vacation Kingdom, the wardrobe department's actual 'client' is not the guest, but the host and hostess who will be interacting with that guest. Or, the accounting department can view their 'clients' as a variety of internal departments. The people in any department might be three or four layers removed from the guest who purchases a Magic Kingdom Park passport. Nonetheless, their attitudes toward service will ultimately affect the quality of service the guest receives—a real domino effect!"*

You can get started by deep-sixing all those convoluted, five-page job descriptions. They just confuse the issue. Replace them with the three questions entrepreneurs live and die by. Call it a "Personal Business Plan." The message is: We all have a business to run. All businesses have customers and products. Therefore you have customers and products. And as with any businessperson, your reward (or lack thereof) will be based on how well you meet your customer's needs. So everyone, from senior manager to salesman to scientist to clerk, has to be absolutely clear on what their products are, who their customers are, and what they have to do to satisfy their customers.

GETTING BACK TO BUSINESS

Personal Business Plan

	INTERNAL CUSTOMERS	EXTERNAL CUSTOMERS
Who are my customers/users?		
What are my products/services?		
What are the standards I must meet to satisfy my customer? • quality • quantity • etc.		

* *Service, Disney Style*, Walt Disney Company, (undated), p. 5.

The number of people "in business" who can't figure out the answers to these three simple questions can be shocking. For some managers and workers in some big companies, such straight business talk will create a totally new mind-set of what their job is all about. Of course, this is the point. This first modest step may not instill the customer/product obsession of Disney or Benz or Toyoda. But for many big companies, it could be a giant leap away from the choke hold of the functional-turned-dysfunctional organization, leading salesmen, scientists, and even bureaucrats back to the basics of enterprise.

Growing the Old-fashioned Way—
with Great Products and
Great Customers

More products to more customers used to be the only way a company could grow. But a lot has happened since we all went to business school. There are a lot of ways to grow today. Mergers, acquisitions, selling assets, and pushing accounting rules to the limit are some of the favorites. In a good year of price inflation, you can get an extra 5 to 10 percent "growth" too—at least on the revenue side. And the 1980s gave us the ultimate double-speak growth artists with the arrival of the asset strippers, those quintessential enterprisers of leveraged buyout fame, most of whom are now sinking in the quicksand of their own debt. And of course some big companies have simply given up on growth altogether. The favorite strategy here is to make a virtue out of not growing. With great fanfare, companies "de-mass" or return to the "core business," a couple of corporate euphemisms for running out of steam. In a classic "same clowns, new circus" routine, it's never quite explained why massing and diversification were such smart strategies last decade—but now it's even smarter to do the opposite.

The old-fashioned way of growing is easier to understand: All you have to do is make more products and sell more customers. To do this you don't need M&A specialists, investment bankers, lawyers, or accountants. But you do have to know the answers to a couple of very important questions: "Can I make it and can I sell it?" Entrepreneurs grow by being able to figure this out—by knowing the straightforward facts about customer needs and their competitive product position. Since they can't afford a $10 million market research budget plus five years to design the product, they keep their ears to the ground and their questions simple. Something like these:

Making Products	Selling Customers
Can I Make It Cheaper and Better?	Can I find them?
At Least Better?	Can I sell them?
At Least Cheaper?	Can I service them?

Sure it's not very sophisticated. You want sophisticated, go to General Motors. Their market research process alone has over six hundred steps!* You want results in a hurry try the simple questions. Get these right, and you're at least in the game. Your final score is going to depend on just one more little question: "How much do you care?"

---

* Is it any wonder that GM is never first to market with anything? If you're now frantic to learn the six hundred steps, read "The Market Research Encyclopedia," written by GM's director of market research and planning. Where can you find it? Need you ask? In the *Harvard Business Review*, Jan/Feb. 1990.

"My Customer, My Product, My Self-respect"

Driving old-fashioned growth are some old-fashioned ideas. The most basic is that entrepreneurs are driven by visions of products and customers. But professional managers are driven by visions of running a business—any business. This seemingly semantic difference, between entrepreneuring and managing, masks a profoundly different view of the world. It blurs over the entrepreneur's near fanatic devotion to his customers and products. At the core of the entrepreneur's love affair with customers and products is a very old idea. The craftsman called it "pride."

Entrepreneurs embrace the craftsman's motto: "My product, my customer, my self-respect." They make the product and they sell it to the customer. This one-two step gives rise to the most powerful emotion in all enterprise—the anxiety-producing, face-to-face trauma of customer judgment. That judgment is aimed right at the ego of the entrepreneur. It can send you to the heights of glory or it can shatter your self-esteem. It doesn't come as a computer printout. It's not a market research study on product features. It's not about a distant department or someone else in the company. It's about your worth as a craftsman and maybe even your worth as a person. Your ego hangs in the balance. It's the grown-up version of the little girl's first, scratchy violin solo—or the little boy's first, nervous time at bat. And the really scary part is, these moments of truth never go away. Ask any concert violinist or any professional athlete. And so it is for entrepreneurs. The lifelong reality: Their personal pride and their personal shame ride on the quality of every product they make and the reaction of every customer they sell.

What does it take to put pride back into work? The one irreplaceable ingredient: becoming *personally* responsible for products and customers. The entrepreneur's moment of truth, lived a thousand times over—the moment when the customer lets you know how good (or how bad) you really are. That's how to re-instill the craftsman's notion about products and customers. These world-class craftsmen set the standard for us all.

▪Karl Benz

It may take some of Karl Benz's fascination with engines, meshed with his belief that customers deserve real improvements in the product. The notion of turning out a new model every year never occurred to Benz. For him the rule was to turn out a new model when you had significant improvements to offer customers. That's quite a different view of the world from the "planned obsolescence" concept hatched in Detroit many years later.

▪Ray Kroc

It could also require a bit of the traveling salesman's instincts of Ray Kroc (McDonald's), blended with his personal obsession for delivering quality and cleanliness a million times a day. From lowly salesman of milkshake machines to absolute zealot of the clean toilet, Ray Kroc epitomizes the value of keeping your eye on the customer and the product at the same time. Visit the top-volume McDonald's in the world, on Orchard Street in Singapore. You'll see spotless toilets. Visit the McDonald's in one of the grimiest neighborhoods in America, near the entrance to the Lincoln Tunnel. Again, spotless toilets. We'll never know how many billions of Big Macs have been sold just to get at a clean toilet—but you and I could retire on it. And it all comes from knowing what customers want and delivering it over and over again.

▪Soichiro Honda

It may even take some passion. Soichiro Honda was passionate about racing cars. He was no less passionate in his self-annointed mission of providing postwar Japan with much-needed, cheap, and reliable transportation. Designed down to the simplest of machines, the Honda scooter still stands as the modern symbol of giving customers exactly what they want. Meeting simple needs very perfectly may be the first *passionate* lesson of customer/product vision.

▪Charles Forte

And it means never letting up, as Lord Charles Forte continues to demonstrate into his eighties. He may be the world's greatest customer/product "nitpicker" since Thomas Watson of IBM. His sixty-five-year obsession with getting the basics right may be monotonous, but it has one redeeming virtue—if you do it long enough and hard enough, you get very good at it.

Creating an Obsession for Customers and Products

No amount of professional management can replace the entrepreneur's adage: My customer, my product, my self-respect. The success of the business is a defining factor in all entrepreneurs' lives, and they really believe that customers and products are the heart and soul of the enterprise. It's not an overstatement to say they are obsessed with customers and products.

Instilling this obsession in the average worker and making it stick takes big changes in company priorities. And since management, not workers, determines what's important, the changes have to start at the top. When senior management gets deadly serious about customer and product priorities, things start to happen. Simple things that everyone talked about for years and didn't do will take on monumental importance. For example, providing an immediate response to all customer requests. Not soon, not I'll get back to you, but right now! Old-fashioned courtesy will no longer be a rare event; it will be the only way customers will ever be treated. Individual worker responsibility for quality will become the norm, not a pipe dream of the quality program coordinator.

No compromises on quality will even be suggested, let alone tolerated. Endless product planning will be replaced by a true sense of urgency in producing real inventions that meet real needs. And ultimately, the cardinal sin, maybe the only sin in the business, will be to lose a current customer. You don't need a Ph.D. in business to figure these things out. They're all commonsense ideas. Many large companies do some of these things some of the time. The entrepreneurial mandate is that all employees must do all these things all the time.

Confucius Says, "Get Yourself in Order"

Getting all employees to do all these things all the time is possible. A visit to fast-moving DHL Asia/Pacific shows how. I've known Po Chung for a little over ten years. Before 1989 the first thing I always noticed displayed in his office was the DHL mission statement. On my most recent visit, I was taken aback by an additional statement of purpose prominently framed and hung on the wall. This was a very personal statement: a full-page advertisement in the *London Times*, written and paid for by Po, denouncing the Tiananmen Square massacre. This was an extremely brave act for a Hong Kong Chinese businessman. Po Chung is, if nothing else, a man ready and willing to set a personal example. Certainly this is how he helped found and expand DHL International. He signed on way back in 1972, when Dalsey, Hillblom, and Lynn were just starting. He was to be the entrepreneur of the Hong Kong business and the manager across Asia as it grew. His story is a great example of creating and maintaining an obsession for customers and products.

Lesson one from Po Chung is to personally feel the need for the product. Po had never heard of DHL, but when he first met Dalsey in Hong Kong, he already knew why Hong Kong companies needed this service: "At that time I was the operations manager for a big U.S. toy company in Hong Kong. We were exporting toys from Asia to the United States. We were the first company to use the whole of Asia as one factory: doll orders here, dress material orders there, Japanese material sewed in Taiwan, dressed on the dolls in Hong Kong. So all of the documents had to flow very smoothly. I was pulling my hair out just trying to figure out which shipment was coming in, whether it was coming in by air, and whether the documents were right and so on. The head office was in Elizabeth, New Jersey, and I was the guy who was chasing after the problems. So when Dalsey talked about a one-day service to the States, I realized that if I spent so much time chasing documents, and my secretary, shipping manager, and shipping clerk spent so much time chasing documents, there must be a lot of people in Hong Kong doing the same thing."

The second lesson is to personally provide the product to the customers. "Dalsey only stayed for three days and left town. Twenty-eight days later I quit my job with the toy company. I was really on my own. Every day I would go to the customer, the only customer, American Express, pick up about fifteen kilos of materials, take a public bus—didn't have a car—down to the North Point Ferry, ride on the bottom part because on the top part they will not let you take parcels, get to the other side, a mile and a half from the airport, jump on one of the little buses, go to the cargo terminal, and ship it all. Then I would eat lunch over there and wait for the incoming material to be cleared. It was usually cleared about one-thirty or two o'clock. Then I would take it down to American Express, deliver it by about two-forty-five or three o'clock, and then go make some sales calls. I started from the ground level. I had only one employee, who was my accountant and who also answered the phone, took messages, and so on. We shared a two-hundred-square foot office."

Lesson three—don't get sidetracked by management theories. "Lynn took more of the accountant-type viewpoint. He said this company will go bankrupt or go 'kaput' in six months because of cash flow. Of course, this made perfect sense to Lynn. There were so many times we were on the brink of going bankrupt. We didn't because we owed people a lot of money. Cathay cut us off, but Pan Am couldn't cut us off because we owed them too much money—$2 million. I kept going, maybe because I was not trained as a business major. I didn't know all those pitfalls. If I had been an MBA, I probably wouldn't have been able to go on because I would have been worrying about this and that. I'd have been spending all my time doing my business plan instead of calling up customers."

Lesson four is about the philosophy, or the company mission. "But Dalsey and Hillblom were philosophers. And so was I. If you prick entrepreneurs, you will find philosophies. The guy in particular who has to introduce a whole new product has to have a product philosophy. IBM is a philosophy. Apple, UPS, and Federal Express are philosophies. And a philosophy has to be held true not only at the top but all the way down to the guy on the floor. It goes from top to bottom. It's like Confucianism. The good side of Confucianism is, it gives you a set of directions about how leaders should work and behave. Rule number one is get yourself in order. Rule number two, get your family in order, then get your clan in order, then get your country in order, and then your empire. Now, big enterprises lose their way when that philosophy becomes ambiguous, and people can't identify with it anymore. Or one part of the company is going one way and another part is interpreting the same set of rules another way—then you have problems. Then they have shaken the glue—the culture or the glue that holds that company together—particularly in a global business like ours."

Lesson five is to pass lessons one through four on to your people. Po Chung goes to extraordinary lengths to drive home the philosophy of DHL, to put visceral meaning into the first point of the worldwide mission statement: "Absolute dedication to understanding and fulfilling our customers' needs with the appropriate mix of service, reliability, products, and price for each customer." Po explains this customer/product vision and how he communicates it: "For a long time we didn't even call them customers. Before we had any marketing people we called them our clients. It's natural to call them clients because you are with them on a daily basis. You provide them with a service. We see ourselves as service providers—like lawyers or accountants. If our client is in trouble, we are in trouble. If he loses money, *we* lose. We feel the twenty thousand dollars of interest they lose if we delay a big package of checks. We feel that it's *our* twenty thousand dollars that was lost. This is what we tell our crew. We say, 'Don't look at that as a package. It is worth twenty thousand dollars a day when you deliver it. If you waylay it for forty-five minutes and miss the plane, that is twenty thousand dollars for our client, or a twenty-thousand-dollar port fine for one of the ships of our clients awaiting documents.' Basically, people would not use our service unless a lot is at stake. And they pay us a premium to transport it, right? If we are late, they are in trouble, whether it's missing a tender, twenty thousand dollars of extra port fees, or twenty thousand dollars a day for twenty-five thousand checks.

"To make this real, the client comes into our training sessions to talk with our couriers and our supervisors. Say the client is a bank. Well, one of their people tells our people: 'We buy canceled checks from the local banks who are *our* customers. They get the checks from tourists, business executives, and Hong Kong factories who get paid by overseas check. There are seven of us here competing for the business. Republic Bank of New York, First Boston, First Chicago, American Express International Bank—we are all competing for this business. Our customers give us the checks, and if we lose money, they lose money. And it all depends on how fast DHL moves the checks. This is how it calculates up; we send X millions worth of canceled checks each day. One day of interest is so much. That is how much you are saving us each day, every day. So by the end of the year, you will have saved us 365 times that. Believe me, this is the only reason we are using DHL.' So if the question is how to pass on DHL's mission, a lot of it is like this. Repeating the same thing over and over."

Po Chung's approach to business isn't Japanese. It isn't American or European. It isn't even Chinese. It's universal entrepreneurship. It's getting personally obsessed with what's important. You might even call it "loving" your customers and products. It's a worthy challenge for any big company.

"Loving" the Customer

I solemnly promise and declare that every customer that comes within ten feet of me, I will smile, look them in the eye, and greet them, so help me Sam.
—Employee pledge, SAM WALTON, founder, Wal-Mart stores

Loving customers comes from seeing them as the only means of putting food on the table. It's hard to hate people who do that for you. It also comes from appreciating those people who admire and use your own product or service. It's also hard to dislike people who admire your work. None of this means entrepreneurs are more friendly or treat their fellow humans any better than you do. But when it comes to customers, they do have a very special feeling for them. Their behavior toward customers comes as much from the heart as it does from the head. Of all the entrepreneurial behaviors practiced around customers, here are four of the most important.

▪Knowing Your Product

Almost always, the first thing you notice about entrepreneurs' behavior toward their customers is that it's all related to how the customer feels about the product. So loving your customer, at least in the entrepreneurial sense, has everything to do with knowing your product! What kind of concern for the customer are you showing if you can't even explain how and why your product will solve his problem?

There's a practical point to be made here. No one really wants to see or talk to a salesman. People go to extraordinary lengths to avoid them. Even if people have a problem, they're hard to nail down for a sales call. This may disappoint the professional salesmen of the world, but it's a fact. Whom do people (prospects) want to talk to? Well, they seem to enjoy talking to their family and friends, a circle that few salesmen will break into. And if they have a problem, people want to talk to an expert on how to fix the problem. Think about what you do when you choose a doctor, or want to buy a car, or need outside help to solve a business problem. Whom would you want to see? An expert, of course. Someone who really knows the ins and outs of solving your problem. Certainly not a salesman—no matter how friendly he is, or how many lunches he might buy. If you're like most people, you'd clear your calendar in a second to get your hands on a real product expert. This may be the best reason of all why knowing your product is the first step in loving your customer.

▪Responding Immediately

The most startling difference between entrepreneurs and big company bureaucrats is in how quickly they respond to customers. This is one area where it doesn't matter if the company is Japanese, European, or American. They all can be, and often are, slow in responding. Think of the last five times you made a complaint to a manufacturer. How long did it take them to resolve your complaint? Are you still waiting for an answer? Or how about the last several check-ins at a big chain hotel. Did the staff behind the counter seem to know every trick to avoid making eye contact and getting sucked into waiting on you? If you had a dollar for every minute you've waited at airline counters, hotels, department stores, gas stations, on the phone with parts or service departments, not to mention renewing your driver's licenses, you'd collect a bundle. I've come to the conclusion that many of these "service" people are either deaf, or blind, or have fused spinal cords that keep them looking down at their desks. Responding quickly to customers is a standard part of all customer service training. It's taught over and over again and nothing changes. Why? Because giving customers an immediate response is not a systems problem or a training problem. It's a deep-seated problem with the priorities of the service giver. Waiting on customers is simply a pain in the neck to most people in most companies. On the contrary, this is never a problem for entrepreneurs. If customers are the only way to feed your kids, you don't need a training seminar to get yourself in gear. This is why Sam Walton insisted that every new Wal-Mart employee take the "So help me Sam" pledge. It at least gets them off to a good start. It's also why he put a Wal-Mart "People Greeter" in every store: the person at the entrance who does nothing all day but greet customers, give them a cart, and direct them to where they want to go. It may not be very scientific, but this is the kind of immediate customer response that has made Wal-Mart the fastest growing retailer in history.

▪ Being Courteous *and* Competent

"When we answer the phone, we're very courteous. That's the good news. The bad news is we don't answer the phone, because the phones don't work." Famous last words from Ramon Cruz, CEO of Philippine Airlines, lamenting the lousy telephone system in Manila. What he was really saying was that company courtesy without company competence will get you nowhere. The most courteous airline in the world (which PAL may well be) can't overcome chronic lost baggage problems and reservation systems that don't work. The opposite is also true. Competence without courtesy isn't exactly going to get you in the winner's circle either. The best-designed car in the world can't overcome Attila the Hun–type sales and service personnel.

Entrepreneurs have a built-in advantage in this department. It comes with the territory. Courtesy, friendly service, and a small thank-you have a certain ring of sincerity from people who run their own shop. You get the feeling they just might really mean it—that they really are thankful for the two hundred dollars you just spent. As for their competence with their product, they at least know how it works. And if it doesn't work, they know how to fix it.

All bigger companies seem to have sterling intentions regarding courtesy and competence. But there's the old problem of functions and specializing. The folks who made this marvelous machine are never the ones you see. The young sales clerk may smile, but he doesn't know a thing about the gas-powered garden tiller you need, or which software is really best for the kind of graphics you produce. At another level, it's just not easy to be courteous to thousands of people you don't know and may never see again. It's not easy to be hired for the sales floor and become an instant expert in computers this month and garden equipment the next. No, it's not that easy to be both courteous and competent. If it's not easy, it will probably never happen. It certainly won't happen if you know in your heart of hearts that it makes damn little difference to your company—and no difference at all for you personally. This is the real nub of the entrepreneurial advantage: A lack of courtesy and a lack of competence make a big difference. They can drive you out of business in a hurry.

▪ Keeping Current Customers Forever

Your best prospect is a current customer, *always*. And for most companies facing higher and higher costs of marketing, all of the profit sits in the current customer base. So why does everyone scream and cheer over getting a new customer and simply shrug their shoulders if one of the current customers slips away. Why do 99.9 percent of all sales compensation systems pay a premium for new business but levy no penalties for losing old business? Why are the best people thrown at new clients and why does the ten-year-old client end up with the "B Team"? And why in so many companies is marketing still the champagne and caviar side of the business while spare parts, repairs, and on-going service feed on a diet of warm beer and grits? By far the most important "marketing" job in any business is to resell and expand those current customers.

This is not an argument against new business—just a common-sense look at growth and profit. The priorities are clear when you're young and small. Losing one or two current customers is an unmitigated disaster. Reorders are golden. They literally keep you alive. But this idea seems to lose its punch as the company grows. And when it goes, the most profitable piece of the business goes with it.

"Loving" the Product

Daimler was completely possessed with the idea of equipping every conceivable vehicle with his engines.
—FRITZ NALLINGER,
Gottlieb Daimler and Karl Benz

Any artist will tell you that no one values their work as much as they do themselves. They will also tell you that trying to sell their first work of art can be an ego-smashing exercise. All of a sudden what matters most is not how beautiful the artist thinks it is, but rather, how beautiful the customer thinks it is. Both of these notions—loving your work and accepting that beauty is always in the eyes of the beholder—are central to the entrepreneur's obsession with products. It's the bringing together of the scientist and salesman in us all that produces winning products. Here, straight from the entrepreneur's handbook, are four of the most basic, common-sense practices of the people who really care about their product and really care that someone wants and needs it.

▪ Knowing Your Customer

Gottlieb Daimler was a salesman who could make cars. It was Daimler, much more than the technical genius Benz, who understood that knowing your customer is the essential first step in producing great products. He was technically competent to be sure, but for him the whole point of making cars was to please and even astonish the customer. Everywhere Daimler went he saw a new market. He went to Paris and licensed his engines to a young man by the name of Peugeot. He went to Coventry and made his engines the envy of Britain. He personally opened a branch in St. Petersburg, where he judged the sales prospects to be enormous. Well, no one's right every time! And Daimler saw everyone as a potential user. He was the first with motorized fire engines, motorcycles, motorboats, and engines for "airships" and rail vehicles. Even the name Mercedes came about to please a customer. His 1900/1901 model, the first Mercedes, was named after the eleven-year-old daughter of his most important distributor. Daimler is hailed, along with other pioneers of the automobile like Benz and Maybach, as a great creator of products. The reality is he was hell-bent on staying close to the customer—sort of a nineteenth-century German Toyoda. And so it should be with the product people in your business.

▪Feeling Old-fashioned Pride

I've never met an entrepreneur who didn't believe that what he was doing was worth doing. And the overwhelming majority of people who work at companies want to feel pride in their products and services. Lately, we've been hearing a lot of "buzzwords" connected with putting pride back into the workplace: autonomy, quality of work life, psychological ownership, and so on. They're not wrong ideas, but they're just not *central* ideas. Having autonomy, quality, and ownership of a completely useless and unimportant job won't make a bit of difference. My grandfather worked in the boiler room of the old Baltimore & Ohio railroad. He had zero autonomy, a rough and dirty work environment, and no illusions that he "owned" anything. Yet he was proud. Why? Because he, his co-workers, and his supervisors thought that keeping those boilers running was important. If they didn't run, the switching station didn't run, and if that happened, the entire B&O Railroad would come to a halt. That's what he believed. That's why his job was important. How many people in today's giant bureaucracies really believe that their job is keeping the enterprise running? How many feel that what they're doing is important? How many even know how their job affects anything at all? These are the things that rip the pride out of work. And these are the things that have to be put back in. To reinstill old-fashioned pride in products—getting employees to believe that what they're doing is worth doing, that it's valuable to customers and important to the company—isn't a bad place to start.

▪Making It Better Than the Next Guy

There's a lot of academic talk today about the "power shift to customers." The theory is that with a global economy and dozens if not hundreds of suppliers for every product, power has shifted from producers to customers. This is advanced as the fundamental reason why quality has become so important. But it will come as a great surprise to entrepreneurs that producers ever had the "power" to shift in the first place. There's absolutely no change in why quality is important. Beating competitors on quality has always been the name of their game.

The entrepreneur makes his living by producing better mousetraps than the next guy. Not the best possible mousetrap in the world, just a mousetrap better than anyone else's. Entrepreneurs do whatever it takes to make their products better than the competition. If zero defects, continuous quality improvement, TQM, or even quality circles help you do this, who is to argue? But the entrepreneur's gut-level instinct of quality comes first. Whatever you do and however you do it, you've got to make it better than the next guy!

▪Making It Faster Than the Next Guy

Ed Penhoet, the founder of Chiron says: The entire biotech industry is a horse race: "Everyone in the industry is smart and knows what needs to be done and everyone in the industry lives and dies on the burn-rate of their venture capital. The winners in the biotech industry will be the ones who can produce the inventions the fastest." Isn't this also true for giant companies in mature industries? Of course! Whether it's Toyota assembling a new model in thirteen weeks or Chiron getting there first with the hepatitis C vaccine, making it faster than the next guy is the only way to stay in the race.

This idea, so clear for entrepreneurs and their start-up companies, must be very unclear for many old-line companies. They may be thinking about it, but they never get around to doing it. But they'd better change, fast. Today, everyone has smart competitors who know what needs to be done. And if the burn-rate of capital doesn't get you, the burn-rate of customer patience will. It's no secret that entrepreneurs love to compete with big companies. The reason is simple: Breaking the tape first is practically guaranteed!

Great Moments in Enterprise

Every so often a customer experience comes along that we can never forget. My favorite, believe it or not, comes from a very large company. The experience has always been a reminder to me that big companies are actually full of fantastic people who, given half a chance, will perform as if their personal honor is on the line. All it takes is to convince them that they are the company. If they do become convinced, they'll behave as entrepreneurially as Disney, Toyoda, and Lever all wrapped into one.

The setting is Teheran, near the end of 1978. It's the end of the line for the Shah of Iran and the "Great Satan" that had propped him up for twenty-five years. Even though the shah hung on for another month, Teheran was no place to be lolling about with an American passport. Especially if you spoke Farsi, which I did. That little business advantage could quickly turn into a major social disadvantage. Almost overnight, speaking the language and being a spook went hand-in-hand.

I was in Teheran to close down an office I had opened just three years earlier. The ride in from Mehrabad Airport had been an eye-opener. This was not the Teheran I knew. It looked like a war zone. We were stopped and searched every few blocks. Tanks, nervous soldiers, and sandbags clogged the streets while a million demonstrators screamed anti-shah and anti-American slogans. It was an angry and eerie sight in a country where such behavior had been unthinkable for decades. Everyone in the country seemed on strike save the troops loyal to the Peacock throne and of course the ayatollah's demonstrators. At the Sheraton, where I was staying, the windows were broken, the staff was gone, and we few remaining "guests" helped ourselves to what food was in the kitchen.

With Dave Johnston, our country manager and an old friend, termination or transfer arrangements were agreed on for the Iranian and American staff. Cars and equipment were conveyed to local employees. Records were bundled or trashed. Events were overtaking the situation, and getting out was quickly shaping up as the number one objective for many Iranians and all foreigners. I recall thinking how absurd, how American it was that we were trying to get documents notarized and the whole place was going up in smoke. In any event Dave and I went through the motions until it was time to move on. Dave and his family were destined for Hong Kong while various Iranian associates ultimately got out to France and the United States.

My own predicament didn't seem so difficult. With passport in hand I headed for the airport. What was normally a thirty-minute drive took about five hours. It didn't make any difference as I found the airport closed, everyone on strike, and no planes allowed to land or take off. I had lots of company. There must have been ten thousand Iranians and all sorts of foreigners trying to get out. Over the next thirty-six hours I witnessed an amazing display of customer service under fire. It came from a lone and very weary Air France employee. All the ticket counters were vacant. There were no Iranian employees of any airline to be seen, and the one or two foreigners I saw seemed intent on avoiding the mass of anxious would-be travelers. All except one, that is: the amazing young Frenchman with clipboard in hand.

He actually seemed to be relishing it all. He was stationed at his counter, looking very tired, but very determined. On the counter a small red, white, and blue flag stood as proudly as the Arc de Triomphe. It seemed to announce, "You have entered the civilized territory of France!" He was handling all comers. He calmly listed names and destinations on his clipboard, making it the only working reservation system in the place. When it was my turn, he seemed particularly interested that I had no preferred destination. "This means you will go any direction?" he asked. "Yes, any direction, any country." He looked me straight in the eye and said the words I was dying to hear, "I may be able to help you. Where can I find you when the time comes?" It was pretty obvious I wasn't going anywhere, so with my "reservation" confirmed on his clipboard, I took up my spot on the floor just like any other refugee.

As the hours wore on, with absolutely no signs of life at any of the other airlines, this young Frenchman looked more and more like Joan of Arc than an airline ticket agent. A full day and more went by. I considered going back to the Sheraton, but I didn't know how many more trips across Teheran were in the cards. And anyway, I clearly wasn't going to get a flight sitting at the Sheraton. In the middle of my second sleep on the floor, like a shining knight in blue, the Air France agent leaned over and whispered, "Come with me. There's an Air France 747 out at the end of the runway. She's been allowed to refuel but cannot discharge or take on any passengers. But I think I can get one person on." He shoved an Air France jacket at me: "Put this on, it's safer." In a daze I followed him behind the counter, through the office area, down several corridors, and presto, we were on the tarmac. No ticketing, no passport control, no customs, nothing. We got in an Air France jeep and shot across the runway heading for a beautiful, gleaming blue-and-white bird, with AIR FRANCE emblazoned across its side. The ticket agent was yelling as we drove, "I can give you no ticket. Everything is broken. I will tell the purser you have to buy your ticket when you arrive." It hadn't yet dawned on me that I didn't have the foggiest idea of where I would be arriving. At the plane, the agent directed the mechanic's ramp ladder to the front cabin door. Up we went, the door opened, and a rapid-fire exchange in French took place between the agent and the purser. The agent turned to me, stuck out his hand, and said simply, "Bon voyage."

The best news of the night came from the purser: "Where do you want to go?" Answer: "I want to go wherever you're going." Reply: "We're going to Bangkok, is that okay?" Answer: "That's wonderful. Let's go to Bangkok." The end of the story is another story about trying to buy a plane ticket from Teheran to Bangkok after you've landed in Bangkok. Explaining this to the Thai Air France agents was practically impossible. After three hours and many discussions among themselves about how to record this transaction, Air France was paid, and I knew I was back in the real world of big business.

I'll never know if the young Frenchman was able to help any others. I do know I'll never forget his help to me. But what sticks in my mind the most is how this one employee responded to the challenge, how he took ownership of the situation. He was on his own, improvising, innovating, doing things that no policy book or training manual ever covered. For a day or two at least, he *was* Air France. This is what entrepreneurial behavior is all about. Watson, Honda, or Benz could do no better. He held the customer, the product, and the company's honor in his hand. And for at least this customer, that ticket agent became a shining symbol of Air France that I'll never forget: a symbol that says caring about customers and products doesn't come from science or from magic. It comes from ordinary people responding to extraordinary moments: those moments when you *are* the company; when it's *your* customer and *your* product, and it's *your* self-respect that's on the line; those great moments that produce great lessons in enterprise.

CHAPTER FOUR

HIGH-SPEED INNOVATION

The Necessity to Invent and the Freedom to Act

We Japanese are obsessed with survival.
—AKIO MORITA, founder, Sony

Living with Crisis and a Sense of Urgency

A recent study found that the cost of innovation, as measured by new products and patents, is an astounding twenty-four times greater at large companies than small ones. Even if these researchers are only half right, it's a frightening statistic. If you're John Akers at IBM, or Denys Henderson at ICI, or Akio Morita at Sony, it's enough to keep you awake nights. Few people today need any statistics to convince them that speed in making and implementing changes is a major competitive factor. And even fewer observers would disagree that small, young, entrepreneurial companies can and regularly do beat the socks off their larger competitors in this arena.

At Sony, still Japan's most innovative large company, Chairman Morita believes that innovation and fast action are lost when companies lose their sense of crisis and urgency. He knows whereof he speaks. Anyone who lived through the nightmare of postwar Japan knows that all people and all companies can move quickly and creatively if their survival depends on it.

Morita goes further. He believes that the ancient value of *mottainai* is really what keeps the Japanese companies moving. *Mottainai* suggests that everything we have is given to us in sacred trust by the Creator. It is precious and we must never waste it. This value fits in with the historic struggle for survival of the Japanese people. Earthquakes and volcanoes, little arable land, no natural resources, and the fury of atomic bombs would give any island people a certain urgency in their daily lives. As Morita tells it, this translated in the workplace into not wasting time or material and constantly looking for incremental improvements.

Whatever the merits of the *mottainai* theory, Morita has first-hand experience in entrepreneurial survival. In a commercial environment where felled B-29s were a major source of metal, spare parts only came via the black market, and bombed-out buildings served as start-up factories, one learned to act quickly and creatively.

Starting with rice cookers and home-sewn heating pads in 1946, the company that was to become Sony scrounged for raw materials, customers, and cash. Morita quickly attempted a giant and seemingly hopeless leap forward. He tried to produce magnetic recording tape—without plastic. Making magnetic tape without plastic, as Morita and his colleagues found out, wasn't easy. They tried cellophane, but paper worked better. On their hands and knees, they cut long strips and lacquered them by hand. Lo and behold, the strips recorded. This is the same company that by 1965 was a primary supplier of computer tape to IBM.

Sony's challenge today isn't a lack of understanding about the sources of high-speed innovation. Morita knows where it comes from. Sony's problem, as with hundreds of other rich and comfortable companies, is how to maintain a sense of urgency when the coffers are full, when complacency replaces necessity. Being innovative is not a genetic trait, a mark of genius, or a skill to be learned at school. It's a normal human reaction—and it can disappear in a hurry.

Of course there are lots of logical-sounding explanations for why entrepreneurs beat big companies to the punch. But the one surefire way to kill off innovation and action is to outgrow your sense of urgency.

Racing Against Time in Biotech

Fortunately, people can get inspired without earthquakes and world wars. A sense of urgency, with its attendant quest for innovative action, can definitely arise in less fearful circumstances. Take America's hottest new industry, biotechnology, or as it is often called, genetic engineering. In the past decade over four hundred biotech companies have sprung up, driven by a new breed of scientist/entrepreneur. This is an industry with few products to date and next to nothing to show on the bottom line. If Americans are such short-term thinkers, why the mad scramble to form and fund all these money-losing companies?

It all started in the 1960s, when most Americans thought the only revolution going on was in the streets. Little did we know that the most profound revolution in the human condition was erupting in the biology and chemistry labs of American universities. The sixties' explosion of biochemistry research has ignited technology and products that promise to shake humanity to its core. In the next ten years, there will be more changes in medicine than we've seen in the last one hundred years. The impact on agriculture will make the green revolution look like child's play. Some of the changes will be dreams come true. Others sound downright scary.

The history is short. The cloning of the DNA molecule led to the discovery of restrictive enzymes and the world's first gene-splicing patent, awarded in 1974. By 1977, the University of California at San Francisco, the hot-bed of the movement, began cloning medically important genes. This led to the production of human insulin and human growth hormones. A tidal wave of university and government research began pouring into the private sector with the historic U.S. Supreme Court decision in 1980 that declared genetically engineered organisms to be patentable. It's been a frenzy ever since. Curing certain cancers has become only a matter of time. Thousand-year-old mysteries of genetic disorders are already being solved. Single tomato plants capable of producing twenty-thousand tomatoes have been genetically engineered.

This is an industry driven by giant hopes, not desperate fears. For biotech companies, every human ailment raises the possibility of a product. Every agricultural sector represents a new market. The flood of new research simply fuels the appetite for more. The freedom and capability to commercialize products with such dramatic possibilities excites people. Exploring "inner space" promises more human benefit and drama than exploring outer space. It's computers all over again, with much higher "tech" and infinitely higher "touch." And it's the ultimate bringing together of the *salesman* and the *scientist*.

This is without question an industry with a sense of urgency —racing to unlock the secrets of life. The market is enormous and the field is wide open. The U.S. Department of Commerce, shedding its usual conservative outlook, is predicting a $40 billion market by the year 2000. *Fortune* magazine reports even higher private projections: "A startling 50-fold increase in sales of biopharmaceuticals by the end of the decade. That would mean $60 billion plus . . . nearly as much as the whole pharmaceutical industry's worldwide sales today." The trick is to win the race. Not surprisingly, the entrepreneurs have won the first leg hands down. That was against the traditional giant drug companies, who are still trying to figure out what happened.

The remaining laps, and they will be grueling, pit entrepreneur against entrepreneur. The field is full of hundreds, soon to be thousands, of like competitors springing up in America, Europe, and Japan. And each company has to win its own race against the "burn-rate" of venture capital. Breakthrough products can take ten years and are running at $50 million-plus to discover, test, and get approved. The key to both these races is high-speed innovation.

Chiron Corporation is not exactly typical of the pack. After ten years it has emerged as one of the big winners in the biotech race. It has actually produced products and is one of only two companies in the industry that are solidly profitable. The first time I met co-founder and CEO Ed Penhoet, I didn't know what to expect. I had never discussed business with a Ph.D. in biochemistry. I knew I couldn't speak his language. I hoped he could speak mine.

It turns out he speaks both quite well. I shouldn't have been surprised. The first thing you notice about Penhoet (and others from his industry) is that he's very smart—smart enough to supply the world with a blockbuster vaccine for hepatitis B that is estimated to have prevented over a million cases since 1986, plus clinical testing of DNA probes, vaccines for AIDS, hepatitis C, herpes, and malaria. He's also smart enough to raise $420 million in a decade, acquire Cetus, another big industry star, and sign distribution agreements with the likes of Merck, Johnson & Johnson, and Ciba-Geigy. And along the way he has managed the company to a solid profit position.

But *smart* isn't enough according to Penhoet: "We're all *smart*. In our field we've already been preselected out, in the sense that by the time you get to people who have Ph.D.s from a major institution—Harvard, UC Berkeley, UCSF—it's a given that they are smart. In this group there are very few people who are really very much smarter than the rest—damn few. . . . In the beginning it was just a race. We all knew what had to be done. We had to be able to hit the ground running and stick with it. Tom Peters is now talking all about speed, right? It is particularly true for biotechnology. It's a race, but I suspect in today's environment, with the world moving as fast as it is, everything is a race to some degree. So I think every company has to come to grips with how to move quickly and how to cut out inefficiencies.

"It may be that speed is more important than cost, in the end, because really—you can't save your way into success. The real value comes when you get some very valuable products in the marketplace. It creates enough margin that you can use that money to keep the other ones flowing through the pipeline. If our history has taught us anything—because we have just been through this decade of a horse race—it is that you have to focus on speed as the key element in building any organization. I wouldn't want to leave you with the impression that this is a theoretical race—this is a very real race. I mean, we knew who the other entrants in the race were. We knew when the starting gun was fired. We tried to keep track of where they were, where we were, and whether they were ahead or we were ahead. So you take a project like factor VIII, for example, the antihemophilic factor, or hepatitis B, or IGF, a number of these things we were working on. The dynamic wasn't, we're racing against the world. No. It was, we're racing against Genentech and Genetics Institute on factor VIII. It's a very personal kind of race, and I think the issue, as a company gets larger, is to keep that sort of personal competition inculcated in the group. I think that was tremendously valuable to us in the early days. Probably it was good for both Genentech and Chiron, for example, that we were competing against each other in several products, because it became very direct and very personal."

Molecular Biosystems, Inc., in San Diego, is still on the edge of greatness. It's where Chiron was five years ago. MBI was founded in 1980 by two college buddies, Ken Widder and Vince Frank. Widder, the young scientist, went to his pal Frank, the young lawyer, to find out how to patent a few research breakthroughs he had made in the lab. The rest is not quite history. For ten years MBI has lived on venture capital and research progress payments from big healthcare distributors who are anxious to get their hands on the ultimate product. Today, MBI is on the verge of getting FDA approval for its first major product, Albunex®, a totally new diagnostic agent to greatly enhance cardiac ultrasound imaging. Patents have been secured. Distribution agreements have been signed in Europe, North America, and Japan. The manufacturing facility has been built. Clinical and human trials have been completed. If approved, Albunex® is expected to create substantial sales.

It's been a fast decade with everything every day aimed at being the first to market—and before the working capital runs out. Vince Frank, the president, says: "Like in any other company, our employees ask Ken and me how to get ahead in MBI. Our answer hasn't changed for ten years. 'Do the absolute best job every minute of every day, on the task right in front of you—that's the only way any of us are going to get ahead.' " The company culture is summed up in one phrase: "making it happen every day." From sharing hotel rooms on business trips to working weekends, MBI looks for every scrap of advantage in this time-over-cost game. And as in the rest of the industry, getting that first product out won't earn MBI a rest period. MBI is on the same frantic track with several other products. Its subsidiary Syngene, for example, is pushing back the frontiers of medicine with DNA probes for rapidly diagnosing various important infectious diseases. It received broad patents for the technology in October 1990. The amazing thing is, when I last visited the subsidiary, Syngene's working capital had only a six-month window. The thirty employees all knew the facts but were forging ahead like marines taking a beach. I asked Vince Frank how the employees could have such high motivation when they were in danger of being sucked out to sea? "Nothing new about this," says Frank. "That's how we live. That's why making it happen every day is the only way to get ahead in this business."

This is the race against time in biotech, an industry that hasn't outgrown its sense of urgency. Can it happen everywhere, even when its need isn't so obvious? Well, a lot of fast-moving entrepreneurs have done just that. If it doesn't come naturally, they find a way to build it in.

Building in Urgency

What if you're not clawing your way out of the rubble of World War II in Tokyo, or not at a company with the potential to change the world of medicine and agriculture? You're practically forced to be fast-moving and creative in those situations. But what if your business is more normal, mundane, one where nobody feels a need for speed or innovation? Where is your sense of urgency going to come from?

You have to build it into the business. It comes from your own perception of what needs to be done. On your side is the helpful fact that urgency is a relative state of being. Regardless of the circumstance, whatever your business, doing it better and doing it faster can be an exhilarating challenge. Even beating your own "personal best" can be thrilling—and sometimes more important than beating the next guy. We don't have to sit around hoping something big and exciting happens to the business. We can *make* it happen. We *have to* make it happen if we expect our people to respond with great speed and great ideas!

Let's be honest—how earth-shattering is it to be a delivery man? Carrying documents you never see, from people you don't know, to other people you don't know. It doesn't sound all that exciting. Yet for Larry Hillblom at DHL every delivery took on the urgency of breaking the four-minute mile. It was the ultimate challenge for him—every day, everywhere in the world.

This is the lesson of DHL—and of hundreds of other entrepreneurial companies that build the urgency into the guts of the business. Hillblom made speed and do-or-die behavior the essence of DHL's service. Less than twenty years old, DHL today has offices in more countries (about 190) than there are members of the United Nations—from Outer Mongolia to the bowels of Wall Street to the jungles of Brazil. In some spots, DHL is the sole foreign presence. The couriers often work in extremely dangerous conditions. Wars, revolutions, and natural disasters are a big part of the couriers' folklore.

From the outside, the business looks simple. From the inside, nothing could be more complicated than promising overnight delivery of millions of documents, to thousands of addresses around the world, 365 days a year. Of course being complicated doesn't make it interesting. The post office is complicated, but hardly interesting. What DHL set out to do had never been done before. But one thing was certain: to pull it off, high-speed innovation had to be the very basis of the business. It had to be built in from day one.

DHL was the brainchild of three young Americans in Northern California. As with most good ideas, they hadn't planned it. They hadn't gone to business school to figure it out. They had no marketing surveys. In fact, they weren't even thinking about starting a business. They were all law students with long nights devoted to reading legal briefs and case studies. They came upon a good way to study and make spare money at the same time: signing up as freelance couriers for shipping companies. Forwarding bills of lading by courier, to distant ports across the Pacific, was a common practice in the industry. Nobody made much of it. It had been done this way for decades.

The ringleader of this band of would-be lawyers was Larry Hillblom. Up through law school, his business career consisted of summer and part-time jobs. As he described it, the high point was raising hell for better worker pay in the food canneries of the San Joaquin Valley. Being a young labor agitator is hardly the expected background for a world-class enterpriser—but then Hillblom is full of surprises. It was during the long flights across the Pacific that Hillblom wondered why no one had ever organized an international courier service. The shipping companies needed it. They all had to scramble around to find reliable couriers. Multi-million-dollar cargoes, often with perishable goods, were at high risk of delay or worse, and it all came down to a bunch of freelance adventurers being absolutely reliable and on time.

Hillblom and his buddies went about passing the word that they were going to set up a "network." *Network* is a pretty fancy concept when you're starting with nothing. Networks take time, people, and money. The young founders had no people or money so they had to leverage their time. They began signing up people wherever they could find them. It was an odd lot in the beginning, to be sure: a taxi driver in Sydney, the manager of the only A&W Root Beer stand in Malaysia, an ex-officer of the Rhodesian army —a classic rough diamond with a heart of gold—and backpacking students willing to stay in strange places. They were looking for people who could ride coach for twenty hours and when the plane landed still move with lightning speed to get the documents delivered. DHL had little to offer these people other than a share of the action. This turned out to be a stroke of luck. The network began to take shape as a string of entrepreneurial start-ups, totally dependent on each other to meet the promise of overnight delivery.

Hillblom had a knack for finding people like himself—people who could be up and running within twenty-four hours. All the early employees of DHL became veterans of carrying the "green bag," the canvas bag full of documents that has become the international symbol of DHL service. In those days the only way to get your DHL stripes was to carry the green bag. Delivering the contents on time wasn't the only challenge. It was getting them there at all. Nobody seemed particularly helpful—not the international airlines, who never fly on time, and certainly not the customs officials with their bureaucratic schedules and demands for "baksheesh." On top of this mountain of inefficiency sat the national post offices. Most resented anyone's delivering "their mail," and they fought DHL tooth and nail around the world. After hurdling all these institutional roadblocks, the real fun began. Green bag veterans could, and regularly did, find themselves smack in the middle of typhoons, wars and revolutions, and even a jail or two.

So just being fast wasn't enough. A large dose of guile and derring-do was standard issue. Call it innovation on the run.

Everywhere Hillblom went, he found a need. After all, he was offering something unheard of. Business documents could take ten days to go from Tokyo to Milan. From Lagos to Mexico City, it could take forever. In a world where postal delivery times between Philadelphia and New York had gone from three days by horse to seven days by plane, overnight delivery anywhere in the world had a terrific appeal. But it all depended on completing the network in a hurry. A half-built network wasn't very interesting to the Deutschebanks and Toyotas and IBMs of the world. DHL had to be everywhere they were, everywhere they had put an office over the last fifty years. And DHL had to be there *yesterday*!

By the late seventies, the DHL network was growing from one country to another, gaining in momentum. There never had been any plans, systems, or procedures. Handshakes were the principal contracts. The manager in each DHL outpost was by default king of his territory. Each fiefdom had one overriding obligation. Whatever comes in, and whatever goes out, handle it with the speed of light. Thus was born a world of DHL mini-entrepreneurs—a world based upon speed, agility, innovation, and at times actions bordering on the unbelievable.

When I first met Larry Hillblom, I was stunned. His reputation as something of an international Howard Hughes, living on the Pacific island of Saipan, was well known. He never granted interviews or made public appearances. Chairman Bill Walton (since deceased) hadn't mentioned him, and I assumed he was skipping this London meeting of his board and top fifty executives. No amount of advance warning, however, would have prepared me for his arrival. Just after I had started my talk to the group, a youngish-looking, red-headed American with a beard strode purposefully to the one empty seat at the front. He was dressed in tennis shoes, Levi's, and a red plaid lumberman's shirt. I'd never seen such a figure at a board-level meeting, especially in London. I carried on, assuming that this wandering lumberjack was only crazy or lost.

It wasn't long before I found out that Larry Hillblom is far from crazy and is never lost. He took the discussion seriously. He had more questions and more ideas than anyone in the room. He got emotionally involved in every point. And he never pulled rank. When it was over he vanished into thin air. No fanfare or good-byes. I later learned this was classic Hillblom. He periodically shows up, gets completely involved, and then disappears on to the next DHL activity somewhere else in the world. I doubt that he still carries the green bag, but little else seems to have changed.

Larry Hillblom remains in my memory as something of a bright red streak of light. The lesson of entrepreneurs like him is clear: High-speed innovation doesn't just happen. People like Hillblom make it happen by sensing a need for it in all they do. An atmosphere of crisis and urgent necessity doesn't have to come from disasters and life-defining products. When you're not blessed with a business that produces tons of adrenaline naturally, or great expectations and wild applause at every turn, you have to find it—to create it yourself. At the base of DHL's success is a built-in sense of urgency, every hour of every day for every one of the forty thousand employees around the world.

Enterprise Bursts— the Amazing Turnaround Power of Innovative Action

In an age when doing it better and faster marks the difference between winners and losers, no one should have to look far to find a need for innovation and action. Morita, Penhoet, and Hillblom set surprisingly high standards for creative action in starting and building their businesses. What can be even more surprising is how powerful and effective innovative action can be in turning around the fortunes of an old and troubled bureaucracy.

Remember John Egan and Jaguar? In the sixties and seventies, Jaguar was going downhill in a hurry. The Labour government nationalized it, ostensibly to keep it alive. But government management wasn't the answer, and by the early eighties, it was ready for the junk heap. Enter Margaret Thatcher with her hand-picked enterpriser to bring it back from the dead and "re-privatize" it if possible. Here is John Egan's record for the first five years.

	1981	*1986*
Customers	14,000	43,000
Employees	8,000	11,000
Profits	(£32 million loss)	£125 million
Market Value	£250 million est.	£920 million

What was the magic? The same sort of actions you've heard about before. Turnarounds do have a certain pattern. Egan's favorite phrase, "making money out of satisfying customers," set the new tone. He got very tough with the sloppy suppliers. Henceforth anything that didn't meet or beat Jaguar's new specs got sent back and invoices weren't paid until the supplier got it right. He immediately leveled with the workers and unions. Everyone's job, including his own, stood in the balance. From now on all rework had to be done at no pay. The entire management team was assigned to dealers to help sell Jaguars. All customers were called for quality and service checks thirty-five days after purchase, and again at nine and eighteen months. Egan promised the workers their fair share if they delivered. They did and he did. In three years they were the highest-paid auto workers in Britain, and under a special scheme, seven thousand of them became shareholders in the company. There were no real surprises in these or any other of the actions Egan took. The same problems had cried out for action for twenty years. The only magic was that Egan took all the long overdue actions in his first twelve months.

Turnarounds are a little-understood phenomenon in business.

They are bursts of high enterprise. Though they don't guarantee the next fifty years will be smooth sailing, they do dramatically change the angle of a company's life cycle. Jaguar, for example, has moved into a more "normal" pattern of performance since its turnaround. But it's operating at a totally different level, a different angle if you will, than it was before the big thrust upward. Some turnarounds, like Jaguar's, are so dramatic that all the lost ground is recaptured and the company ends up at a historically high performance level. Others only halt the slide downward and start the company growing again at ground zero. All these companies would be history, however, if they hadn't undergone a turnaround phase.

Turnaround masters like Egan all have one thing in common: They move like meteors to do the things that have to be done. At the heart of these "enterprise bursts" is a massive and quick dose of innovative action. The obvious question: If taking a lot of innovative actions in a hurry propels companies upward, why do we wait to do it until our very survival is threatened?

Enterpreneurs don't wait. Moving fast and breaking new ground are the most consistent and visible characteristics of entrepreneurs. High-speed innovation is the entrepreneur's number one competitive weapon—and it's virtually free. Every entrepreneur dreams of competing with the biggest and the slowest. It's the closest thing in business to legalized highway robbery.

Larger companies are superb at discipline and routine. But they're ill-suited to encourage innovation and terrible at taking quick action. As swiftness and agility are hallmarks of entrepreneurship, being slow and ponderous are telltale signs of bureaucracy. In fact they're often the first symptoms. IBM comes to mind—the same IBM we grew up thinking was the best-managed company in history, the same IBM that produced more profit than any company in the world. Or *is it* the same IBM really? Did IBM cross the Rubicon into a world of bureaucracy and a fight for survival? John Akers seems to think so. Listen to his recent pronouncements just before he announced the virtual splitting up of the company: "We missed a beat in midrange systems, badly. . . . We were late with the lower end of the 370 line. . . . We were late in workstations. . . . We have lost share in the personal computer business, partly because we were late with laptops. . . ." That's a lot of "being late" for one paragraph. Judge for yourself, but it has that ominous ring of a company that has lost its sense of urgency.

There are many reasons why urgency fades—why complacency conquers action and indifference overpowers inventiveness. They're all "deadly sins" against high-speed innovation.

The Seven Deadly Sins of High-speed Innovation

Everything that can be invented has been invented.
—CHARLES H. DUELL, director,
U.S.A. Patent Office, 1899

Short of hiring Mr. Duell to run R&D, what are the biggest roadblocks to new ideas and rapid-fire movement? With all good intention, bureaucracies commit numerous "deadly sins" against speed and innovation. There's always a "good reason" for another procedure, another committee, or another control point. All such rational-sounding steps underlie the very different purposes of managing and enterprising.

The reason giant organizations keep shooting themselves in the foot over high-speed innovation goes to the heart of twentieth-century theory about how to handle size and complexity. The scientific method says we can manage anything if we analyze it enough, plan it enough, and implement the plan like clockwork. Five seconds into pursuing this fantasy, you're knee deep in planning, controlling, systematizing, and generally smoothing out any bumps and covering any potholes in the road ahead. Man conquering chaos may be a noble pursuit, but it misses the innovation point by a mile. Fast-moving and creative enterprise is not about removing rough edges and eliminating surprises. With rare exception, in fact, it's the bumps and the potholes that contain most of the real gold.

This, then, is the dilemma: Laudable efforts to run a tight ship have the perverse effect of sinking the ship. Here are some specific illustrations of well-intentioned efforts to "run a tight ship."

▪I'm Okay, You're Okay

Mr. Duell's complacency is at the top of the list. Insisting we're all okay, another gift to business from psychology, produces terminal inaction for companies in the heat of competitive wars. Mr. Morita's point is that we're *not* okay, we're *never* okay! *Crisis* and *stress* have become bad words in business. But everyone knows that more gets done in an hour of crisis than in a month of feeling good. These "bad words" mine the gold in the rough edges and surprises of enterprise, in the bumps and potholes of opportunity. They scream out that we're not okay, and we'd better fix it in a hurry!

Eliminating stress has become a corporate obsession. How many stress-management courses does an already lifeless bureaucracy really need? Too much stress may be bad for the arteries, but when was the last time you did something really great with no stress at all? "I'm okay, you're okay" is the first sure step to killing innovation and action. Believe it long enough and your business fails and the factory closes—not an okay result for anyone!

▪One Best Way

If you want to silence workers forever, you can't go wrong with the "one best way to do the job" mentality. This ranks as the original sin of "scientific management" and comes straight from the granddaddy of all industrial consultants, Frederick Taylor. Way back in the 1890s, this Philadelphia cost-cutter popularized the idea that there is one optimum way to perform every task. Whether it's turning a screw on a motor mount or timing the toilet trips of assembly line workers, everything could and should be optimized.

Taylor, the first great efficiency expert, learned his trade as a mechanical engineer. He conducted over thirty thousand tests using varying speeds and shapes of cutting tools to find the one best way to do any metal-cutting task. So far so good. He then took a leap of logic that would shape the thinking of business for a hundred years. If the optimum way of calibrating machines can be scientifically discovered, why not do the same for human performance? Why not optimize the output of entire factories, even entire companies, through scientific analysis? After all, there has to be "one best way" to do everything. Voila! The birth of scientific management.

Twenty years later Henry Ford closed the loop on Taylor's thinking. Ford asked why waste time optimizing human performance—the most efficient strategy is to get rid of humans altogether and replace them with machines at every step of the process. Workers should be relegated to keeping the machines running. All this was great news for mass-production fanatics, but it was the death knell for worker innovation. Taylor and Ford had one powerful bond. They shared a deep and abiding mistrust of workers. Taylor talked about the "high-priced man" (the efficient one) and Ford proclaimed the "five-dollar day" (for fewer and fewer workers), but neither man could tolerate the notion that workers might be *thinking* contributors.

Even so, it wasn't the *theory* of "one best way" that did the damage. After all, Taylor, Ford, and their ilk had profound and positive impact on straight-line forms of output. And that's not bad. As with most breakthrough ideas, the real trouble started with the implementers who didn't know when enough was enough. "One best way" evangelists began applying it to everything in business. The *best way* quickly got translated as the *only way*—and deviating from the standard was a cardinal sin. In a world where everything was figured out to the third decimal, worker initiative and innovation weren't needed or appreciated.

The bottom line? Scientific analysis and controlled performance may do wonders for metal-cutting tools, but they're not much help in inventing products, beating deadlines, hitting new levels of quality, or fostering employee commitment. Most damaging of all, they simply paralyze employee innovation and self-directed fast action. Taylor's words still hang in the air: "A 'high-priced man' does just what he's told to do and no back talk." Contrast this sentiment with Soichiro Honda's belief in "the genius of the worker." Taylorism gets you worker uniformity forever, while Hondaism gets you sixty thousand employee suggestions a year. Who's really optimizing the output of workers?

▪ Out of Touch

The odds are very high that the idea for your next great product or service will come from a customer or a competitor. This is why being out of touch is so damaging to successful product and service innovation. Losing contact with customers and losing sight of competitors can take many forms. However, this particular sin always starts at the core of the business and spreads outward. If you spend enough time in enough company headquarters, you can actually "feel" the disease. The signals of a company's openness to or isolation from the real world of customers and competitors are easy to spot.

I first met Fredy Dellis when he was president of Hertz International. He had done a magnificent job of keeping Hertz number one in the wildly competitive international car rental business. Dellis was right for the job. Athletically handsome, he looked like the Hollywood version of a European Grand Prix champion. And the place he called home was right for the business. Hertz International headquarters sits too close for comfort to heavily trafficked Bath Road, leading right into London's Heathrow Airport. So for starters, Hertz HQ is located right in the middle of its biggest market. The building is one of those ghastly British office structures that ought to be on Prince Charles's list of architectural carbuncles. The noise and fumes of the traffic fill the reception room. Hertz cars are jammed on the side and back of the building. It looks more like

a rental location than a headquarters. The upside is that real customers are forever dropping in on headquarter's personnel with
problems or questions. Busy-looking staff in Hertz uniforms or
nameplates come and go. The constant roar of Heathrow takeoffs
and landings replaces the quiet pitter-patter of other corporate headquarters. There is no carpeting to soften the sounds. And of course
all the competitors are within a stone's throw. From president to
clerk, no one can miss this daily reminder that Hertz has a ton of
competition. There is an unmistakable feel here that says: "We're
in the thick of the battle. Everyone in this headquarters knows what
customers and competitors look like, smell like, and think of Hertz."

Today Dellis has a bigger job and a bigger challenge. As president of Burger King International, he's got to close the gap in the
eternal battle with McDonald's. He's certainly got a bigger building
to do it from! A first visit to Burger King's headquarters is indeed
a stunning experience. Somewhere outside of Miami, through what
seems like miles of orange groves, an enormous pink coliseum takes
shape in the distance. Driving closer one gets the feeling of approaching the Acropolis—or at least Persepolis. Eventually the
structures square off, revealing wide drives and a beautiful manmade lake at the rear. The three or four buildings stand alone in a
gigantic clearing, completely ringed by citrus orchards. It's a
breathtaking sight and the interior is more of the same, but too large,
too elegant, and much too quiet. Perhaps as a sign of the times, few
people are in sight. The design style is somewhere between Mormon
Tabernacle and early CIA. The staff cafeteria, the only place to eat
for miles around, is sort of the Russian Tea Room version of a fast-
food joint. A different world from the Burger King you and I know.
As I said, a stunning experience—and a stunning sense of isolation
from the real world of Whoppers and Big Macs.*

---

* Don't sell your stock just yet. Burger King's new owners, Grand Met in the UK, have
big growth plans for the company. They have brought in British turnaround wizard CEO
Barry Gibbons to make it happen. Gibbons, Dellis, et al. have strong entrepreneurial instincts
as big company managers. They'll need them to fix the mess they've inherited. As *Fortune*
put it: ". . . he [Gibbons] knew the fast-food chain had lots of problems—bad marketing,

Of course it's only a "feeling." But the contrast between Hertz on Bath Road and Burger King in the orange grove is striking. When any company looks so *untouched* by customers or competitors, you have to wonder where the ideas for innovative new products and radically improved services will come from? I'm not making the case that executives should work out of tacky and cramped facilities. But keeping the decision makers and the imperial bureaucracy in splendid isolation can't be the answer either. Feeling out of touch can soon get to be more than a feeling.

▪ Centralized Everything

"When in doubt, centralize" is an idea that easily takes on a life of its own. If it happens to work in one area, it gets applied to everything in sight. And wherever it's applied, the trade-off is always innovation and speedy action.

At the heart of centralizing are two very appealing goals: Do it more efficiently (the old economy of scale rubric), and make sure it's done right. Either one of these two perceived benefits is enough to carry the day in the centralize/decentralize debate. Both rest on shaky ground.

What about doing it more efficiently? Are big factories more productive than small factories? Does central purchasing really get things cheaper? Is the big R&D center the most efficient (or effective) way to invent products? And what does corporate personnel actually contribute to the bottom line? Cost savings? Improved worker performance? Higher employee commitment? Every company and every function have to make these judgments for themselves. But they may have to find a new reason. Destroying a sacred belief of big business, the evidence to date tells us that bigger is rarely cheaper, and centralized is almost never more efficient.

---

dirty restaurants, an unimaginative menu, and poor service. . . ." Whether they keep their pink "Pentagon" of hamburgers or not, the thing they have to do is get the company back in touch with customer desires and competitor actions, fast. Early signs are good. An "enterprise burst" in the making? Stay tuned.

But somebody does still have to make sure it's done right. That's a heavy statement about who knows best and who does best. At its core, it's about who trusts whom to do what. It's a form of control, no doubt about it. But *controlling* is not the problem: it's what's getting controlled by whom that causes concern. Some things in enterprise need a lot of control. Being true to the values of the company, for example. Oddly, this is out of control in most companies. Nobody checks it. Nobody gets promoted or fired on account of it. We devise elaborate systems for controlling costs, but not for commitment to the cause. Or how about a little control over losing current customers, the single most costly failure in business? Compensation experts in headquarters create airtight sales incentive systems for selling new business, but when an old customer is lost, everyone shrugs their shoulders. Or why run cost analyses on five-minute toilet breaks in the factory, but not on five-day executive strategy sessions in Bermuda? Are toilet trips a bigger deal than setting strategy? On and on it goes. You get the point. The least we should expect, then, is that the controllers are controlling what's important. But don't hold your breath for central command to get the picture. In another affront to big company logic, it turns out that making sure it's done right isn't a "higher you go, the better the view" game. Score one more for decentralizing!

Whatever the merits of centralization, you can be sure that fostering innovative action is not one of them. This statement rests on my own little theory that corporate creativity and speed are in inverse proportion to the number of "checkers," "passers," and "deciders" in the loop. A checker is the person who checks your new idea for errors of fact or questionable judgment. A passer is that important person (usually a middle manager) who reads the checker's analysis, studies it all, and passes it up, sideways, or back down to you. Passers are corporate versions of air traffic controllers. Once your idea is aloft, they have total logistical authority. In large companies, there may be several levels of deciders. At each level, four things can happen. Only one of them is good news for you. All deciders can

- Say yes, and send it on to the next level.
- Say no, and your idea is history.
- Do nothing, and your idea is also history.
- Send it back for more checking and passing.

There are no scientific studies to prove my theory. But there's plenty of visible evidence that the total number of checkers, passers, and deciders increases along with the level of centralized authority in the company. To get a handle on how you're doing, try this "rule of thumb" scale. You won't be that far off!

CHECKERS/PASSERS DECIDERS	INNOVATIVE ACTION RATING
One	This is Mach 2—hang on!
Two to three	Be patient. Rome wasn't built in a day.
Four to five	Nice try, but the opportunity passed.
Six or more	Learn your lesson? Next time don't ask.

▪Lab in the Woods (the Big Bang Theory of R&D)

To see a big R&D lab in the woods is to see a company with big innovation problems. Shortly after World War II the idea of moving entire research and product development functions off to the woods caught on. Big business was very impressed with war-era achievements like the Manhattan Project, the U.S. effort to manufacture and deliver the atomic bomb, which was done in great secrecy in White Sands, New Mexico, an isolated if not idyllic spot. Of course the Manhattan Project was not about R&D. The horrific secrets of nuclear chain reactions had already been discovered. What was going on in New Mexico was implementation in a time of high crisis—not invention in peaceful isolation. Such asterisks to history seldom deter attempts to get a leg up in business. So the era of programmable corporate invention, the "Big Bang Theory of R&D," was launched on a false premise.

By the 1960s, if you didn't have a big research center, where quiet and serious invention could take place, you just weren't "blue chip." It didn't look serious to have product development operating out of a dirty factory—or across the hall from a bunch of rowdy salesmen. And heaven forbid that such important work should be interrupted by naive customers. And in a total misreading of the reasons for America's economic dominance, the whole world (Germany and Japan included) began building their own labs in their own woods. In big companies everywhere, product innovation moved to the mountains.

Over the decades, however, it was becoming painfully apparent that a lot was going into these labs in the woods, but very little was coming out. At least very little that could be manufactured and sold. Even so, such practices die hard. Just as everyone in the world was rediscovering that saleable products can get invented almost anywhere but R&D centers, along came the 1980s hottest buzzword—*innovation*. As if innovation was a brand-new thought, corporations raced to organize it, make it the latest corporate "value"—and put it in a separate building! The lesson seems to be, if an R&D center can't produce the products the customers want, change it to an "innovation center" and see what happens.

▪Marketing Takes Over
(Striped Toothpaste and Big Fins)

All along, the marketing people have complained about "engineers in ivory towers." Some CEOs, particularly those who came up the marketing side, thought they had a point. Why not turn over the product innovation business to the marketing folks? They know what the market really wants. They do all the market research. They hold the focus group sessions. They're "in touch with the customer." Another very rational idea.

Marketing had a heyday and we got such memorable products as striped toothpaste and giant fins on already oversized cars. It all looked very promising until customers discovered that striped toothpaste didn't clean teeth any better than the old white toothpaste. And while the fins were impressive, the engine was still a piece of junk. Giving marketing full rein on product innovation was great—until the customers began demanding *real* product improvements. The best that can be said for this "revolution in product innovation" is that it was mercifully short.

But hope springs eternal in the marketing department. And sure enough, their run at being innovators has gotten a new lease on life. The opening came when everyone hopped on the "customer service" bandwagon. All of a sudden, customer service became an integral part of the product—many said the *most important* part. This increased attention to service innovation was certainly long overdue in most industries. It also got the marketing function back in the innovation business—this time creating bells and whistles for the service component. The reasoning was familiar. Marketing knows what customers really want, so redesigning customer service is clearly a marketing job.

Unfortunately, everyone in marketing was reading the same book. The service innovations that emerged were mainly copycat cosmetics, often with a distinctly "California" feel. Take, for example, the recent insistence in some companies that all customers get called by their first name. What's the point here? Is it really more courteous to use first names, even for people you don't know and who are twice your age? Does it make the customer forget that the kid calling him "Willy" still doesn't have the foggiest idea of how to solve his problem? In too many companies, hip courtesy has become the marketing answer for old-fashioned product competence.

In the same vein, how about the now mandatory script followed by every perky waiter or waitress in certain "marketing driven" hotel and restaurant chains? You've heard it. The memorized script, delivered with a large and seemingly permanent smile, turns out to be a long-winded sales pitch for exotic drinks and dishes you know you don't want. The real rub is that the script, the artificial smile, and the presumptive sell of the "Tahiti daiquiri" don't make the cold T-bone any hotter and the weak coffee still tastes like weak coffee.

Yes, there are plenty of marketing-inspired innovations most of us can do without: scripted smiles and phony courtesy, five-minute conversations with a recorded message, twelve-page airline questionnaires, handed out just as you fall asleep. So why does marketing, the function directly focused on customers, spend so much effort on fringe nonsense? Why don't they go right to the core of the matter and make fundamental improvements in products and services?

It really isn't for lack of trying. Marketing innovators try very hard. But marketing-style innovations, whether they be automobile fins or scripted courtesy, suffer the same defect as R&D labs in the woods. Marketing and R&D are both prisoners of the artificial functionalizing of business. A lifetime of separating product/customer innovation has given us too many experts and too few craftsmen. Companies have to back up and work as one to create improvements that customers really want.

▪ Senior Management Disconnected

A recent survey of CEOs asked, "What function in your company do you trust the most?" Dead last on this list was R&D—a vivid example of the distance between many senior managements and the supposed innovative process of the company. When upper management disconnects itself from the innovative action of the company, the game is really over. Of course putting new ideas into play at the speed of light is anathema to running a tight ship. Yet tolerating and encouraging some chaos is central to fostering action and creativity. This rests very uneasily with the rank-and-file executives. Who could blame them, really? For one hundred years we've been taught nothing about chaos except that it must be stamped out.

The twist here is that most senior managers got to be senior managers precisely because they were able to "beat the system" throughout their careers. The play-it-by-the-rule-book type, the ultimate risk avoider, rarely does anything spectacular. And rarely does a corporate wallflower rise to the top. Much more often, it's the guy (or gal today) who turned several divisions upside down, broke some rules along the way, and has some battle scars from hand-to-hand corporate combat. These are not wallflowers. They are human, however—and once at the top, the last thing they want is a lot of unpredictable chaos beneath them. It's as if they decide they will be the last cowboy in town! Whatever the reason, when the top of the company stops practicing and fostering high speed and innovation, bureaucracy and slow motion can't be far behind. A disconnected senior management has brought down many a fast-moving, innovative company.

Speaking of disconnected senior managements, I may have found the "mother of all" examples in that fabled land of supposedly connected management, Japan. This is a story of committing every deadly sin in the book. This can happen when a Japanese Goliath and an American Goliath get together to sell a little fried chicken. But it has a happy ending—because it's the story of one little Japanese David, who proved a few *golden rules* are more powerful than all those *deadly sins*.

Colonel Sanders Goes to Japan

"I hadn't the slightest idea to become a chicken man. Then I heard about Colonel Sanders and how he made quite a few franchise dealers millionaires. Then I happened to see the paycheck of my regional manager and the amount was not what I expected. Much less! So I decided to try to become a small independent entrepreneur. The quickest way was to become a restaurant owner or a franchisee. So I made up my mind to join Kentucky Fried Chicken. But I found there was no company in Japan. There was only Lloyd Weston."

This is Takeshi Okawara, talking a mile a minute and wearing a bright red jacket emblazoned with WE'RE NUMBER ONE and a KFC baseball cap. He's also the founding spirit and CEO of the one thousand-plus outlets that produce just over $1 billion in sales for Kentucky Fried Chicken, Japan. KFC was the first fast-food business in Japan and today has more outlets than anyone, including McDonald's. KFC in Japan is second only to the U.S. operation in sales. But getting to this lofty position required innovative actions above and beyond any call to management duty. Okawara's story is one of heroic "intrapreneurship" under the leaden foot of Japanese and American industrial giants like Mitsubishi and Heublein and R. J. Reynolds. But let's backtrack to Okawara's first discovery of KFC and his chance meeting with one Lloyd Weston.

In the late sixties, Takeshi Okawara was a young, mid-level employee of Dai Nippon, today the largest printing company in the world. In his own words, he was just "an average working guy with enough pride to want to improve my situation." The company was working on the Canadian government's exhibit for the upcoming Osaka International Expo. Okawara was sent with two cameramen to travel across Canada and get pictures for the exhibit. This was his first trip to North America and his first introduction to Kentucky Fried Chicken: "We landed at Vancouver and rented a station wagon. We started out across Canada to Victoria, Manitoba, Calgary, all the way to Quebec. We also went down into places like Jasper in the United States. Since our budget was limited, we stayed at Howard Johnson's and picked up lots of hamburgers and fast food—McDonald's, Burger King, Kentucky Fried Chicken, Dunkin Donuts, you name it. I don't remember the McDonald's or Burger King wrapping except that they seemed cheap. But as a printing company employee, I was very impressed with the high-quality paper and printing of the KFC box.

"Back in Japan, one day I happened to see a bulletin board message from a Dai Nippon man in Europe. It said that a guy named Lloyd Weston was coming to Japan to start Kentucky Fried Chicken with the Mitsubishi Corporation and that someone should try to get the printing business. I later learned that Weston was a friend of John Brown's, the owner of KFC, and his job was scouting international markets. I immediately recalled that KFC box, and, as I said, I had read about Colonel Sanders and was thinking about the restaurant business. Well everyone in the office ignored the message. So I just took it and called on Lloyd Weston at the Okura Hotel. From him I learned that KFC was also putting up a small exhibit at the Osaka Expo, and I got the printing order for the KFC boxes. I later learned that the Mitsubishi people were furious about this because they had their own printer, Topan Printing, which was a fierce competitor of Dai Nippon. So now both Weston at KFC and the Mitsubishi guys knew who I was."

That fateful meeting with Lloyd Weston resulted in something far more important than another printing order. From it, Okawara moved rapidly to learn the restaurant business. At age twenty-seven and with no experience in the fast-food business, Okawara became the first employee of the Mitsubishi/KFC Japan joint venture: "There were no stores yet, just a lot of ideas about how to start the business. I joined them in September 1970 as the first store manager. I didn't want to work at Mitsubishi headquarters because my goal was to become a sole owner. I wanted to learn how to cook chicken and how to run a restaurant. Mitsubishi had invested in shopping centers, and their plan was to put a KFC in each. They tried to put the first store in a big shopping center in Nagoya, on the corner of the parking lot. This first KFC in Japan was scheduled to open on November 23, 1970. I was the manager. When I got there on November 10 and went down to the store location, there was no building yet. Then I learned I had to find bread and chicken suppliers myself. And I had to find employees. Nothing was set up! It was such a shock. Mitsubishi was such a gigantic organization that I thought all I had to do was go there and run the store. But there was nothing there. Then a KFC man, Mr. Connors, came by and told me I could stay in the hotel only three days. It was too expensive. So I also had to find a place to live.

"I thought the first thing to do was find employees. But in those days nobody dared work for a foreign company, especially with a name like Kentucky Fried Chicken. On a map of the town, I saw a culinary school was nearby. The school allowed me to come and talk to the students. I talked about a new revolution in food service—all the things that KFC had told me. The students asked me questions about this and that and really made fun of me. Anyway, I said I would wait outside for anyone who wanted to try. Only two guys came out—and I hired them. They are both still with me. One is my managing director and the other is still on my board. These two guys were able to convince some other classmates, so at least we had some employees.

"When we finally opened, we put flowers and bouquets all around and had a ribbon-cutting ceremony. All of the local housewives were there, and I was so excited. As soon as we cut the tape, the housewives grabbed the flowers and disappeared! Nobody was left. So next we decided to have a "free test trial" for the new Kentucky Fried Chicken—the "world famous chicken." People came and tried the free chicken, but when I tried to sell them some, they disappeared again! Still, the first few days we did sell some. The first day we sold about three thousand dollars, which was good. By the fifth day we were down to fifteen hundred dollars. It kept dropping. Within a month the volume was down to about seven thousand yen, which was twenty-five dollars. At that volume, if we cooked one box—two halves—it was more than enough for a whole day. But we could hold the chicken for only two hours. So the more we cooked, the more we discarded and the more we lost.

"At that time, there were no American fast-food restaurants in Japan. Only one Mr. Donut. McDonald's came in six months later, and they opened in the Ginsa, in the heart of Tokyo. They were smart. We opened a store in a remote city, in a parking lot. There weren't even many car drivers in those days. Many people were riding bicycles. So our drive-through didn't mean anything. And it only took nine months to eat up the initial capital, which created a $1 million loss. Fortunately, KFC was being acquired by Heublein so they had no time to look at what was going on here. Otherwise they would have shut us down. Mitsubishi was so big they could tolerate it, but they were unhappy. This was their first venture into this kind of retail business, so once things went wrong, there was lots of grumbling in the Mitsubishi organization about the chicken business. The next thing I knew all the managers above me at Mitsubishi headquarters, up to managing director, quit. They all got out before any new money had to come in, and also they didn't want to end up doing carry-out work. You know, carrying the KFC box to customers. So I had myself and the few kids from the culinary school. A sinking ship, obviously."

Is the picture coming clear? Here's our hero Okawara and a couple of students caught on a sinking raft, between two distant ports. On one side of the ocean, KFC Corporation had become a hot Wall Street commodity. It was acquired by Heublein, which was taken over by R. J. Reynolds, who eventually tossed it to PepsiCo. And, of course, with this wild succession of American owners, came four different management crews, each with their own nutty ideas about selling fried chicken in Japan. On the Asian side of the Pacific, much closer to the action, was the giant trading group Mitsubishi. The behemoth of heavy industry knew nothing and cared less about a string of fast-food joints started by a colonel in a white suit from Kentucky.

But a funny thing happened on the way to the bottom. Takeshi Okawara was getting the entrepreneurial bug. He was beginning to see it all as his own little baby, and his pride of ownership began to overwhelm his sense of imminent disaster: "So starting as store manager, by the next spring I became corporate management because there was no one left, and then six months later I was on the board of directors. But it reached the point where Mitsubishi was considering abandoning the business. Then I really began to fight to keep it alive. Mitsubishi didn't know what to do, but I was insisting so hard they just said, 'Okay, okay, go ahead.'

"See, when I ate the chicken I thought it was so good. And when I gave it away free, people loved it. And once in a while they would even save up money and come back. So I thought that since it was so good, if we could find people who have money, they would buy the chicken. We needed another store. Of course there was Ginsa, but it would have cost us so much and we were in the great big red! We did find one good location, a little bit off center, but it was a business center. A busy spot. I knew the people there had money. So we found a space, about half the size of my office now, and in a small car we moved the equipment from the shut-down store in Nagoya to the new location.

"My guys and I sold chicken in the day and painted the shop ourselves at night and lived in the back of the store. It all seems funny now but in those days we were sort of desperate. The company was on the verge of bankruptcy. I was sending reports but still no one from headquarters came around.

"I began negotiating with Mitsubishi and KFC to loan us a small amount to open more stores. They told me to go to the Mitsubishi Bank. But I was shocked when the Mitsubishi Bank refused to give us a loan. The Mitsubishi Bank is an entirely different part of the organization, but still it was shocking. And then Mitsubishi's livestock business refused to sell me chickens on credit. KFC Japan was under the New Business Development Department and the Livestock Department had nothing to do with them. The general manager of Livestock said, 'It's silly to sell you chickens, because my receivables won't ever get paid.' Well, without money and without chickens, things were very desperate.

"Then I got an idea. My brother worked at Sumitomo, a big competitor of Mitsubishi. He introduced me to the district manager of their livestock business. I went over and told him we were a company of the Mitsubishi family, and we were doing okay. Of course I was talking about the future. He believed me because he thought that if Mitsubishi had invested in us, we must be good. So Sumitomo agreed to sell us chickens on normal credit. Then I jumped to another big supplier and told them about Sumitomo and they agreed to sell us chickens too. Finally I went back to the Mitsubishi Livestock manager and said, 'Hey, Sumitomo and others are selling us chickens. They're your biggest competitors, so is that good enough for you?' Then he said he would sell us chickens. I used the same trick with Sumitomo Bank and Fuji Bank to get loans. So that's how we got chickens and money."

I had to ask Okawara why he never jumped ship. It all sounded so frustrating: "Well, my goal from the beginning was to be independent, you see. I thought I could learn more in a difficult situation than in an easy one. And Colonel Sanders, on his first trip to Japan in October 1972, gave me good advice. He said, 'The easy way becomes harder and the hard way becomes easier.' I really like those words. So I thought that by solving all these problems I will be preparing for my own business. I felt I had already seen hell, and after hell, everything else would be heaven!

"But of course I never left KFC. I achieved the independence I wanted right here. Today KFC Japan is a separately listed, independent company on the Tokyo Stock Exchange. Mitsubishi and PepsiCo are still the two largest shareholders, of course. But there are various independent shareholders, including me and some executives and some of our franchisees. I should explain that, in the Japanese system, because of Mitsubishi's large share, KFC Japan is considered a member of the Mitsubishi Group or family of companies. And today, not including the Mitsubishi Trading Company itself, of all the affiliated companies in the Mitsubishi family, and there are 482, KFC Japan is the second biggest money-maker."

Finally, I asked Okawara if I should refer to him as the founder of KFC Japan: "No, just call me a chicken cook who somehow ended up being CEO of the whole company." Whether chicken cook or entrepreneur, Takeshi Okawara had to learn the hard way how to keep moving and shaking the boat with two very heavy anchors. But maybe, as he said, that's the best way to learn the rules—especially golden rules!

The Golden Rules of High-speed Innovation

He that will not apply new remedies must expect new evils; for time is the greatest innovator.
            —FRANCIS BACON, "Of Innovations," 1625

High-speed innovation is hardly a new concept. Francis Bacon was no entrepreneur, but he hit the nail on the head in 1625. Improving things is not a static game. Time does bring "new evils" and changing challenges. Standing still doesn't keep you in the same spot—it puts you at the back of the pack.

So why all the recent hullabaloo in business circles about being innovative and fast-moving? Look at the current crop of business books. It seems every other one has the word *innovate* in the title or subtitle. It's as if we've just discovered that innovation is good for business. And moving fast is some brand-new trick to conquer the world. Even Peter Drucker got on the bandwagon in the mid-eighties to publish his zillionth book, with the up-to-the-minute title *Innovation and Entrepreneurship*. Could it be that big business has finally figured out why 90 percent of the growth in the world comes from small, upstart competitors? Maybe so, and that's terrific news, isn't it?

Well, yes and no. Take a closer look. This all has the familiar ring of old-fashioned common sense, long ridiculed and forgotten, being repackaged as modern management genius. Drucker, for example, makes the remarkable assertion: "Management is the new technology (rather than any specific new science or invention) that is making the American economy into an entrepreneurial economy." Do you detect just a bit of defensiveness about the science of management? He concludes the introduction to his book with a truly scary thought: "This means that the time has now come to do for entrepreneurship and innovation what we first did for management in general some thirty years ago: to develop the principles, the practice, and the discipline." Really! Is this the unabridged embrace of innovation (or entrepreneurship) you were expecting?

No one's against understanding innovation. But let's not do to it what "we first did for management in general some thirty years ago." Especially if the "we" Drucker talks about is who I think it is. The truth is that it was largely "we" management gurus who killed off innovative action in corporations in the first place.

Rediscovering the importance of agility and fleet-footedness is obviously a huge positive for big business. They need to be exploded out across all industries and in all facets of an operation. But the thing we don't need is the management experts to "develop" au courant "principles, practices, and disciplines" on how to do it. Such thinking has always been part of the problem—not the solution. Maybe we should first *stop* doing some managerial practices (deadly sins?) and see what happens. Maybe we should remember the most famous Francis Bacon quote of all—beware those things that "Cure the disease and kill the patient."

Here's a more modest (and innovative) proposition. If high speed and innovation have been dead in big companies for decades, yet very alive and well in entrepreneurial companies, why not look there first? When you do, you won't find innovation departments, or seminars on creativity, or rules and committees to reduce bureaucracy. You certainly won't see a list of principles, practices, and disciplines to follow. When you look at entrepreneurial companies, what you do see is a rip-roaring combination of urgent necessity and the freedom to do something about it—the necessity to invent coupled with the freedom to act. If you want principles, try these, the entrepreneur's two "golden rules" of high-speed innovation.

The Necessity to Invent

Remember this bit of old-fashioned wisdom: "Necessity is the mother of invention"—*Mater artium necessitas?* We've been saying it since the time of Caesar—because it's true. It's based on the historical fact that anyone can be innovative if his life depends on it. Current management insight notwithstanding, we're not about to change history. Programming innovation, absent necessity, is doomed to failure. *Managing innovation* isn't even the issue. What has to be *managed* is the belief that things absolutely, positively have to be improved—that it is a matter of great and urgent necessity. Whether it's solving old problems or capturing new opportunities, theories and procedures are no substitute for burning necessity. Here's the enterprise version of *mater artium necessitas*.

▪Feeling the Heat of Burning Necessity

Feeling some heat is a burden borne by all entrepreneurs. This is a "problem" that most big companies don't have. Inside a bureaucracy, you can't find anybody who feels much heat about anything. From sales clerks who shrug their shoulders, to recorded messages and form letters, to faceless bigshots who haven't seen a customer since 1954, absolutely no one seems accountable. This would be unfathomable behavior to any entrepreneur. When it's down to putting food on the table, someone has to be personally accountable.

It doesn't have to be this way, and it can't be if we expect employees from top to bottom to feel the pressure and adrenaline of necessity. First, they've got to know there's a competitive war going on. They can't be sealed off in corporate time capsules for forty years. They've also got to feel some personal pain, as "unenlightened" as that may sound. They can't have their raise and Bermuda conference too, while the customers are leaving in droves. And they can't brush it off by blaming "the company" when they are the company. Everyone has to have their feet in the fire. Feeling the heat of burning necessity may in fact be the first necessity.

▪Creating Crisis and Urgency

Work for an entrepreneur, and you earn your stripes in the art of crisis command. Many I've watched and the couple I've worked for seem to leap from crisis to crisis—and from success to success. Watch enough of this and it begins to sink in. Few really great things ever come from careful planning. Most great leaps forward come on the wings of crisis. Is this weak planning or great inspiration? I don't know, but I do know that it's complacency, not poor planning, that's killing big companies everywhere. Most CEOs would happily trade a pound of planning for an ounce of urgency from their bureaucracy.

Before you jump on this tiny bandwagon, be warned that operating with crisis and urgency is not exactly a company picnic. It's sort of the managing equivalent of watching your own angioplasty. There's a lot of anxiety, a little danger, some real pain, and a burning desire to get it over with. But, lo and behold, in a matter of minutes those little balloons can wipe out years of neglect—and when it's over you're healthier than you even deserve to be. And so it is with corporate crisis. Not a pleasant experience, but where would we be without it? Of course—fatter and more complacent than ever. Next to nothing gets done when times are good, but let disaster strike, and corporate energy and ingenuity know no bounds. The trick, of course, is to dole out the crisis in small, regular doses—creating tiny tremors, not giant earthquakes, if you will. It still may not be a lot of fun, but the entrepreneurial message is clear: A little crisis a day keeps the complacency away.

▪Do Something, Anything, Better Each Day

The best definition of innovation is the broadest. Everyone should come to work determined to do something, anything, better each day. Franklin Delano Roosevelt was no businessman, but he knew how to get things moving. Promising an all-out attack on the depression gripping the country, the presidential candidate laid out his "method" in 1932: ". . . the country demands bold, persistent experimentation. It is common sense to take a method and try it. If it fails, admit it frankly and try another. But above all, try something." Every shred of research into the process of innovation says the same thing: The way to innovate is to try something, anything, again, again, and again.

Doing "something, anything, better" doesn't just mean R&D. Inventing products isn't the only "necessity" in business. And a hundred people trying is a hundred times better than one lonely innovator. It all takes a new mind-set about what employees are really paid to do. Maintaining the business, which most people are programmed to do, is really losing the business. Growing and prospering demand that all of us do something, anything, better each day.

The Freedom to Act

If you can only follow one "golden rule" at a time, you'd better make it the freedom to act. Innovation without action might get you a Nobel prize, but it won't get you a customer. History is replete with great ideas that got implemented by others. Ask the British. They invented a million things that made fortunes for German, American, and Japanese companies. From chemical dyes to automobiles to radar, British industry had a habit of doing only half the job.

Today, it's no longer the British getting clobbered by the Germans—or the Americans losing out to Japan—or even the Japanese being taken to the cleaners by Koreans. It's muscle-bound big companies everywhere that are suffering from the old British malaise. And it's not just getting inventions to market where fast action counts; it's keeping markets you thought you owned from being stolen as you sleep.

While corporate committees analyze them to death, entire markets are gobbled up by smaller and hungier entrepreneurs. Example: A nonplayer in Japan, Soichiro Honda beats Nissan and Toyota to the punch in America and produces the biggest-selling car in the biggest market in the world. Honda is also years ahead of all importers in meeting the "made in America" demands of the U.S. government. Nobody in Tokyo says, "Soichiro who?" anymore.

Example: British Airways may call itself the largest, but British passengers call Virgin Atlantic the best. Led by Richard Branson, a music-producing and balloon-flying entrepreneur, Virgin has stolen the show across the Atlantic. While the supercarriers form alliances and fiddle with their reservation systems, Virgin has taken a major slice of the market with rapid-fire customer-oriented innovations.

Example: A breakthrough in science occurs in San Francisco, and presto, four hundred new biotech companies are up and running, dominating the market. While the big pharmaceuticals slept, entrepreneurial "gene-jockeys" created an industry that may equal worldwide pharmaceutical sales by the year 2000!

Example: An old industry gets deregulated and like lightning bolts, hundreds of small, start-up carriers take a major piece of the lucrative long-distance telephone market. If you're waiting for the mighty AT&T to come roaring back, remember this is the same elephant that after a decade still can't figure out how to make a dime from computers—a business that made millionaires out of every Tom, Dick, and Harry in Silicon Valley. The fact is, the examples are endless. It's gotten so bad in the biggest of the big, that just taking action, any action, is a truly innovative event.

Can big bureaucracies do anything to match the speed of their smaller, more enterprising competitors? Of course they *can*. Entrepreneurs aren't action-oriented because their genes are different. Entrepreneurs move fast because they personally feel the necessity and they don't have to ask six layers of management before they move off the dime. They have the freedom to act. But this isn't how bureaucracies operate. Even if they sense a necessity, the analysis and approval can take years. And in a world where rocking the boat usually gets you tossed overboard, who's going to buck the system? These are manmade impediments, not laws of nature. So it's all the more a mystery why dismantling them seems to take an act of God.

Thomas Edison, still the all-time record holder of American patents and the founder of scores of companies, was famous for saying, "Invention is 10 percent inspiration and 90 percent perspiration." So here's a short list of enterprising possibilites to raise the "perspiration level" in the business.

▪ Freeing the Genius of the Average Worker

Entrepreneurs simply don't buy the notion that you have to be a "rocket scientist" to run a business. Business runs on common sense, and the bulk of the common sense resides in the bulk of the people—in other words, the average worker. Soichiro Honda called it the "genius of the average worker." It's these people who know the product, inside and out. They're the ones on first-name terms with customers. It's the average worker who has to deal every day with every stupid form and time-wasting procedure in the company. None of this is surprising, of course. What's surprising is how little we use their genius.

Why don't we strip clean this gold mine of good ideas and mass of energy? A big part of the trouble seems to be with the reality of who's average. The average people come to work on time, go home on time, and in between do their job. They do what we expect them to do. They're not the superstars in the company. They're never going to become vice presidents, let alone CEOs. The average also aren't the bums of the business. They're not drug addicts, thieves, or lazy no-goods. They don't come to work every day determined to wreck the company. Average means average, which means a busy management doesn't think about them much.

Not only do we not tap their genius, but many companies seem absolutely determined to deep-six any innovation and initiative from average workers. The ghost of Frederick Taylor still stalks many a factory floor and sales office. Putting good human relations aside, what do we lose when the bulk of our people go mentally comatose as they walk through the factory gate? What is the cost of freezing out the action-taking instincts of 90 percent of the people? The answer is obvious. You get companies full of "Rivetheads"—the half-angry, half-sad label coined by Ben Hamper, GM assembly line worker turned writer. From his own experience in the factory, Hamper says you get to the place where "working the line at GM was like being paid to flunk high school the rest of your life." This is why it's good business to free the genius of the average worker. This is why every employee has to believe he can make a difference.

▪Action with Customers, Products, and Inside the Organization

Where should we aim our high-speed innovation? If *everywhere, all the time* sounds too ambitious (or a little nutty), how about focusing on the core of what keeps you competitive? The one place you can never go wrong is combined customer/product innovation. The overlap is a throwback to the craftsman—the enterpriser who has to make and sell his own products. This may seem obvious, yet it boggles the mind how many companies maintain a self-defeating functional separation of product and customer innovation.

Every single action directed at customers and products is a step in the right direction—not big, across-the-board changes, but a hundred little experiments in a hundred places. They won't all work out, but there's no faster, cheaper way to learn. The thing big companies have to get over, however, is arrogance. Believing customers know more than we do about buying, using, and servicing our products is a good starting point. Innovative actions with customers, above all, have to tap into their expertise as buyers and users of your products. And you have to take it all seriously. Forget questionnaires that no one reads. Forget slogans that no one believes. Forget advertising claims and expensive client lunches. The actions that change your core competitiveness are always the "sleeves rolled-up" efforts to make buying, using, and servicing your product a faster and better experience for customers.

Actions directed at the internal workings of the organization are surefire winners also—with one giant caveat: They've got to be connected to the business of making great products and keeping customers coming back for more. Unconnected internal improvement projects take on a life of their own, chewing up precious time and resources. Entrepreneurs are often absolutely astounded by what they see when they get acquired by bigger companies. Hundreds of committees, thousands of meetings, and millions of sheets of paper are expended on ideas and projects that have nothing to do with the business. It's as if the really hard thinking and the most determined actions are reserved to feather the nest of the bureaucracy or the executives.

Beyond this caveat, there is serious work to do on the internal workings of the company. Almost all of it involves getting rid of something—getting rid of dysfunctional procedures, out-of-date forms, and out-of-touch committees. Actions attacking all of this are worth their weight in gold. It's called bureaucracy bashing.

▪ Bureaucracy-Bashing Bosses

In most organizations, the first battle is to wipe out fifty years of bureaucracy. Only the bosses can clean up this mess. Stop to consider that the fundamental purpose of rapid action in business is to beat the competition to market with better products and services. Ask yourself what's going on that doesn't help you reach that goal. Then stop doing all those things. Don't worry—the company won't implode into a black hole. What you learn is that all those extras are just bureaucracy run amok.

For sure, taking a sledgehammer to the bureaucracy isn't the fun part of being boss. But it may be the single most heroic act any CEO can ever take. Getting everyone's attention is a necessary ingredient in successful bureaucracy bashing. Try taking the very first swing of the hammer right down the middle of corporate headquarters. After that it gets a lot easier. Just keep at it till knocking off committees and knocking out photocopiers becomes a company habit. For speeding up action, it's a habit with golden results.

Golden results usually come from following golden rules. The business of fostering high-speed innovation is no different. But feeling the necessity to invent and having the freedom to act aren't "spiritual happenings." They're practical, everyday conditions that must exist to encourage and permit a fast-moving and creative spirit of enterprise—the kind of red-hot spirit I found at a place called Chili's.

Chili's Recipe for Red-Hot Growth

For restaurant results that sizzle, you don't need to go all the way to Tokyo. Just go to Dallas. In one bubbling pot, you'll find all the ingredients of high-speed innovation and super high growth; a legendary entrepreneur at the helm; the hand-picked protégé, an MBA-turned-enterpriser, to run it; the constant battle against "deadly sins" and bureaucracy—all fired by a burning necessity to improve and an extraordinary freedom to act.

I first came across Chili's—recently re-named Brinker International*—when it was still on the *Forbes* list of "The 200 Best Small Companies in America." One of the fastest-growing companies in the United States, Brinker passed through midsize like a meteor and is now zooming toward the billion-dollar mark. No, it's not another high-growth computer company from Silicon Valley. Brinker International means Texas-sized growth in fajitas and

---

* Chili's was founded in Dallas in 1975 by Larry Lavine. Norm Brinker acquired the twenty-three existing units in 1983. Original entrepreneur Lavine stayed on, a practice Brinker strongly encourages. Brinker has repeated the process twice more. In 1988 he bought Grady's Goodtimes (re-named Regas Grill), with five restaurants in Knoxville, Tennessee. His most recent venture was to buy Romano's Macaroni Grill, a single restaurant in Leon Springs, Texas. Today, all three are rapidly expanding under the Brinker International flag.

chili, macaroni and cheese, and juicy prime ribs. High growth in the restaurant business, a market that experts say is saturated to the point of drowning? And from Texas, an economic basketcase for the past five years? That's right—straight from Dallas, Texas, the best restaurants either side of the Rio Grande. And they're sweeping across America with a tenfold increase in units and a whopping twentyfold increase in sales and profits in less than a decade. In the process, Chairman Norm Brinker and President Ron McDougall are rewriting the book for high-speed innovation in the food service industry.

Norman Brinker was a farm boy from Roswell, New Mexico. His first brush with a much bigger world came when he rode for the U.S. equestrian team at the 1952 Olympics in Helsinki. He later married Maureen ("Little Mo") Connally, Wimbledon champ and America's reigning queen of tennis. He also suffered through her early death from cancer. Professionally he's done it all: from an entry-level job in hamburgers (Jack in the Box), to chairman of Burger King, to owning a single coffee shop, to creating one big-name chain after another. Along the way he has become a living legend in the restaurant business.

For openers, he invented the full-service chain restaurant business back in 1966, with the hugely successful Steak and Ale, which spawned Bennigan's, his second successful chain. Both chains were big winners, an unmatched feat at the time. Pillsbury bought his business and asked him to work his growth magic on their ailing giant, Burger King. He promptly initiated the famous "Battle of the Burgers" against McDonald's. Sales skyrocketed (the last good news at Burger King), and his reward was to be promoted ever higher on the bureaucracy ladder, becoming chairman of Pillsbury's massive restaurant group. A year later he quit to get back to doing what he loves best—entrepreneuring. Apparently no one told Norm Brinker it was a lousy time and place to make another run in the restaurant business. So he took over a small, struggling group of restaurants called Chili's in Dallas.

Ron McDougall first worked for Brinker way back in 1974 and

has more or less been with him ever since. An MBA from Minnesota, he put in his time on packaged goods at giants like Sara Lee and General Foods. With Brinker, he got his chance to move into high gear. Shedding the image of "those noncreative MBA types," he was deeply involved in the concept and start-up of Bennigan's. He rode the Pillsbury and Burger King circuit with Brinker, a trip that was more detour than desire. When Brinker asked him to run his new venture, as president, he headed straight for Dallas.

Their odysseys in and out of the corporate world have left Brinker and McDougall with a profound preference for fast-moving innovation—and appreciation of the competitive value of getting everyone involved. Brinker is famous for letting customers and employees tell him what needs to be done: "Before I walk into one of our restaurants or a competitor's restaurant, I wait for a group of people to come out, and I ask them, 'How was it? Is this place any good?' " At company headquarters he almost never calls meetings, but spends a big part of his time just talking to people. He likes to wander into someone's office and explore any new idea on their mind. The industry chronicle, *Restaurants & Institutions*, says it best: ". . . and he has seen to it that Chili's sends a message to all its staff: Ideas Wanted. Good suggestions are rewarded with spot bonuses, or at least letters of appreciation. He tells managers who have just come into the Chili's system to look around and point out anything they think can be done better before they become 'Chilized.' Almost 80 percent of the current Chili's menu came from suggestions made by unit managers. As a former chairman of Burger King, Brinker knows the importance of taking good advice from the people in closest touch with the customer and the dangers of stifling employee creativity."

To get the *real* Brinker International message, I went to their busy headquarters, right off the LBJ Freeway in Dallas. Ron McDougall is a classic "medium-is-the-message" kind of guy. He speaks without commas or periods. Just a continuous flood of exclamation points! Listen to him breathe fire on the necessity to keep improving (pauses and punctuation, courtesy of your editor): "We believe here that if you stay the way you are today even if you're successful, down the road you're not going to be working well anymore, because you're going to be yesterday's news at some point. So we're not afraid to change here! We're not afraid to challenge! We're all challenging the system! No matter how good this thing is, we *never* think we're in first place. We always play like we're in second place trying to get that extra edge to get back into first place. Our biggest enemy is probably ourselves—that's this company, which is us! And so we challenge the system all the time: whether it's more efficient operating procedures, better quality products, better ambiance in a restaurant . . . better service systems. Whatever it is, we're always trying to find a better way to do it. So where we are today, that's like your benchmark—now *beat it* somehow—or we fail! You know what I mean?" With McDougall it's pretty hard to miss the message.

Big company innovation? Here's a front-line description from McDougall, the innovator who's seen all sides: "I think the larger you get, there tends to be a rigidity that sets in—through time, I think. When you're small you're scrambling and flexible—quicker on your feet—because there aren't that many things to change. The larger you get, if you change one thing you've got to change—you take a McDonald's, with twelve thousand restaurants. You change one thing, you've got to change twelve thousand restaurants, all the hundreds of thousands of employees. You have to change procedures, whatever." So there's more to change in big business. Can't argue with that. But aren't there a lot more people to help make the changes? What are they all doing about it? Here's what they're doing, according to McDougall: "[But] bureaucracy tends to set in, in the larger systems. . . . There's a lot of little links in the chain, I guess. A lot of departments. They tend to become little fiefdoms out by themselves, and doing things for their own department—Internal projects. Never have any impact on the business! Some of the larger companies I've been with—I've seen those things happen. These projects become a project within themselves. They never have an application outside your four walls. Never impact the business. But it's a real neat project to work on—or it's a lot of fun—or you get strokes out of it—but it's not moving the pea ahead." At this point, he came up for air and sensed I was a couple of thoughts behind him. The McDougall approach to slowing down is to repeat his last point—several times—until you're caught up: "The pea! You know, the pea! Like moving the pea across the table? Get it?"

Like Brinker, McDougall places great store in the ideas of employees: "The key isn't to change for change's sake, obviously, but to keep looking to find a better way to do it. And we don't care where the idea comes from. Whoever has the idea—bring it up—we're gonna make this thing happen! So a 'not invented here' syndrome hopefully doesn't happen in this environment. I don't think of every idea myself, nor does Norman. You know, a lot of great ideas come from the waitstaff—from the unit managers. You know, employees throughout the whole system, because they're actually closer to the firing line, and they can see the opportunity better than we can see it. We try to foster an environment where you can get those ideas up, surfaced, so you can see them and grab them—capture the idea and work with it!"

An amazing amount of employee participation goes on at Brinker. Take what happens when employees leave the company, for whatever reasons. McDougall tells it in a isn't-this-what-eveyone-does tone: "We've got a few of these people leaving, and instead of replacing them, other people come forward and say: 'You know, the three of us can split that one job up into three parts,' and we don't replace that person. We have people coming forward with these ideas, and what we do is—we raise their pay and don't hire a new person. So these people get a job expansion—they get a salary expansion—and we eliminate a position." I allowed as how I didn't think people at most companies would come forward to offer to do more work to eliminate a hire. "They come forward here," McDougall fired back. "I guess there's some tentacles there, because one of the things that they believe is that we'll take care of them. If they come forward with an idea like that—it's a good idea—we don't say, 'Okay, take more work on, see you around.' If it's worth it to us, we'll cross their palms with it. Also, everyone in the company including the home office is on profit-sharing—*everyone*! All the way down to the person who walks in the first day, they're on profit-sharing. . . . I've got a whole team here that's looking to save money! And you don't need a hundred-thousand-dollar idea to contribute. If you can save one thousand dollars, that goes back into the profit pool. So if someone's going crazy on the copier machine, we have a lot of policemen around!"

To McDougall, the possibility of failure is an integral part of taking action. Promoting initiative but forbidding failure has tripped up many "wanna-be" innovators. At all three Brinker chains—Chili's, Regas, and Romano's—decentralized action taking is an article of faith. McDougall tells how thay keep the faith and deal with the inevitable mistakes: "At most companies it's red tape, or levels. You've got approval levels you have to work your way through to get something through a lot of the doomsayers. A big company is more people saying how you can't do something than how you can do it. And what we have around here is kind of we-don't-like-to-fail, but we're not afraid of running hard and hitting the wall once and bouncing off and getting up and going again. It's a belief that you have to try things, and if it doesn't work, don't be a fool and stay with it and drive it in the ground. Try—if it doesn't work—back off and come again! We tried a lot of things that didn't work very well; we retreated and attacked again in a different direction."

So there you have it—all the ingredients to keep a growing company growing; creating a high sense of urgency, encouraging constant improvements, fostering innovative ideas, keeping employees involved, fighting bureaucracy, and permitting some failure along the way. Underpinning these practices are those two "golden rules": feeling *the necessity to invent* and having *the freedom to act*. The spectacular success at Brinker International isn't just because Norm Brinker and Ron McDougall live by these golden rules themselves;

they've also mastered the art of pushing them down deep in the company. It's their recipe for red-hot growth—big portions of innovation, served at high speed.

Sir Brian—
the Whirlwind of Wembley

One of the shortest discussions I've ever had about speed and innovation in enterprise came at Wembley Stadium outside of London. It was also one of the most profound. This isn't surprising as I was talking to Brian Wolfson (recently annointed Sir Brian), the whirlwind chairman of Wembley, Plc. Wolfson can say more of value in five minutes than some of us say in five years. He is without doubt the fastest-moving entrepreneur I've ever met. At the drop of a tuppence he could be off to Colorado forming a new company, or forging new strategies as chairman of the UK's National Training Task Force, or simply taking the time to help an acquaintance meet the right person in Timbuktu.

I've been on the receiving end of Wolfson's helpful nature numerous times: He's given me good, solid advice, a valued introduction to the British Institute of Management where he serves on the board, and one of the unforgettable weeks of my life as the business guest of the unforgettable Chief Aboderin in Nigeria. Most astonishing is that Wolfson asks nothing in return for taking time to help others—a rare trait in the world of commerce.

Wolfson has founded several successful international businesses over the years. However, his acquisition of a major interest in, and management control of, Wembley, Plc. is something of a high-profile departure from his previous ventures. Constructed in 1923, Wembley may well be the most-recognized British "product" in the world today. It's hard to keep a low profile with events like the

Olympics (1948), the World Cup, the Beatles, the Rolling Stones, Madonna, and such serious business as Nelson Mandela's first worldwide TV speech after his release from prison. So I asked Wolfson what got him interested in Wembley, Plc. He surprised me by rattling off three things that don't show up on his public CV. First, he had always been keen on sports and was in fact a four hundred-meter champion runner in the UK. Second, he enjoyed working with Peter Ueberroth on the new concept of using corporate sponsors to finance the 1984 Los Angeles Olympics. And third, as chairman of the UK committee to get the 1992 Olympics to the UK (which Barcelona won), he saw up close some things that needed changing in the UK sports and leisure field. And then the Brian Wolfson I know best added the clincher: He knew that Wembley was getting run-down and needed a lot of work—and had tremendous untapped potential.

And tap it he did! In typical Wolfson fashion, in the five years he's been running the show, he has turned the place upside down and inside out. Sales have leapt from a stodgy $44 million to $254 million. Profits have gone from a negligible $175,000 to $15 million. This magnificent growth is nourished by nearly $140 million in capital improvements—$115 million of which has gone directly into the core business at the Wembley complex. And with the famous stadium and arena now setting all-time records for events and profits, Wolfson has pushed out internationally to Germany, Japan, and the United States. New international operations, such as computerized ticketing services and racetracks, are all extensions of Wembley's know-how in the sports and leisure business. This is no Maxwellian financial house of cards. Sir Brian still believes in making money the old-fashioned way: growing on the backs of products and customers, with constant innovation and blinding speed.

When I arrived at Wembley, Wolfson's long-time personal assistant, Margaret, said what she always says: "Larry, it's another hectic day. We'll have to play it by ear." Then Brian rushed in, asking if it would be all right if we talked in snatches and, before

I could answer, ordered up the Bentley and two security guards to give me the behind-the-scenes tour of Wembley. When we did get down to the business at hand, I asked him the obvious question of just what it is that keeps Brian Wolfson moving. The instant response: "A, it could be that I'm just inherently restless. B, I have a lot of energy. And C, I actually believe that in a private relationship, in a deal that you're trying to fulfill, or indeed in the energy cycle of a business, the most critical thing is the establishment and maintenance of momentum. When you lose momentum, it takes enormous energy to reclaim it."

For years, Wolfson practically lived on airplanes. He had set up a worldwide business of television leasing and seemed intent on being everywhere at once. I asked him about it: "Well, you don't build a business in thirty countries from scratch without moving. We actually took thirty greenfield sites, which had never existed before, and created in those thirty countries a business from scratch. You must know three things to start a new business: there's the widget, the environment, and the people. It's all right if you know the widget and the people—you can try a new environment. It's all right if you know the environment and the people, you can try a new widget. But if you have the situation where you need to learn more than one of the three, you lose your ass. This has to be anybody's philosophy who wants to start a business. So take what I was doing: I knew the widget and I knew the people I put in each country—but I had to learn the local environment. You have to move a bit to learn the local environment in thirty countries."

And how does it feel, after all those years of incredible hustle, to now have reached success? "No, I don't believe I've been successful. I think success is a very, very fraudulent concept. Failure is real. You know where you are if you bloody fail! What does success do? Make you smart? Get you a beautiful woman? I mean what's success? It's a very short-term horizon." I said, "Most people would say you've been very successful. You've certainly made Wembley a success." Automatic retort: "No, it isn't. Not yet. Maybe ten, fifteen years from now it will be successful." Now we were getting down to what keeps Wolfson moving—sort of the entrepreneurial version of a Japanese "continuous improvement" quality program.

Suddenly I realized Brian had been standing up at his desk the whole time we'd been talking. He didn't say so, but I began to feel he was getting antsy to do something more practical than expound on himself. So I let fly with a last question on how he found so much time to help other people: "I enjoy people. I always have. I take and give energy in relationship to people. I enjoy the inter-relationship, the interaction. I believe that busy people, if they're effective, are brokers in time. And the only gift of self you ever give another human being that means anything is time. Anything else, you can pay someone to do for you. But the thing which is a gift of *self* is time."

Maybe Frances Bacon was right. Time *is* the greatest innovator. But maybe Brian Wolfson is also right: that the end-of-the-day point is, time is a gift, not the enemy that brings "new evils" but a limited resource to "apply new remedies." If time is the denom-inator of *high speed* and *innovation*, isn't it time to stop acting as though we have all the time in the world? Isn't this the most timely lesson from Morita and Penhoet and Wolfson and a thousand other fast-moving enterprisers?

CHAPTER FIVE

SELF-INSPIRED BEHAVIOR

Ordinary People Doing Extraordinary Things

I'm looking for people who love to win. If I run out of those, I want people who hate to lose.
—H. ROSS PEROT,
      founder, Electronic Data Systems Corporation;
      founder, Perot Systems Corporation

On Wings of Eagles

Finding people who love to win is easier said than done unless you're a believer like Ross Perot. This Texas billionaire, the quintessential American entrepreneur, is a big believer in winning—for himself and for his troops. Like Confucius, his first rule is to set the first example. Return for a minute to Teheran, early 1979. When Ross Perot learned that wild-eyed revolutionaries had thrown two EDS executives in prison, he went ballistic. He formed his own commando team, hired a real Rambo, Arthur "Bull" Simon, to lead it, and rescued his people from Evin prison in Teheran. All of this made great headlines and even a great book and TV movie, *On Wings of Eagles*. It also makes great people management, if you're looking for extreme performance and commitment from your employees.

Right up to his current crusade to "save" America from its politicians, Perot has always created headlines with his brand of example setting. Over twenty years ago he personally went into Laos trying to get supplies to American POWs in North Vietnam. He bought the Magna Carta for $1.5 million and promptly gave it to the U.S. National Archives to be a national reminder that individual liberties only come from individual action. Amid great controversy, he headed a commission to get Texas education out of last place in the country; his thanks was the eternal resentment of most educators. He pleaded with fellow Naval Academy graduate Oliver North to stop taking the Fifth Amendment and tell the truth about Iran-Contra. Perot says: "I told him . . . that I felt that a man who was prepared to die for his country should be prepared to tell the truth for his country and that it looked terrible for a Naval Academy graduate to take the Fifth Amendment and that if they [North and Admiral Poindexter] would simply tell the truth, put all the facts on the table and get this over with in a few days, I would pay his legal bills, take care of his family if he went to jail and help him get started when he got out." And after he sold EDS to General Motors, in a bitter and public battle, they paid him another $750 million to get him off the board and shut up about their "contempt" for customers and employees. All these headline grabbers have made Ross Perot a bigger-than-life character. Like most people willing to take strong stands on controversial issues, he has ended up in the love-him-or-hate-him category of opinion polls.

But in the opinion poll that counts most with Perot, there's no ambivalence at all. There's no CEO in the world who has the kind of respect and loyalty of employees (and even ex-employees) that Perot enjoys. Perot has been out of EDS since 1986, but the admiration lives on even there. Recently in Brazil, two EDS employees almost choked up in describing to me how Perot had inspired them. The commitment of his people borders on the un-believable. It's out of step with the modern world. One executive gave up $900,000 in GM stock to go back and work for Perot Systems. It may sound corny, but "soaring with eagles" is what Perot people really want to do. "One for all and all for one," a phrase in Perot Systems' statement of goals, really means something when you work for Perot.

What would it be like to work for a CEO who built a company worth billions, but set his salary at $68,000 in 1965 and never gave himself a raise? If you were a "Rivethead" at GM, how would you feel when the largest shareholder went public with the very things you'd been saying all your life? Odds are you'd be cheering when Perot unleashed his take-no-prisoners attack on the entire GM board: "Get rid of the committees and consultants and MBAs. Stop showing contempt for your dealers, your employees, and your customers. Give up the corporate dining room, the chauffeured limousines, the hefty bonuses in hard times. Get back to the trenches. Listen to the troops. Take care of them first, and they'll take care of you." And most dramatically of all, what would you do for the CEO who hires commandos to rescue you from an Iranian prison?

This is the stuff that gets the attention and respect of employees. It's also the stuff that Ross Perot is made of. It's called self-inspired behavior. Entrepreneurs rely on it in building their enterprise. It's personal inspiration that drives them to "get themselves in order," to find a little self-motivation to do the right thing. And great entrepreneurs not only inspire themselves—they inspire others. Passing it on comes mostly through example. Ask youself again. If you're ever thrown into a foreign prison, would your boss come and get you? Would you be inspired to go the extra mile for the boss who did?

The New Entrepreneurs— "They Are Us!"

Aside from the occasional superstar like Perot, most self-inspired entrepreneurs are not much different from you and me. All the statistics show they're a pretty average lot. Most never even planned to be entrepreneurs. It happens because of circumstance—often a crisis, like being dirt poor; or full of frustration; or getting fired, the number one reason that people go into business for themselves. Yes, these are ordinary people who simply find themselves in extraordinary situations.

This is important to remember when the press and TV bombard us with entrepreneurial myths. It's absolutely necessary to keep in mind if you hope to instill the spirit of enterprise in your own people. The Boeskys and Maxwells and Bonds of the world, billionaires one day and bums the next, are not quite the example to follow. We can't let tabloid hype discourage average workers and average companies from pursuing the old-fashioned basics of enterprise. Here are some of the more damaging myths about those people who create and build businesses.

▪ Myth Number 1

Entrepreneurs are born, not made. It's in their genes. They all invented something in a garage when they were twelve, wear strange clothes to work, and are generally unintelligible at cocktail parties. This is the "nerd" theory of entrepreneurship.

▪ Reality Number 1

The average entrepreneur is thirty-five to forty-five years old, has ten years plus experience in a large company, has an average education and IQ, and, contrary to popular myth, has a surprisingly normal psychological profile. As a group, they look and talk like you and me—a fairly average bunch.

▪Myth Number 2
The entrepreneur's overriding goal is to be a millionaire. He does it for the money, pure and simple.

▪Reality Number 2
Every shred of research denies this myth. Relatively few entrepreneurs ever earn the kind of bucks paid to CEOs these days. The entrepreneur's real obsession is to pursue his customer/product vision. Money is the necessary fuel to do this. Venture capitalists, shrewd evaluators of the entrepreneurial quotient in people, can spot the "get-rich-quick" types and avoid them like the plague.

▪Myth Number 3
Entrepreneurs are shady characters, ready to take legal shortcuts, and are generally on the prowl for suckers to screw.

▪Reality Number 3
Compared to the Sumitomo Bank scandal or the German chemical makers selling to Libya or the American CEOs making one hundred fifty times their average worker's salary, entrepreneurs don't seem so greedy after all. In such a sorry state of affairs, the Hondas and Bransons and Waltons of the world look more and more like saintly protectors of old-fashioned virtue. The unhappy fact is that low ethics and illegal tactics seem pretty well distributed throughout the population.

▪Myth Number 4
They're high risk takers—real dart throwers.

▪Reality Number 4
Entrepreneurs may be innovative, but that doesn't make them fools. Remember, it's their money they're risking. The reality is that big

company executives regularly take greater risks with shareholders' money than entrepreneurs are willing to take with their own. As to the "risk" of leaving a secure job and starting out on their own, all risk is relative. The entrepreneurs I've met are uniform in their belief that the greater risk is to leave your future reward and satisfaction in the hands of a series of corporate bosses, all of whom have their own agendas to push. Betting on the corporate lottery for the next thirty years is a risk most entrepreneurs aren't willing to take.

▪Myth Number 5
Here's the latest one to hit the street: Too many entrepreneurs spoil the national brew. Everyone can't go off and just "do his own thing." Who's going to mine the coal, produce the steel, and make the cars? Every country needs its foot soldiers too.

▪Reality Number 5
No one's suggesting that everyone just go do their thing, or that the whole world should work in a garage. What is suggested is that everyone needs to become competitive, including the folks in giant corporations. For mavericks and foot soldiers alike, a strong dose of old-fashioned enterprise isn't a bad place to start.

Too Many Managers
Spoil the Scottish Brew

The reality is, most enterprisers are former foot soldiers. Big corporations, yesterday's employer of choice, have become the breeding ground for tomorrow's entrepreneur. In a massive shifting of circumstance, our parents' dream of "the good and secure job" has become for many a nightmare of frustration and insecurity. It's not too many inspired entrepreneurs that are spoiling this brew; the evidence says it's too many uninspired managers. Take the case of Fraser Morrison in Edinburgh. His is an amazing story of self-inspired behavior that saved his family's company from the clutches of big business.

"In 1948, my father started the business with absolutely nothing. It was very small, what we called a jobbing contractor. He slowly built up the business, virtually on his own, within a very small radius of his hometown, a place called Tain, Scotland. When I joined him in 1970, the business was still quite small, working within this radius of perhaps twenty-five miles from our home. In that kind of situation, you can get involved in everything that's going on. So I might have been setting roads or houses one day and going home that evening and helping prepare the accounts. It was an all-hands-on-deck situation.

"Anyway, in 1974 we sold 80 percent of the family business to Mining Finance House, a large public company in London. We were still small, working only in Scotland, turning over maybe two million pounds. But the company's offer was terribly difficult to refuse. We retained 20 percent partly for sentimental reasons, and, well, 20 percent gave us a continuing attachment to a business which bore the family name. My father retired—I think he stepped down as managing director two or three years after he sold the business. One of the reasons we sold to this particular company was that they had no other construction interests. So we felt we were not going to be swallowed up by a major international construction company. Well, two years after they bought our business, they bought a major international construction company. So we were in the situation that we had tried to avoid. We were backed into this large international company, Shand, who had operations all over the UK, and the Middle East and subsequently in Malaysia and in the States. They were huge compared to us. After we became a part of the Shand Group, we had quite an uneasy relationship with the Shand people because we didn't want to be there and they couldn't really split us up and absorb us because we still owned 20 percent. That 20 percent turned out to be hugely significant."

It was a long, miserable journey to 1989, when Morrison finally regained his business. Along the way, everything that could go wrong in a big conglomerate went wrong. The holding company changed hands four or five times. The Shand Group began bleeding, with huge losses in Asia, the United States, and even in the UK. And of course dozens of corporate managers came and went, each with their own agenda. Meanwhile, Morrison Construction remained profitable and minded its own business in Scotland as best it could. But the losses from Shand, now being run by finance people, were overwhelming the whole construction group. No one in London seemed to have the foggiest idea of how to fix it. The last of the holding companies became disillusioned with the entire construction business and wanted to chuck it all. Morrison's nightmare of being sold off to unknown buyers as part of a losing group appeared imminent. He tried to buy back the 80 percent of Morrison Construction but was flatly rejected. The holding company wasn't about to "sell the only good part and keep all the dogs." Instead, they "promoted" him to run the entire construction group. He hesitantly agreed but asked for an option to buy back the company if it were put on the block. Another rejection. The board didn't know what they were going to do but were testing the market. Not surprisingly, there weren't a lot of buyers for a hugely unprofitable construction group. So in a let's-stick-it-to-the-Scots offer, Morrison was told he could buy "the bit in Scotland but only if he took the bad parts of the dog along with it." The Scotsman decided to go for it as the only way to regain his company. But to avoid financial collapse, he would have to turn around the losing and much bigger operations practically overnight. His plan was simple. Start running the big business the same way he'd run the small business.

"So we ended up in March 1989 buying back the 80 percent of Morrison Construction—at long last restoring family control. But we also had to buy our parent company, Shand, along with it. So I had a business with overall U.S. dollar sales of about $220 million but with very big losses. Still, we owned 100 percent and

I thought I knew how to turn it around. Thankfully, my hunch was right. In our first year, we turned over about $265 million and made $7 million! Last year we pushed on up to $300 million and $11 million in profit."

So the Morrisons of Scotland beat some long odds, selling their company at $3 million, and getting it back at $300 million. Of course, for fifteen long years Fraser paid his dues to a long parade of uninspired managers. No one was trying to motivate him. In such a demoralizing environment, you have to tap the source of all entrepreneurial motivation. It's called inspiring yourself.

Inspiring Yourself

From bigger-than-life characters like Ross Perot, to corporate refugees a la Fraser Morrison, to the corner shopkeeper, enterprisers are self-inspired to do their thing. No one makes them do it. No one beats them over the head to put in the extra effort. And they certainly don't need a motivational speaker to get them going. They motivate themselves. They're self-inspired to do their thing because doing their thing is exactly what inspires them!

This is not as rare as it may seem. Everyone gets inspired by something. Some people are inspired by gardening; others by a good game of tennis. Still others can be greatly inspired by reading a good book. It just so happens that entrepreneurs are inspired by their work. So there's nothing mysterious about it. It sort of depends on what turns you on. However, the most common denominator in life is that you and I and 99.9 percent of the world have to work to survive. We don't have to garden or play tennis, but we have to work. And if you can't figure out how to get yourself inspired at work, you're headed for a pretty dull life.

An Ordinary Man
Doing Extraordinary Things

"I think it's the freedom. Yes. I wanted the freedom. Of course, the lesson I learned is that for freedom, you have to work hard. You have to build something. Then you've got freedom."

Meet Christopher Lin, an ordinary man doing extraordinary things in Taiwan. Framed on the wall in his office hangs his motto in Chinese: "Don't Let Life Discourage You." It certainly never has for this Taiwanese wunderkind. With the most ordinary of beginnings, in forty-three years he has inspired himself to reach extraordinary heights. After ten years in industry, and several prestigious government assignments, he founded his business empire in 1983. The flagship company, Excellence Publishing, publishes Taiwan's leading monthly business magazine among numerous other titles. Excalibur Business Development, operating through separate divisions, provides a range of services to business from consulting to recruitment to PR. And recently Lin opened Excelsior Securities, his own registered stock brokerage firm. Lin is also involved in a thousand other things, from serving on government advisory committees to producing "Business Forum," a TV show, to founding Taiwan's Montessori School. And recently he established Taipei's Young Child Education Center. This is a busy man.

I've known Chris since 1984. All that time I assumed he was part of a wealthy, upper-class Chinese family. He is polished, articulate, and knows everyone from the premier of the Republic of China on down. Not until I asked him to open up on how and why he became an entrepreneur did I learn of his extremely humble beginnings. Chris Lin is a Chinese Horatio Alger. His is a story of keeping his eyes wide open and his spirits sky-high. He had all the qualities you might expect: obsessed with getting himself educated; working till he dropped at any job; maybe even being a bit lucky, or at least being in the right place at the right time; and gratefully accepting help from anyone who would give him the time of day. But the quality that most stands out about Lin is his childlike wonderment at it all—almost a naiveté in trying to better himself, only to learn time after time how much further he had to go. His self-inspired behavior is pure and simple—with an unusual innocence. Even today he often exclaims, "Wow, I'm so lucky. How can I be doing all this? It's so great!" From working hard to going to fortune-tellers, this is obviously a man who knows how to inspire himself.

"I am very optimistic, but also very conservative. I was born in November 1949, the year of the ox. You know the ox is very conservative. So inside I'm conservative, but outside, I am very outspoken and look always to the future. I was conceived in mainland China but born in Taiwan. This is special to me. My father and mother came around April—in the retreat of the Chiang Kai-shek regime. They were average people. Not wealthy. We lived in a factory dormitory. I remember the floor was cement, but not very smooth cement. There was little to eat. Some people from mainland China—important military or government people, or people who spoke English and had good relations with Americans—they had a better chance. My father was not that privileged. He was working class.

"My father was a very hard-working man, not only in his job, but also in the family. He always went to the factory earlier than he should and came back always after hours. As I can remember, he also helped my mother do the housework. Our family was poor. Six brothers and sisters. I could see he was trying to be promoted, and finally he made manager level. But he couldn't go further because he couldn't speak very good English and also he was not a graduate of the university. That was the struggling stage. I can feel now how hard it was.

"We lived in Hsinchu, in the southern part of Taiwan. Whichever school I was in, I always felt it was the best I could have. Half the students were barefoot in the school, but I felt lucky to be there. After my fourth year we moved to Taipei. I felt, 'Wow, good, now I'm really lucky to be in the capital of the country.' But the north and south are very different, and I wasn't prepared for the educational system in the capital. I failed the examination for academic school, so I had to go to a vocational school. I didn't know it then, but it was sort of a second-class school. The students were local and because of that I learned the Taiwanese dialect. My family only spoke Mandarin. Today it's a big advantage to speak Taiwanese, so this experience was good. In all my classes, my scores were top flight. I had to go to vocational high school also, but because my scores were high, I got into the best one in the whole country. Again I felt I was lucky to be there. But then I remember very clearly, one day reading a newspaper column about attitudes toward Taiwan's vocational schools. All the people said they didn't want their children going to vocational schools because they were secondary to the academic schools. Before that I loved my school. But suddenly I felt, how come our school is being classified as second-class? Also something else happened. There was this girl I liked very much, but nothing ever happened when I asked her out. It seemed her family thought I was not good enough. This also made me start thinking.

"Anyway, competition made it very difficult for students from vocational schools to go to the university. I used the last semester there to study very, very hard. I bought the academic high school material at the bookstore and I studied it by myself because the vocational school was not preparing us for the university entrance examination. I had to get up very early and go to bed very late, but I prayed to God to help me get through this. I should add that my father took me to church a lot. We were Christian. I listened and it gave me strength. Anyway, I passed the university examination right after graduation. Vocational school students weren't even supposed to take the exam. This gave me great confidence. I didn't compare to the top graduates of the academic schools, but I was average. I went to a public university, not the top one of course.

But the tuition was lower, and with my family's financial condition, it was best.

"I stayed active in church. Every Sunday I taught Sunday school. One of my friends at church was the son of K. T. Li.* And he was very kind to me. I felt very honored. In Taiwan, if K. T. Li asks you to sit down together—well, it was like walking in the clouds. Also, about that time I went, just out of curiosity, to a fortune-teller. You know a Christian cannot go to a fortune-teller—but I went. The fortune-teller told me I would meet a lot of people of great accomplishment in my life. I've always remembered that because I only knew K. T. Li then, and I didn't believe the fortune-teller. But now I can see that through coincidence, or fate, this has happened. I have always been inspired by high caliber people. I've been lucky enough to meet people like Henry Kissinger, Malcolm Forbes, Caspar Weinberger, Akio Morita, Premier Hua Pei-tsun, and so on. So maybe there is something to fortune-telling."

Lin went on to graduate school in finance and accounting. He then took a very ordinary position with giant Asia Chemical. During his tenure there he took time off to go to the United States to study for his CPA license at Northern Illinois University. After ten years at Asia Chemical, he had worked his way up to executive vice president. "At Asia Chemical I worked very hard. I never indulged myself. I never allowed myself to forget hard work. And my chairman was very good to me. He partially subsidized my U.S. study. But I wasn't a chemical man. I thought very hard about my future. I even went back to the fortune-teller, who told me I would have *my own* things to do in life. So finally I decided to quit and form my own company—to try something I could really be expert at. I was thirty-four.

"While I was thinking about starting my own company, some

* K. T. Li eventually became Taiwan's legendary minister of economic affairs and minister of finance. He is often called the architect of Taiwan's economic miracle.

interesting things happened. It really goes back to K. T. Li. When I was in the States, I learned the CPA system—and the market system as a whole. I studied hard and passed the CPA examination in the United States. Years before I had failed it in Taiwan. About that time, 1983, the Taiwan government was trying to set up a new financial market system. So one time when talking to K. T. Li, I started telling him about problems in the Taiwan market. He thought what I was saying was right. So I did a report for him, which he brought to the Economic Planning Council, and they thought it was right also. Well, I felt so great, so stimulated that I could even suggest things to the government.

"Because of my report, K. T. Li recommended me to the minister of finance, L. T. Shu. After I spoke with Minister Shu, he invited me to the meetings. I was very honored to participate at the government level. Of course, at that time my hair and clothing weren't so proper—because I didn't have proper guidance. But I improved myself little by little. In the meetings, you have to say something valuable, and sometimes that's very difficult. But I tried very hard. Minister Shu asked me to be on the government committees trying to set up a sound CPA system and a sound capital market. I was the only one on both these committees. And without really knowing me well, Minister Shu, who was also chairman of the Chinese Management Association, appointed me as deputy secretary general of the CMA, which shocked everybody, especially the business professors. I really don't know why I was appointed, but Minister Shu wanted me to promote the CMA and bring it to modern life. Finally, I was offered the job of advisor to the chairman of the SEC."

So Chris Lin, the factory worker's son from Hsinchu, found himself in the midst of the sharpest economic minds in Taiwan. Not bad for a vocational school graduate. But Lin had his sights set on something other than a government career: "All this was happening just as I was forming my own company. I had some ideas to raise the international level of Taiwan management and industry. This was my vision. I could not give up this new company. So I decided to give up all these government opportunities and stay in the private sector. The start-up was not what I expected. It was very difficult at the beginning. I thought it would be easy to pull people together and do things like productivity consulting or international recruitment. But there was little business and very limited talent. At that time, when friends asked me about my plan, I would say, 'Well, there is no plan. It's only my imagination.' I knew how to do a plan, I just didn't do it. I think I would do it over again the same way. If I had worked with a plan, I'm sure I would have been out of business. I really believe that!

"But it was a struggle. To help Taiwan industry, I needed talent and expertise, not just my imagination. So I went looking for the expertise. The first thing I felt good about was the PA Consulting* connection. When I contacted PA, they gave me two heavy volumes about what PA does. I said, 'Wow, I cannot do even one of these things—productivity improvement, strategy, nothing.' I had to admit, we didn't have the know-how. But we got it. From PA, and from others. We learned!"

The publishing business started more on impulse than insight. The Chinese Management Association had started a management magazine after Lin convinced them that they needed a visible, high-quality magazine to circulate important business ideas in Taiwan. After a couple of years, CMA lost interest, but Chris Lin took it as a personal mission to keep the idea alive. He had no money but he bought out the magazine with promissory notes—his first step into publishing. "At that time the magazine was deeply in debt, and I was trying to do everything myself. But I knew that if I didn't, the magazine would die and people would blame me. The magazine was difficult to run. Again, I just had an idea. But I didn't have the know-how. I read a story about Henry Luce. I dreamed I could be a Henry Luce type in Taiwan—or even China. China with 1.2 billion people! Wow! So I went to New York to see the

---

* The worldwide British consulting and recruitment firm. It was through PA in fact that I first met Chris Lin.

senior vice president of *Fortune* magazine. I walked into his office. He didn't know me. He was just showing courtesy. By luck, we had a common interest in Montessori schools. He began telling me about business publishing. How *Fortune* finds a story. How *Fortune* develops and delivers the story, all this. I raced back to our editors to tell them: '*Fortune* does this and that, we have to do it too.' Today I'm proud to say *Excellence* magazine is at a world-class level. But it has been difficult. After a while I realized *Forbes* was really the right model for Taiwan. Again I went to the States. I called them. It was a cold call. Nobody recommended me. And today we publish the *Forbes* Chinese-language edition. I suppose this is my problem. I find an opportunity and I just do it. I get a vision. Then I go in and find a big hole. A lot I don't know, so I learn it. Really, it's been the same with all my businesses."

One of Lin's most endearing qualities is that he doesn't pretend to know all the answers. It's not self-doubt, just a continual thinking through of options. He ended our discussion with a common concern of entrepreneurs—whether they should pay more attention to "managing." After Lin asks the question, he seems to answer it for himself: "I love to deal with people—mingling with employees and customers. But also I have that conservative character. I will say, at my age of forty-three, maybe I should become more conservative, more down-to-earth in my management style. Perhaps what I should do is use more strategy, more figures, look at the numbers and the audits—become more a business-minded person than an opportunity finder, more of a 'coldblooded man'—very cool, you know, with the policy and the figures." Chris lifts his eyes and stares at the ceiling. Slowly, he starts up again: "Of course, that way I would never have started any of these businesses. I think if I had started out coldblooded—with the figures, with the budgeting—I wouldn't even have a business today."

Whatever Lin tackles next, you can be sure he'll bring a ton of self-inspiration. It's hard to read Chris Lin's story (much less to hear it in person) without getting strong signals about making yourself smarter and being ready to work harder. It's not surprising—

working smarter and harder is the secret of ordinary people who do extraordinary things.

Working Smarter *and* Harder

It was quite chic a while back to go around the company saying "work smarter not harder." That turned out to be bum advice. The people and the companies who get to the top do both. It's a tough combination to beat when people can outthink *and* outwork the competition. Ask anyone who's come up against Chiron—a certified champion in the smarter and harder league.

According to Homer's *Iliad*, the centaur Chiron was the creative source of medical knowledge. Chiron tended the wounds of heroes and taught the healing arts to the god of medicine, Asclepius. As reward for his good works, Zeus placed Chiron in the heavens, forming the stars of the constellation Sagittarius. Chiron Corporation in Emeryville, California, is certainly living up to its namesake's fabled reputation. Co-founder and CEO, Edward E. Penhoet, a Ph.D. in biochemistry, has guided this star biotech firm to its heavenly heights since its founding in 1981. Of the four hundred-plus entries into the brave new world of genetic engineering since 1980, Chiron ranks number three (after Genentech and Amgen) in market capitalization, at $1.5 billion, and is one of only two solidly profitable firms. Penhoet and his two co-founders, Ph.D.s William Rutter and Pablo Valenzuela, scratched out their first business plan on Easter Sunday 1981, in Penhoet's living room. They chose their name because the centaur Chiron, half-horse and half-man, was a true recombinant organism—and a wonderful symbol of their genetic engineering technology for using recombinant DNA to produce materials in human health care. Since that day, these three scientists-turned-entrepreneurs have turned an abundance of self-inspiration into both a medical and a financial miracle.

As I sat down across from Ed Penhoet at Chiron's headquarters, he was thrusting a book titled *Invisible Frontiers* into my hands: "Read this! The subtitle's 'The Race to Synthesize a Human Gene.' This book is in fact about a race between Bill Rutter at the University of California at San Francisco, the co-founder of Chiron, and Wally Gilbert at Harvard, who was associated with Biogen and Genentech, to do the first cloning of the insulin gene. The book does a very good job of giving you the essence of the competition that existed between these groups. See, in order to understand the dynamic of the industry, you also have to understand the dynamic of the academic schools who founded this industry. I think probably the biggest misconception that the American public has about being a scientist is that it is an occupation which is somehow fundamentally different from any other. Scientists are not viewed as highly competitive people. The typical American view of scientists comes from Saturday morning cartoons, crazy guys working in labs and being isolated from each other in a corner doing their little bizarre things. But, in fact, this science in particular, molecular biology, biochemistry, has been a tremendously competitive enterprise, whether or not it is going on in the universities or in a business environment."

Penhoet charged ahead, explaining how the field exploded after the major advances made in biochemistry in the sixties. Getting the perspective seemed important. The key dates:

- 1967. Discovery of restriction enzymes—no practical value in itself but gave scientists the technology to clone molecules.
- 1974. Boyer and Cohen receive DNA gene-splicing patent.
- 1977. First cloning of medically important genes (insulin and human growth hormones) at University of California at San Francisco.
- 1980. U.S. Supreme Court rules that genetically engineered organisms are patentable, and America's hottest new industry is born.

"So before these companies were started, and that is what you will read in this book, the scientific enterprise was a tremendously competitive one. The field is populated by a lot of hard-charging, aggressive, very hard-working people. I'm talking about the academic world. And San Francisco was probably the epitome of that. The biochemistry lab at UCSF during the seventies was a place where you could find people at work seven days a week, twenty-four hours a day. Anytime that you went there, there were people working, competing, moving the science along. So there has been a dynamic of hard work and competition in this field going back to the sixties. Over time it became increasingly competitive and less what the worldview of 'academic' was. In a sense, individual professors were entrepreneurs. Universities supplied them with lab space and with some support services. But every one of these guys, myself, Rutter, and all the others in the field, were basically small businessmen. You had to get your own grant money, you had to set up your own lab, you had to get the work product out, which was generally publications. So there was a tremendous drive for publication. All this grew out of an entrepreneurial environment, not entrepreneurial in the classic sense, because the product was not money—but the behavior was there. The behavior of the people who were key to the scientific enterprise didn't change when they moved from the university environment to a commercial environment. They still competed aggressively, worked hard, and had a strong drive for success. What distinguishes the various groups today is the different dynamics they established before they started a company, as much as what they established in the company itself. And in our company, of all the people I know, Rutter is one of the most hard-working. He enjoys working seven days a week, sixteen hours a day; he always has. His style of working permeated UCSF because he was head of the department. He built the department and recruited a lot of the key people. So many of us in Chiron worked for Bill at some point. I got my Ph.D. in his laboratory. Pablo Valenzuela, the third founder and our research director here, was a postdoc in Bill's lab. Pablo's another guy with no energy barrier. You can discuss a new line of research one afternoon, and the next morning he's already got experiments going. And so in many ways this enterprise is an extension of Rutter's lab at UC San Francisco, especially in terms of people's work ethic and competitiveness.

"Still, we wanted to stay well-plugged-in to the university. We were quite sure that the academic world was going to continue to create new knowledge that would have practical applications. This is crucial. See, in the sixties, there was a big political schism between business and academia. Also, there was very little need for each other in the sense that the traditional pharmaceutical companies were developing drugs based more on serendipity than on knowledge. They screened thousands of chemicals to find ones that would do a certain thing, and in general, many drugs got to market, still do in fact, without a deep understanding of how they worked. Therefore, the pharmaceutical companies themselves did not have a great need for the knowledge that was being built up in the universities. This was changing slowly in the seventies. Merck was probably the first to change. Roy Vagelos, the chairman, was recruited from academia to run Merck research, which was atypical in that Roy brought with him some deep knowledge of biochemical mechanisms. Merck's success today in large part is a reflection of what Roy brought to the company in the mid-seventies. Anyway, in 1981, we thought we could bridge this gap. We had good reputations scientifically, and at the same time, we had personal skills which allowed us to be seen as acceptable partners for commercial organizations.

"So we had a very strong work ethic and a good knowledge of what was going on in the field. Now that wasn't unique to us . . . sure, compared to the average person walking around on the street, the whole community of these biotech people is very smart. But once you get inside the community, well, you are just another guy in the community. What distinguishes them is really the degree to which they focus their energies and the degree to which they apply themselves to their tasks. So it's really hard work that in the end is an absolutely crucial competitive factor. It's impossible to go around every company and analyze this. But as I look around at who has been successful in our field and who hasn't, there is no question in my mind, for example, that the UCSF work ethic was a significant factor in Genentech's success and in our success. And I think the difference is bigger than it seems between people who work extremely hard and people who just put in an average week. That is, somebody who works sixty hours probably gets more than twice as much done as somebody who works thirty. They may get four times as much done. Maybe it's the square of the work, because it's a matter of total focus on what these people are doing.

"Also of extreme importance, we had an ability to get people to join us and believe in our vision of creating real value from the science. Employees had to believe in the vision enough to work in a way they wouldn't in a normal commercial environment. So a fifty- to sixty-hour work week is true not only for us as leaders of the company, but also for a large fraction of people who work here. Chiron got hepatitis C for only one reason—the entire company started working very hard on it way back in 1981. I mean it wasn't an accident. It didn't just fall out of the sky one afternoon."

At a meeting some months before, Penhoet had told me that he believed the tenured university professorship was "absolutely the best life in the world." So what was it that really caused him, Rutter, and Valenzuela to give up the life of university scientists to become entrepreneurs? And what have they learned about enterprise along the way? Well, there were two main reasons for the move from academia to business. First of all, the scope of the science was dramatically increasing. It became clear by the end of the seventies that very large sums of money, investment money not grant money, were going to be devoted to the practical application of this technology. So if you wanted to stay competitive in the science, it was important to participate in this growth phase. Second of all, and somewhat related, we had as a group of people a strong interest in doing something practical with the technology. In one sense, it was almost an explosion which occurred because all of this technology had been building up in the academic world, and not much of it had gotten transferred to the traditional drug world. The traditional pharmaceutical companies, even today, are somewhat skeptical. But then they were tremendously skeptical! The attitude was: 'There are only going to be one or two products that will come out of this that are worth anything.' None of them really wanted to wade into this in a major way. For us, on the other hand, the technology was maturing, but people weren't using it as aggressively as it could be used to solve real important medical problems. And then a third thing was, when we saw the situation, we had to analyze whether we were going to make a significant impact on it. After looking at our own strengths and weaknesses as a group, we thought we saw some opportunities that were not obvious to others and we also had some skills that were not broadly distributed at the time. So it really was a drive not only to remain competitive in the field, but to expand our competitive base and apply that to really doing something meaningful on the practical side. That's the underlying dynamic of why we started Chiron.

"Naively, off we went into the wild blue yonder. There is no way to do this except naively, because if you had experience in doing it, you would probably do it differently. So by definition, almost all entrepreneurs are naive. I guess that's both the strength and the weakness in the end. You are willing to try some completely new things, and at the same time, you undoubtedly make a lot of mistakes. But I think the critical aspect is to have built up a lot of 'capital' before you start one of these businesses. I talk to young students all the time and ask them what they'd like to do. The common answer: 'Well, someday I'd like to start a biotech company.' Well, why? 'Because it sounds like a real exciting thing to do.' Unless you have an edge on the field when you start, you can't just say: 'Oh gee, biotech, or computers, or whatever looks like a good industry—I think I'll start that kind of a company.' No, you have to have a key competitive advantage going, somehow, by virtue of your previous experience. You see, you have never heard me say that I did any of this to make money. I can't say I don't enjoy the financial rewards that come with building a successful enterprise. That would be foolish. On the other hand, I know very few people who have been successful in any environment who simply went at it as a way of making money. People who think, oh gee, it says in the paper that Herb Boyer just made $100 million starting Genentech. Well, gee, maybe I'll start a biotechnology company too. That's almost a certain recipe for disaster.

"It's the same with MBAs. I've seen a string of very unhappy young MBAs from very good places, who are very talented, who go and take CEO jobs in small companies and almost always flop. They're not trained to be entrepreneurs. They're trained to manage enterprises. They will function well in large organizations . . . but to be successful early on in a small company, well, the management of it is the least of your problems. You will never be successful with just business manipulations in these kinds of enterprises. You succeed because you create some value. You feel a need in the marketplace, and unless you create that value, no amount of business razzle-dazzle or training is going to overcome the fact that you have not created any fundamental value. This is crucial. You don't have to be a scientist. If you're a business person, you align yourself with somebody who can contribute technically, an engineer or whatever, and together build one of these teams. But people who just want to start a company because it's a good way to become wealthy—well, they almost always fail."

High Commitment and High Performance

Do self-inspired entrepreneurs like Perot, Lin, and Penhoet share any common characteristics? What are the fundamental qualities they demonstrate as workers? It's really a very short list. One characteristic of all entrepreneurs I've met is that they like what they do. This is why working harder comes so easy to them. They're *highly committed* to what they're doing. In addition to liking what they do, they're really interested in doing it well. Working smarter is a reflection of the constant effort to do it better. In personnel lingo, they're out to achieve *high performance*. So the self-inspired behavior of entrepreneurs rests on two rather basic qualities—high commitment and high performance. In plain English, entrepreneurs love what they do and they're good at doing it.

Life can get very complicated around commitment and performance. For one thing, these qualities have great impact on each other. It's much more likely, for example, that you will become great at something if you're doing something you love to do. Conversely, most people who really hate a particular job are not good bets to ever become great at doing it. But these two qualities also have their own separate roots. It is certainly possible to like what you do but not be very good at it. New hires often fall into this group. On the other hand, some people are very good at what they do, but simply hate doing it. Or at least they hate doing it at the particular company or working environment they're in. Then, there are those sorry souls who both hate what they do and are bad at doing it—the perfect opposite of entrepreneurial behavior. Corrective action for these various possibilities can become totally confused. Training, for instance, is an action to improve performance. It presumes that a lack of knowledge is the issue. If someone hates his job, training him won't change his commitment.

It doesn't do much good if the founder of the company (or the hired CEO for that matter) is the only one with high commitment and high performance. To go beyond a one-man shop in anything, some enterprising, self-inspired behavior has to be instilled in the workers. This is where the rubber meets the road for many aspiring entrepreneurs, and it's the bottom-line "people problem" for all managers. Inspiring yourself is laudable. That's where it has to start. But inspiring ten thousand workers is the real trick. Creating a company full of highly committed, high performers is the key test for entrepreneurs and managers alike.

Inspiring Others—
Creating Mini-entrepreneurs

Most of us can figure out how to inspire ourselves. But can we inspire others? The successful entrepreneur as well as the successful manager has to be able to do it. But both entrepreneurs and professional managers have a spotty track record on fostering commitment and performance in others.

The entrepreneur's excuse rings a familiar bell. Like great, natural athletes who make lousy coaches, entrepreneurs are often unaware of what they do. They don't think about it much and thus have a hard time passing on their natural ability at enterprise. By the time they recognize that they're developing a house full of bureaucrats, the company is well into its life cycle, heading straight for the professional management phase. This usually means the founder gets suitably brainwashed into thinking that he now needs a real personnel department. The company reaches into the available pool of professionally-trained personnel people, and it goes downhill from there.

With company managers, it can be even more of a challenge. Not only are they unaware of entrepreneurial behavior, but there's a whole world of professional personnel people, in and out of the company, giving them a lot of bad advice. On the inside, the personnel department has usurped large chunks of the line manager's relationship with his workers, often leaving him with little responsibility and even less authority for doing much of anything about worker commitment or performance. And while it's slowly changing, it's still the personnel function that attracts the most non-business-minded people in all business. On the outside, there's no other area of management training or consulting that is so riddled with charlatans, incompetents, and just plain crazies as the "how-to-manage-and-motivate-people" crowd. It's little wonder, then, that most of what passes today as progressive people management in many companies has little to do with either common sense or the spirit of enterprise.

But the situation is far from hopeless. Workers want to get inspired, and a lot can be done about it. We can't *make* people more enterprising, but self-inspired commitment and performance can be fostered in 99.9 percent of all people. As with everything else in this book, the best answers about how to get people to love what they do and to be good at it come from watching and understanding entrepreneurs themselves—or, more precisely, understanding the circumstances and environment that inspire them in the first place. To a large degree, this environment can be duplicated in any company—an environment that draws out the inherent self-inspiration in us all. So the best way—maybe the only way—to inspire others is to get them to inspire themselves. The best thing you can do is show the way through personal example. And for showing the way, you'll never find a better example than Soichiro Honda.

Who Says Americans Can't Make Cars?

"The young people idolized him. For example, in 1983, when Mr. Kume was introduced as the new president, which in Japan means CEO, we had a big party. Thousands of employees came. When Mr. Honda introduced Mr. Kume, he made a wonderful speech. He said: 'This company, Honda, we always seem to have a kind of sloppy person for president. A person just like me. Have you noticed? Yes, only sloppy kinds of people become president at Honda. Well, Tadashi Kume is a very sloppy person and that is why he now becomes the president.' Then he turned straight to the audience and said: 'So I'm sorry but because you have a sloppy president, you have to work harder or the company will collapse.' And the young people just cheered and cheered. They loved it."

This is Tetsuo Chino remembering Soichiro Honda. He remembers him well. Chino was president of Honda USA during the record-breaking 1980s. He was the man who started the production of high-quality Hondas with American workers in the Marysville, Ohio, plant. And he was also the man who pushed the Accord to become the number-one-selling car in the United States. I was meeting with Chino at Honda headquarters in Tokyo. He may have risen to the stratosphere level of Honda management, but he's as down-to-earth as any automobile man on the production floor. He had recently entered semi-retirement, a phase at Honda known as "soft running": "This is quite usual at Honda, but it is unusual among Japanese industry. We call it the soft-running phase, that time between day-to-day operations and retirement. I am still an advisor to the company—the Honda Motor Company of Japan and also the Honda Motor Company of America." Chino is also the current president of the America-Japan Society in Tokyo, a tribute to his intimate knowledge of the United States.

Honda is called the most international of all the Japanese car manufacturers. It was the first to produce outside of Japan (in Marysville), and today nearly half its employees are "foreigners." But Honda is probably most famous for its attention to customers. It has, after all, won the prestigious J. D. Powers Customer Satisfaction Index in America six years running. It also has the well-deserved reputation of being the automobile company run by real automobile lovers. Soichiro Honda was the son of a blacksmith who at sixteen began his working career as a mechanic. As a young man he was a champion race driver until a near fatal accident in 1939 ended his career. The company has remained deeply involved in racing and holds many Formula One records. All this adds up to putting Honda ahead of the pack in technology. It was the first company anywhere to meet the tough U.S. emission standards, and it's years ahead in engine efficiency with its recently announced 100 mpg model. It's no wonder little Honda now has the top-selling car in America. But none of this extraordinary show of enterprise could have happened without enterprising people. Maybe the only untold story of Honda is how the legendary founder inspired his people—even those American auto workers who everyone said couldn't make a competitive car anymore. Everyone, that is, except Soichiro Honda.

"We decided to produce in America in the mid-seventies. Before any other Japanese car company. And long before any talk of quota restrictions. The reason we decided to go to the States to build cars was that the Honda philosophy says we should make products where the market exists. Of course we were a little bit hesitant at the time because so many people were saying the quality would be bad, or the community would be tough on us, or the unions would be difficult, and so on. Anyway, in 1977 we decided to start with motorcycles in Ohio. We bought a huge piece of land to expand to cars. We didn't ask for any incentives or tax breaks. We did ask for a road to approach the property, but other than that we didn't ask for any special treatment. In '79 we were producing motorcycles and we started automobile production in '82."

And what about the Ohio plant and the American workers? "You know, when we first announced the Ohio plant, a journalist in the States, in Dallas, I think, asked me, 'How will you deal with the alcoholism and the drug abuse?' I did not understand his question. I asked him, 'What do you mean, the alcoholism and drug abuse?' He said it was the biggest issue in Detroit. I was shocked. But none of those bad things happened. The workers are as good as any Japanese. The cars are the same quality."

Well, why can't all companies in America say that? "That is a very good question. Take the concept of quality. Some companies, in fact some component suppliers we had, said if you achieve 98 percent good quality, that is a good result. But what about the 2 percent failed rate? It's unfortunate for you if you buy that 2 per-cent. So Honda is always concerned about the 2 percent. We always aim at 100 percent quality, not 98 percent. The employees in Ohio know this, and they have no trouble doing this. But I don't know exactly the answer to your question.

"I think it comes down to trust. If management and workers stop trusting each other, the working environment becomes dis-torted. If you want to have good-quality products, you have to establish understanding and trust between workers and manage-ment. So the first thing we aimed for was to establish that good relationship with the workers. If you have trust, then you don't need any third party to intervene, like a labor union. Because you have direct avenues of communication. Honda is not against labor unions, actually. We would accept them as we do in Japan. But in Marysville they tried twice, and both times the employees voted them down because they didn't think they needed a third party. How to make mutual trust is very important.

"Now I always told our American workers, Honda doesn't have any magic wand to say one thing and change the world. It takes daily effort. For example, the top manager of the plant is supposed to be on the line at least once a day. Twice is much better. He has to observe himself how the line is moving and chat with the workers and encourage them. But in some companies the big office suite is the land of the manager. He lives up there above the workshop where the real work is done. Also, at Honda we wear the same uniform in the plant, from the president of the company to the line workers. And they have the same cafeteria. They eat together. So at lunch they can talk with the president and the management. All of this makes for trust."

Chino didn't do it all by himself. The example of Soichiro Honda, occasionally in person and always in spirit, is the constant companion of any Honda executive—at least for those like Tetsuo Chino, who grew up under his leadership. What was that example? What kind of man was he? "Soichiro Honda was a self-made man. He was also a very unique Japanese. He thought that performance at work is the genuine thing. He always wanted to make a break-through with a new idea. So he didn't want to be guided by somebody else. You know our MITI [the powerful Ministry of International Trade and Industry], the Japanese bureaucrats? Well, MITI said that if Japan had too many automakers, then Japan could not compete with the big American or European companies. So when Mr. Honda tried to diversify from motorcycles and enter the auto business, MITI said no. So Soichiro Honda fought with MITI. He told them: 'MITI is not our shareholder. Why can you decide my destiny? I want to make automobiles, and certainly you cannot make any decision for me. You are not my shareholders or my customers.' This was a great fight in Tokyo, you know. Honda entered the auto business in spite of MITI. Yes, he was a very unique Japanese.

"He was also a humanitarian. He always said the technology is just a means to make people happy. So the company was a people-oriented company. Mr. Honda always said there are five important groups surrounding the company. One of course is the shareholders. The second is the trade people, the vendors and the suppliers and also the dealers. The third category is the people in the community. And the fourth category, of course, is the customers who use our products. Finally, the fifth group is the employees. Mr. Honda said we must treat this fifth group, the employees, very well because that is the basis of a people-oriented company. He was interested in the people in the community also. For example, he founded two or three plants in Japan specially designed to employ only handicapped people.

"So he was very people-oriented himself. He was very easy to talk to and kind of an entertainer actually. He played music for people and entertained them. He tried to make everybody happy. When he was inducted into the American Automotive Hall of Fame, all the dealers said they appreciated his efforts and his products. But Mr. Honda said, 'It's not me. All merit has to go to you, the dealers.' Then he disappeared from the table. He asked for the wine waiter's uniform, dressed in the uniform, and reappeared. He then served wine to all the dealers. He was saying to each, 'Thank you, thank you. It is only because of you I'm in this Hall of Fame.' That is the type of man he was.

"But he was also a very business-minded person. If you made any mistake in business, he could get so mad. But the next day he would recover and try to correct it. He was kind of a teacher. He would come to us and ask how we could all improve the situation. He was aggressive about the business, but he would always try to help us. He did this especially with the young people. They knew he was serious but also there to help them.

"Mr. Honda thought the genius of the company was in the workers. And they knew that he trusted them. He always liked the workshops and the plants best. He went there a lot himself and discussed things with the workers and the technicians and the engineers. He would make his comments and he listened to their ideas. He strongly inspired employees about the product. When he was young, he raced cars. He had a very bad accident and quit, but he was always keen to develop race cars. Developing new ideas and new technologies is very good for the engineers. Working on racing engines is very good for timing, for faster learning. Mr. Honda always said, 'Beating the clock is the most important factor to becoming number one.' That kind of spirit about high performance cars was very inspiring to the engineers and even the production workers. See, Mr. Honda believed technology has no end. You can always improve it. That's why we produced the all-aluminum-body car and we're now testing the 100 mpg engine. These things are difficult, but our engineers are always encouraged to challenge limits. Automobile employees are very motivated by making machines no one else can make!"

Few company leaders could match Soichiro Honda's near mythic proportions in the eyes of his people. The more you learn the more you see that his method of inspiring others was by being inspired himself. He was fascinated by cars and so are his people. He trusted his people so they trust their company. On and on it goes, even up through his retirement and recent death: "When he retired, he announced, 'The reason I am retiring is I've gotten too old to understand today's technology—your technology. This is the computerized age. It's your age. I know the mechanical movements, but I cannot see the electronic movements so I am too old. Now is the time for me to retire because the work you must do is too complicated for me to understand.' The employees were very moved. And after he retired, he did the right thing. He would come to the office two or three days a week, but he would not involve himself in company business. And even though he founded the company, he didn't allow any heirs in the company and none of the executives were allowed to have their heirs in the company. This was appreciated by the employees and it's very unusual in famous Japanese companies. Normally Japanese companies make a very huge funeral with receptions and ceremonies when their founders die. But Mr. Honda had forbidden any funeral ceremony for himself. He did ask for a big party to thank all the people who helped make the company great. So we did that and invited everyone on behalf of Mr. Honda. As I said, he was a very unique Japanese."

One can argue that Soichiro-san wasn't out to create "mini-entrepreneurs." Surely, he wouldn't have put it that way himself. But the fact is that he inspired Honda employees to extraordinary levels of commitment and performance—extraordinary commitment to the business of making the best motorcycles and cars in the world, and extraordinary performance in product innovation and customer service. At the end of the day, call it what you want, this is what leaders of enterprise are supposed to be able to do—whether it's a factory in Japan or Marysville, Ohio.

And speaking of those Americans in Ohio who are turning out the most competitive car in America, why do they do so well with the Japanese system? In a soft dropping of the other shoe, Tetsuo Chino's final thought suggests it could be because underneath it's really as American as apple pie: "You know it's like I said about eating together in the plant cafeteria. They don't have any special place in line. Or special tables to sit. It's a first-come, first-serve basis. This is kind of basic democracy. Everyone is equal. This we were taught by you Americans. We are only following your system!"

Inspiring Entrepreneurial Commitment

Commitment comes from the *heart*: from believing that the company mission has value to feeling you have a personal stake in it all. And from commitment flow pride, loyalty, and plain old hard work. Entrepreneurs are extraordinarily committed to what they do, bordering on the obsessive. There's a lot of motivation theory floating around on how to inspire commitment in big companies. But why not go straight to the most committed people in business for some answers? Here are three practices, straight from the entrepreneur's handbook, that are virtually guaranteed to inspire others to higher commitment.

▪ Love What You Do

Entrepreneurs love what they do. They're proud of their enterprise. They see challenge in every mundane step. They'll work night and day to see it succeed. A little of this would go a long way in all big companies. Of course it's not a perfect world. Everyone can't "love" every job they ever have. But that doesn't change the principle. The number one rule in commitment remains that you have to like what you do. Every job can be made more important. Challenges can be created in the smallest of tasks. And companies can find purpose in most anything, from Kentucky Fried Chicken to cures for cancer. The long-term payoff for getting this spirit instilled in employees is simply enormous.

▪ Share Fortune and Misfortune

Entrepreneurs have little choice but to pin their future on the future of their company. They have to share the fortunes as well as the misfortunes of the business. And so it should be for everyone. What's good for the company should be good for the workers. And if it's good for the workers, it should be good for the company. It's called shared destiny, and without it, you can forget about a committed work force. How could it be otherwise? Nowhere in the world will employees commit to a company that isn't committed to them. That's simple common sense.

Shared destiny also means if it's bad for the company, it's going to be bad for employees. This is the ultimate entrepreneurial mindset, but it rarely works at big companies. Maybe it's just habit. Could it be that neither fortune nor misfortune has ever been shared? This has to change dramatically. Until companies and their employees truly get in the same boat together, there can be no real commitment.

▪Lead by Example—Always

This is the rule everyone agrees on, but few really practice. How can you inspire others to new heights of commitment if you yourself don't care? It's the height of arrogance to expect more of others than you can personally give. The hard advice comes down to this: If you're not committed, if you don't like what you do, move on before you infect the whole barrel. Find something that turns you on. You owe it to your people—and you owe it to yourself.

Inspiring Entrepreneurial Performance

High performance depends on knowledge, skill, and working smart. It comes mostly from the *head*. All kinds of techniques and training have been invented to improve the performance of employees. They may be useful—if employees are truly inspired to perform. Entrepreneurs look at performance as a matter of survival—not scoring points for the next merit review. Here's what helps them produce high performance, and it can work for everyone.

▪Get Better at Doing What You Do

Continuously raising performance standards is a habit with entrepreneurs. This happens when you know you're in a battle of survival. Working smarter takes on dramatic new meaning when it's the only thing standing between you and bankruptcy. Raising the ante to stay competitive is the lifeblood of enterprise. It ought to be the lifeblood of everyone in enterprise.

▪Save Your Best for Customers and Products

Entrepreneurs save their best shots for making great products and serving real customers. It's called focus. In too many companies, too many people save their best shots for internal battles. Enormous effort (and expense) can go into these turf wars, but at the end of the day, the only performance that builds the enterprise is that directed toward products and customers.

▪Lead by Example—Always

You don't need a treatise on the meaning of leadership: It's patently obvious that the top of the company has to personally set the company's standard of performance. There's just no other way. This may mean different things in different settings, but getting your hands dirty with real customers and products once in a while is a terrific way to start.

What If I Do and What If I Don't?

Finally, we get to the crux of the matter, the missing link in this business of inspiring others, of creating "mini-entrepreneurs." Transforming bureaucrats to entrepreneurs is a tall order. What if they don't want to be transformed? Is there some fail-safe button to push? Believe it or not, there is. It's a button called self-interest, and every human being walking the face of the world has one.

It all comes down to how you answer this question: "What are the real consequences for good performance and the real consequences for bad performance?" It's the old *"What's in it for me if I do"* question with an added twist: *"And what will happen to me if I don't?"* The reality is that entrepreneurs are self-inspired by the immediate, often severe, and always personal consequences of their actions. There is no place to hide. There are no six-month probation periods. Your kid's next meal is on the line. On the up side, there's no supervisor stealing your glory—or otherwise deciding whether you did well or not. If you do well, you'll get immediate and powerful feedback from where it really matters—your customers. Entrepreneurs exist in an environment where their actions count personally. The consequences, positive or negative, are clear. And they come from where they're supposed to come from in enterprise—not from bosses but from customers.

Bureaucrats just don't live in this world. Big modern bureaucracies are notorious for their ability to insulate employees from both the positive and the negative results of their work. This is probably bad psychology, and it's certainly bad business. Too many companies, with too many personnel theories, are hopelessly stuck in neutral—no personal positives, no personal negatives, just the clear signal that individual commitment and performance really don't matter much. Directing employee consequences would seem a reasonable thing for bosses to do. Everyone knows that just giving personal feedback can be powerful—and it doesn't cost a cent. Unfortunately, "progressive personnel practice" has all but torpedoed the real potential of instilling strong consequences. For starters, we've become so obsessed with the minutiae of job descriptions, it's pure chance if the sacrosanct annual performance review has any connection to the fortunes and misfortunes of the company. This all-powerful connection seems hard to make so no one talks about it.

Second, giving positive recognition has reached the status of moral principle, while negative consequences float in perpetual limbo. In the very progressive companies, it's as if everyone's doing their best—nobody's performing poorly, even if the company is on a collision course with bankruptcy. The cruelest and dumbest personnel scenario comes with the inevitable layoffs, when every single employee says, "Gee, why me? I got a great rating last year!" At the other extreme, somewhere along the line we've convinced ourselves that salesmen like special recognition but no one else really needs it. Elaborate sales commission schemes and trips to Hawaii are devised to recognize the sales force, while the factory workers and clerks get to read about it in the company magazine. And of course, underscoring the imbalances in most companies' handling of consequences is the wacky and wonderful world of executive compensation and privilege. A very special system with three self-interest buttons to push: high, higher, and highest! But there is hope. An alternative exists between Karl Marx and Attila the Hun. It's called enterprise. But for it to work, companies have to start giving straight, meaningful answers to the eternal question, "What's in it for me if I do, and what happens to me if I don't?"

For most big companies, this will require a major overhaul in their performance systems. A more entrepreneurial performance environment sends a very direct message. Both good fortune and misfortune are felt by everyone, starting with top management. The bureaucratic notion that no one is responsible dies a natural death. When a client or market is lost, it won't do for everyone to just stare at the ceiling. And when a client or market is won, everyone wins. Not just the salesman, but the factory worker and the processing clerk too. And top management, just like entrepreneurs, will live or die on how well the company satisfies customers. Therefore, to create an entrepreneurial performance environment, a few basic ideas have to be in place. The four most important are:

▪ Consequences Determine Behavior

Employees do things where they perceive the consequences will be positive or at least neutral. They avoid doing things where they believe the consequences will be negative.

▪ Everyone Has a Business to Run

Every employee has products or services to offer and customers or users to serve. The only test of success is how well those products satisfy those customers.

▪ Customers Give Consequences— Bosses Give Feedback

The boss's job is to make sure workers know the consequences of their performance and that something happens because of them.

▪ The Company and the Workers Have a Shared Destiny

The consequences to workers and the company must be in sync. What's good for the company should be good for the workers— and vice versa.

Customer Consequences at Brinker International

I had just reminded Ron McDougall that, with close to twenty thousand employees, Brinker International isn't exactly a small company anymore. Yet it's still chewing up the market like there's no tomorrow. Rolling out three separate chains simultaneously has never been done in the food service business. Norm Brinker is already the only man to ever do two—Steak and Ale along with Bennigan's. Now he's going for three—driven by the unbridled cheerleading of President Ron McDougall. If they're all successful, and the signs are good, Brinker and McDougall will have accomplished what all other giants in the industry have only dreamed about. But doing this means getting bigger in a hurry. Anyone could keep twenty-five people focused on customer consequences.

But how do you do that when you've grown from nothing to twenty thousand employees in less than a decade?

"All right, we're not a small company," McDougall replied, conceding the obvious. "But what I attempt to do is have every individual's project tied back to the customer somehow. Anything you're working on, see if you can find a strand back to the customers. I don't want a corporate staff against the field. That's not the battle. We're all on the same side, trying to give the customer better service out there. So if my MIS department can find a better way to schedule labor in the unit and save the manager time—which they've done, they've saved the average manager five hours a week on scheduling—that's a thing that's driven right into the manager's hands and helps him at the restaurant level. Every project that we do like that hopefully has some tentacle to affect the customer out there. We try to stress that everyone is here to make the operator's job easier—to make him more efficient—take the paperwork off his back—get him out taking care of the customers and the employees! If you're working on a project here, it can't be simply to make your desk look neater. It's got to have a tail that eventually affects the customer. It's an on-going challenge for us to keep focused, though. It's focusing and re-prioritizing all the time."

And what about the field? It's highly decentralized and spread out into hundreds of little entrepreneurial-style businesses: "In a smaller company, you know, it's an open-door policy. But I can't handle twenty thousand employees walking in with ideas. As we decentralize, we have the regional directors and the regional vice president take more and more of the corporation with them. And it focuses down. Everything can't come through my office here. We *really* try to delegate and decentralize. And the field stays focused on what they're doing because it's in their self-interest. Everyone's in profit-sharing. The waitstaff runs their own profit-sharing—tips. All the managers in the units get bonuses—based on what their restaurant itself does in profitability. Sales and profit goals. So they're kind of self-contained little businesses out there. Each restaurant is like a little two-to-three-million-dollar factory.

And if they hit their goals they get bonuses on their goals. So they're very focused within their four walls to make it happen."

Brinker and McDougall want their people to want to succeed. And they want them to enjoy succeeding. But there's a downside, and it's a big one. In this super-charged growth environment, there's no room at all for what McDougall calls *the laggards*. The humor disappears as he gives the bottom line on preserving the sonic pace of the business: "The laggards? They set bad examples for the people that are working for them and with them. Tough as it sounds—it's bad for morale to keep the laggards around. So you've got to be proactive. You've got to prune the tree. Dead branches make the whole tree look brown." McDougall paused, and I got the feeling he meant it.

If inspired leadership will make it happen, Brinker is home free. Listen one more time to McDougall, waxing incredulous at the opening salvos at Romano's: "Macaroni Grills? Going crazy! It's explosive right now. Very successful—got a two-hour wait on the weekends to get in. Our challenge right now is how we accelerate our expansion plan. Our biggest constraint right now is getting enough managers—quality managers trained—quality training time—that will roll the expansion plan as fast as we can go. We've got the money—we can get the real estate—we can build the restaurants. When Macaroni gets a few more restaurants open, it'll automatically open up more slots. We gotta move quicker, but Macaroni Grill is going to be a smashing success. You know we don't want to take just one business—grow it and say: 'We're done! And all you people in our system, betting on a growth company, and your job progression, sorry.' We don't want to run a business that just runs into a wall."

Every company must find its own way to create mini-entrepreneurs. Brinker International's amazing record says it has found several: energetic commitment from the top; everyone on some form of profit-sharing; decentralized, with small entrepreneurial units; both headquarters and field performance tied into customer needs. Entrepreneurial practices are all hard at work in a big company, designed to do one important thing: keep everyone inspired.

Good for the Business, Good for the Soul

Tremendously important to me is the feeling that we were doing something that had a significance far beyond building a company or what the financial rewards could be. I was convinced we were doing something that had tremendous importance in the world.
—BENJAMIN BAINBRIDGE TREGOE,
co-founder, Kepner-Tregoe, Inc.

Self-inspired behavior has as much to do with how you live as how you work. It's obviously good for business, but it's also good for the soul. It defines the character of people, of companies, and even of nations.

The goal is to take Ben Tregoe's quote as your own—after a lifetime of effort, to really believe you've made a difference—big or small—in the world. I used to think only powerful people like corporate chieftains could make a difference. Today I know that's not true. For the real purpose of being inspired is not to move mountains, but to move yourself: to motivate yourself to make your life matter; to believe, when all is said and done, that you did good work and gave it your best. It can make you a great worker, no doubt about it. But even more important, it can make you a great person.

The transforming power of self-inspiration has created many a business and human miracle. For example, we wouldn't normally think of a man with a Ph.D. in classic literature as a role model for business. But I guarantee you that Robert Howard Allen could teach your employees a thing or two about motivating themselves!

Robert Allen used to run an upholstery shop out of the back of his farmhouse. But his story isn't about the upholstery business—or about business at all. It just makes a powerful point about getting yourself inspired. By all accounts, Allen had little to be inspired about. At the age of six he had been abandoned by his mother to be raised by elderly relatives. His great aunt taught him to read the Bible, but he was never sent to school. He lived in rural Kentucky in a run-down farmhouse with no plumbing. Rarely had he ventured more than a few miles from the spot where he was born. Poorer than poor, he'd never been to a movie, or ridden a bicycle, or been on a date. With holes in his shoes and his front teeth already missing, Allen seemed a picture of the least that life has to offer. Then, in 1981, at age thirty-two, this country bumpkin who had never seen the inside of a classroom took a college aptitude test just to see what he had missed. To everyone's amazement, he blew the lid off the exam. Once he entered college as a freshman, it quickly became obvious that Allen had more raw knowledge of his subjects than any of his professors. He graduated in three years, summa cum laude. Today, with a Ph.D. from Vanderbilt University, Robert Howard Allen is a full professor of classical literature and one of America's rising folk poets.

What was he doing all those years, isolated in the backwoods of Kentucky? What he was doing was reading every book he could beg, borrow, and steal—from Donald Duck to the Bible, from Homer to James Joyce. Allen had a burning passion to learn and had become a walking encyclopedia of history and literature. With virtually no contact with the outside world, he had no idea how special he was. He assumed all educated people would know more than he did. This is self-inspired behavior in a virtual vacuum—twenty-five years of effort with no pats on the back and no material gain in sight, driven only by his own sense of challenge. If Robert Allen can become an expert on world history and classical literature all by himself, what does that say about the power of self-inspiration? It says to me that we'd better find out how to tap into it—in ourselves and every employee in the company.

It is the power of self-inspiration that drives Ross Perot, Akio Morita, Charles Forte, and Buel Messer—and a hundred others that fill these pages. The truth is, when you go looking for self-inspired people, it's a sure way to get your standards raised. Take Messer, for example. It's hard to be too proud of yourself when a blind man can outperform you at every turn. You begin to wonder how your career would have gone if you had no eyes. You discover how much can be achieved with so little. It can make you wonder at how little is often achieved by those with so much.

CHAPTER SIX

TRANSFORMING BUREAUCRACY TO ENTERPRISE

Dismantling the Twentieth-Century Corporation

Dismantling and Starting Over

Transforming today's bureaucracy into tomorrow's enterprise doesn't start with adding something new. No new strategies, techniques, departments, or committees are needed. These can't be the solution because they're already a big part of the problem. They're just more of the excess baggage you've been carrying around for years that's got to be unloaded.

So the first drill is to start tossing stuff overboard: dismantling the mass and weight you've carefully added over the years; keeping it *small* by trimming all of the fat and some of the meat of the twentieth-century corporation. After you've taken it apart and torn it down, keep it that way. Keep it *personal* down the line—keep it *honest* up at the top—and keep it *simple* everywhere in between. If you feel the load lightening, you're well on your way to doing what enterprisers are supposed to do. You're ready to *start over* with the old-time basics of the *spirit of enterprise.*

Starting Over in Scotland

Remember Fraser Morrison in Edinburgh? He's the man who got his family company back but had to take its much larger, money-losing parent along with it. Starting over with the spirit of enterprise wasn't a slogan for him. It was a matter of immediate survival. In chapter 5, I recounted his achievements, but I didn't provide details on how he did it. Here's Morrison's own account of how he transformed bureaucracy to enterprise—overnight.

"So we bought this business that was losing money. We made an awful lot of changes on day one. The first day we retained two directors and the rest, eight or ten, went. We restructured the company so that it was operating on lines similar to the business that we had in Scotland. One of the great difficulties we found, when we added up all of the contract delays on the sites, was the sites were cumulatively eight years behind contract schedules. When you think of the overheads on our construction sites, they can be anything from £10,000 to £100,000 a month, and we were eight years behind schedule! So I focused peoples' attention throughout the business on bringing those eight years' delay back to zero within twelve months. Everybody said it couldn't be done. Well, giving people impossible targets sometimes works. In fact, we got it back to plus thirty weeks in the twelfth month."

▪ Keep It Small
"We split the business up into relatively small—I call them family-size—units. So a director will have a business between only £5 to £20 million turnover. They have a team of between thirty and sixty

staff plus the hourly paid employees. That way they can get to know all of their people quite well. It's worked well for us. The people enjoy a small operation more and take a huge amount of satisfaction from it. You can get the team spirit, which I think is very, very important. The Shand Group [the larger company he bought] just didn't have it. The same with commitment. I think you tend to find it in the small companies. As we grow, we *must* create the structure in which people can continually achieve high commitment. It comes from a desire to do well. From being successful and making some money. But it's not only a money-oriented thing. It's about having a lot of pleasure and satisfaction out of seeing something that you personally developed and built."

▪ Keep It Personal

"I learned a lot of lessons from seeing them try to run our company. They always gave us the feeling that they knew what to do and that we weren't important. It was a huge lesson to me on how to run a business. You have to let the people feel that they are the key element of the business. Hopefully, our structure now is such that people have got a strong personal interest in developing the business. A strong sense of feeling important and that they themselves have a strong entrepreneurial input to the business."

▪ Honesty at the Top

"The main factor that contributed to our success is the enormous commitment that I and the people around me have. When my brother and I bought the business back, we sold about 18 percent of it to the executive directors. So we have about fifteen senior people who have a shareholding in the new company already. I told all of them we want to run the business in a way that's in their best, long-term interests also. So at some point we will think about a public flotation or taking in outside shareholders or whatever to secure it as an organization which is going to generate and build up its own managers. Business needs that kind of personal commitment at the top, and I'm sure we have it today."

▪Keep It Simple

"You've got to try to make it simple. The simpler it is the easier it is to be understood by everyone. The single most important thing that I've learned throughout this process—and I haven't found a situation yet where it isn't appropriate—is that if you forget about the nuts and bolts of the business, you're lost. When we were part of the big holding company, the senior people had lost touch with what was happening in the business. They didn't understand what the people thought. In any situation, even if you are in a financially difficult situation, if the day-to-day operations are working well, you'll be in a strong position. The more effort that the Shand people put into the politics and what was happening with the holding company, the worse the situation got down on the sites and the weaker their overall situation became. Every day you see companies who are having constant changes at the top or companies that are in an endless restructuring process. Again and again, you see the focus going away from the operation of the business. I think concentration on making sure that the nuts and bolts are right will get you into a strong position in the long run."

▪Start Over with the Basics

"For a long time, I'd been telling the parent company I knew what needed to be done to sort this business out, but they decided that they knew better. They were running it as one big business. So when we got it, we split the thing up. And very, very quickly we really refocused the attention of the people away from looking toward the parent company. We put new directors in who we knew would focus their attention on the sites and the operations of the business. We had to very quickly focus the attention of the business toward the only place we make money in construction, which is on the construction site."

Fraser Morrison fits nicely in the long line of legendary Scottish entrepreneurs. His great uniqueness, however, is that he has seen it from all sides—from enterprise to bureaucracy and back to enterprise. And he's determined to avoid the mistakes of his former masters. There are a thousand things companies try to do to transform their bureaucracy to enterprise. But few of them actually work. The five suggestions here come from the masters themselves, and they directly attack the deep-down differences between entrepreneurial and managerial behavior. You may find more elegant or exciting things to try, but skip over these at your peril. You'll never regain the spirit of enterprise if you can't revive the enterprisers.

1. Keeping It Small—
Dismantling Size and Structure

> The advantages of smaller size are becoming very great.
> —PETER F. DRUCKER

Just days before I completed this manuscript, I came across a pronouncement that stopped me dead in my tracks. In one fell swoop, the great Peter Drucker, that icon of twentieth-century big business, wiped out fifty years of management thinking. In a special report by *Fortune* magazine titled "What I Want U.S. Business to Do in '92," Drucker came to grips with the obvious: the dismal results of "bigger is better." His complete statement should have been carved onto the board tables of every major corporation in the world decades ago. Alas, it's too late for that, but it's worth repeating here:

> The advantages of smaller size are becoming very great. Young graduates go to work for giant companies because they have a recruiter on campus and a training program, and three out of five leave within five years. They used to go from one big company to the next. Now they go from a big company to a medium-size company. When you look

at who is exporting, it is not the big companies. Yes, GE has done very well with aircraft engines, and Boeing with aircraft, but other than that, practically all the exporters of manufactured goods are medium-size companies, highly specialized. I don't think big companies will disappear. I think that in the future it will be a strategic decision whether you want to be bigger or not, when in the past bigness itself was the goal. Some businesses will have to be very big, but I see more and more businesses where medium size is much better and where it simply diffuses results and destroys profitability to try to be big. It is becoming increasingly important to think through what is the right size.

For big companies, suffocating under their own weight, Drucker's advice is a dollar late and a penny short. They made their strategic decision a half century ago. And since that time they've lock-bolted into place a rusting functional structure designed to help them grow ever bigger. What are they supposed to do now? Unfortunately, their only option is to take apart and tear down the monstrosities they've built—those "engines of prosperity" that have run out of steam. We're talking about nothing less than *dismantling the size and structure of the twentieth-century corporation!*

And this is just what GM and IBM have concluded they must do. It's no small matter that the biggest company in the history of the world (GM) and the most profitable company in the history of the world (IBM) are simultaneously shrinking their empires. Their recently announced plans, politely referred to as restructuring, are not just more re-organization exercises. They are radical, revolutionary steps to dismantle their corporations—something they should have done years ago. And GM and IBM are only the tip of the iceberg. Repudiating much of twentieth-century management thinking is becoming the dominant strategy of giant companies everywhere as they prepare for the competitive battles of the new millennium.

General Motors' announcement in December 1991 was greeted

with headlines like THE END OF AN ERA. And it certainly is. If CEO Stempel does what he says, and he has virtually no choice, General Motors will never be the same again. The closing of twenty-one North American plants and washing out of seventy-one thousand jobs (nearly a quarter of all positions) will be the shock of a lifetime for the eighty-three-year-old organization. Stempel promises that the new GM will be more responsive to customers and less mired in its own bureaucracy. To back that up, nine thousand of the first twenty-four thousand layoffs will come from the company's black hole of white-collar employees. While this is a bitter pill, everyone but GM seemed to know this should have been done years ago. Even Douglas Fraser, president of the United Auto Workers, said, "They should have bitten the bullet earlier." GM's reputation as a centrally controlled, procedure-driven, bloated bureaucracy has made it a caricature of all big companies stumbling into a cycle of survival. With this history, we have to hope there's more to the GM plan than just getting smaller. Real structural change is desperately needed too—like lopping off the heavy executive hands at the GM Building that so love to wield power from the center.

IBM's announcement just two weeks earlier, attacking both size and structure, is truly revolutionary and holds great promise. Not only does it go much further than GM's, it also comes much earlier in the company's cycle of big troubles. IBM, after all, did earn $6 billion the year before, again making it the most profitable company anywhere. But the signs are bad in Armonk, and CEO Akers says he is ready to bite the bullet. In a proclamation that eerily mirrored the breaking apart the Soviet Union, IBM will spin off its divisions to become independent and much smaller companies. Getting products from research to the market much faster is one of the major goals. Twenty thousand jobs are scheduled to go, but unlike those at GM, layoffs are not the centerpiece of the effort. The new, freestanding businesses will produce startling changes. For example, the mainframes group and the workstation group will likely become real and fierce competitors. IBM may hold major or lesser shares of these newly formed companies. The one sure casualty will be

Armonk headquarters, with its massive and deeply entrenched bureaucracy. Akers may end up, as Gorbachev did, sitting in the Kremlin with no country left to run. This can happen when you dismantle the old guard and create legions of sovereign enterprisers down below.

We're left to wonder how such smart companies got into such troubles. One thing is for sure: Stempel and Akers couldn't wait around any longer for the likes of Drucker to tell them what to do. Nor can the hundreds of other giants around the world who are in various stages of "restructuring." One of the earliest to see the light was Jack Welch, the CEO of General Electric (USA). Since he took over in 1981, he's been dubbed the man who wants to run GE like a small business. He flattened GE's nine levels of management, cut pay levels from twenty-nine to five, obliterated the corporate staff, and—you guessed it—cut one hundred thousand jobs. "Neutron Jack" also got rid of all product lines that weren't first or second in their market. And, as described earlier, he's now taking dead aim at the old functional structure with GE's new salesmen/scientist idea to get products to market faster. The result: In the past decade, sales and profits have climbed steadily while GE's market value has streaked skyward from $12 billion (eleventh in the United States) to $65 billion (second only to Exxon).

Welch's advice for would-be dismantlers: "Picture a building. Companies all added floors as they got bigger. Size adds floors. Complexity adds walls. We all built departments—transportation departments, research departments. That's complexity. That's walls. The job all of us have in business [today] is to flatten the building and break down the walls." This is what dismantling or restructuring gets you: flattened buildings and broken walls—and a 500 percent increase in market value in a decade.

A few big companies never build up that much that needs to be knocked down. Like Toyota, which unceremoniously collapses management levels and any new functional walls every couple of years as preventive action. Or Marks & Spencer, which still runs its empire the way a Main Street merchant used to. Or Johnson &

Johnson, which really lives by its motto: "Growing Big by Staying Small." None of these companies has ever thought that greater size and complexity was the path to greater enterprise. J & J's method of avoiding the pain of tearing it down has been to break it up early. When a new product hits a certain, modest size, presto, it becomes a new company, with its own board, its own management, and its own survival at stake. If you're running a growing business, its obvious which approach makes the most sense.

Like most CEOs and all entrepreneurs, Ed Penhoet at Chiron has given this problem a lot of thought. From the university lab, to his billion-dollar biotech start-up, to forging relationships with the giants like Merck and Johnson & Johnson, Ed Penhoet has pondered the double-edged sword of size: "It's our number one challenge right now. We are at a new size which is entirely different from the band of sixteen that we were, and I think I'd be lying to you if I told you we were as productive per person today as we were ten years ago. We are not. There is no way as a practical matter that could be the case. First of all, we have recruited much more broadly. Second, the company has already established a somewhat different dynamic than in 1981, when we were living from day-to-day, almost hand-to-mouth. So I think you have to accept a certain reality that as a company grows larger, the dynamic will not always be the same.

"For us, then, the key issue is to continue to create smaller units within the larger environment, and there are ways of doing that. We have a subsidiary, for example, which is about 125 people. They are just focused on biotechnology in ophthalmics. It's sort of like the Johnson & Johnson approach of splitting things up. We actually like the J & J model. We have two big programs with them, and we think it is not a bad business model for us to follow. So, if there is any company that we might choose to emulate, we would be probably closer to J & J than many others, because they have this decentralized aspect to their business. When we deal with Ortho Diagnostic Systems (a J & J subsidiary), for example, who is our partner, there is some overlay of J & J, but basically we are dealing with a company about the same size as Chiron, although it is part of this gigantic company. The dynamic in Ortho Diagnostics is not tremendously different from that in our organization. So one thing is to keep the units as small as you can. The other thing is to continually reinforce the separateness to the whole group and to set a style of entrepreneurism and focus on getting things done."

Keeping it small sooner or later bumps into keeping it personal. Penhoet had just said it would be harder for five thousand people to keep up their productivity than it was for his original sixteen. My question back was, "Why? You're a scientist. Why can't five thousand people be as productive as five hundred or fifty or sixteen? Logically, they should be. What's going on?" This brought forward the "Penhoetism" of the day, one of those answers that seems so clear you wonder why you asked such a dumb question: "It's harder to keep it personal for five thousand people, because once they view themselves as one over X, where X is the large number, then the degree to which they feel the personal connection to the success or failure of any given day's work goes down. You know, none of this comes by years. It comes by minutes. What I do with this minute, the next minute, etc. So I think in that sense, it's harder to keep that personal connection to results."

2. Keeping It Personal— The Heat of Consequences Down Below

> If you had to reduce it all down to one thing, it's how to make it personal. So it's their soul that's involved and it's a very personal thing.
> —EDWARD E. PENHOET, PH.D., co-founder, Chiron Corporation

"Personal meaning to every worker," continued Penhoet as I was still mulling over his previous answer. "I think that is the critical thing. How can you get people who are in the organization to feel the competition themselves, personally? I don't have the whole answer, but you must find an answer. If they see themselves as one grain of sand in the mound or one ant carrying things back and forth, and if they know that their dropping out won't make any difference, collectively the whole organization will slow down. So to some degree every individual who works in one of these enterprises has to feel the personal heat of the competition. But at the same time, when the company wins, they must somehow win as well. They must be rewarded by the whole set of reward mechanisms. We think ownership is crucial. We have a strong belief that subsidiaries should have their own equity structure so they can have ownership in their own enterprise. It's difficult to do for accounting reasons, but we still like to reward people based more on the things that they control than on the performance of this larger, amorphous mass over which they have relatively little influence. So if you had to reduce it all down to one thing, it's how to make it personal."

Ed Penhoet saved his most unconventional wisdom for last. His vote for the organizational model that wins the "keep it personal" trophy was the best tip-off that Dr. Penhoet has never been to a management course: "You know, the other enterprises that we see where people work hard and are productive are all individual, personal enterprises. The groups that we've interacted with since we started the company that are the most hard-working and productive, believe it or not, are in the service sector: lawyers, investment bankers, etc. Whether you like this group of people or not, the facts are, their compensation is pretty much directly related to their output. It's very personal. As a result, working with these groups is quite different than working with many other groups—especially large companies. Again it's this personal aspect. Success or failure on a daily basis has a lot of deep personal meaning to these people."

Why is such straight talk so rare in personnel management circles? Why have monetary reward *and* punishment always been pooh-poohed? Why do *any* kind of reward and punishment hang in perpetual limbo in most large companies? It's clear that keeping it personal means something personal has to happen to someone. The consequences have got to be there, pure and simple. We can argue whether the consequences should be financial or a friendly pat on the back. But the bottom line is, as Penhoet states, success or failure on a daily basis has to have a lot of deep personal meaning.

There are at least three proven ways to keep it personal for managers and workers. They can become real owners or shareholders of their company. They can own a little piece of the business like an "intrapreneur." And everyone, everywhere can at least be the owner of their own job. All three ways are quantum leaps over bureaucracy in answering the eternal question: "What's in it for me?"

Miracles can happen when workers become true owners. It's obviously not that they get smarter or more skilled, but that for the first time, they have a personal stake in the success and failure of the company. There are examples every year of employees purchasing their company and miraculously saving it from bankruptcy. All the evidence says that any form and any level of employee ownership has a positive effect on morale, productivity, and profits. In 1974, the U.S. Government enacted the Employee Stock Ownership Program (ESOP). The most recent study of ESOP companies shows that their average annual gain in stockholder's equity is running just under double the Dow Jones average for the same period. In another analysis on competitive performance, covering five years before and five years after instituting an ESOP, the results are even more striking. Between the two five-year periods, the ESOP companies *tripled* their own growth rate against their competitors. There's no mystery to keeping it personal when it's really your company. With less than 10 percent of employees owning some of their company, the only mystery is why so many businesses still don't do it.

Intrapreneurship is an old idea with a new name. It's giving a small group of people total autonomy, and a real share in the ups and downs of their venture. For the big company, it provides the chance to create some entrepreneurial business and, in the bargain, not lose their entrepreneurs. 3M has practiced a version of it for years. At 3M if you invent a product, you get to run the business yourself. This is the core reason why 3M is called the most innovative big company in the world, and why it has the highest percentage of new product revenue (25 percent plus) of any big company in America. Letting employees taste the up-and-down consequences of their ideas is far more important than all the pop innovative techniques you've read about.

As with most good things in life, "intrapreneuring" has its limitations. The first is that only a relative few can play. Second, it's bound to be little more than a PR conversation piece if only silly little projects and products become its province. The intrapreneurs or new business group or whatever you label them have to be working on something that makes a difference to the company as well as themselves. And the biggest pitfall of all is that enemy number one, the corporate bureaucracy, always wants to help. They offer up purchasing rules, accounting help, and personal policy books, none of which can possibly help the intrapreneur. When they can't keep their helpful hands off, the project is as good as dead. Even with these disadvantages, though, intrapreneuring is still a good way to make the job personal.

Whether or not your employees own the company, or a piece of the company, they'd better own their jobs. And I don't mean some theory about psychological ownership or making everyone feel good all the time. I mean feeling the heat of consequences all the way down the line. It takes a living, breathing, entrepreneurial performance environment, where employee output is answered by unrelenting consequences, both material and psychological, both positive and negative—the same kind of operating environment that drives entrepreneurs to extreme levels of commitment and performance. If you take only one idea from this entire book, this is the crucial one. It can do more good, for more people, in more organizations than any other single step you might take. If this doesn't revive the enterprisers out of their bureaucratic sleep, start taking pulses—they may be dead!

Keeping it personal is a personal thing. You know your people and what's going to work. Whatever way you choose to do it, with these ideas or your own, it's one of those few things you probably can't overdo.

3. Keeping It Honest— Integrity and Consequences at the Top

> Companies should begin to focus on a new bottom line: making moral decisions.
> —ANITA RODDICK, founder,
> Body Shop International

"When the Body Shop needed a soap factory, it would have been easier to attach it to our headquarters in England. We put the factory instead into an area in Scotland with 70 percent unemployment, giving work to folks who had been idle for nine years. We now provide jobs for over one hundred people, who make some 20 million bars of soap. Twenty-five percent of their profits go back into the community. The stroke you get is not in the shares going up another bloody five pence, but rather in an enthusiastic work force that's proud of what you do and is motivated by it."* Meet Anita Roddick, who founded and runs Body Shop International, the most successful retail business to come out of the UK since Marks & Spencer. And she also has the products to go worldwide, which even venerable M&S has found difficult to do.

Roddick has a missionary zeal about her, what some would describe as a high sense of integrity with a decidedly liberal bent.

---

* "Making Morality the Goal," *Fortune*, 30 December 1991.

It has to do with things like saving the environment, making products with only natural ingredients, and sending employees off to Romania to work in orphanages. I called her up to ask what she thought about CEO pay in America. Her office said she was "somewhere in Africa on hunger or the environment or something like that."

Plato said there must not be a spread of more than five times between the highest- and lowest-rewarded person in a group. More than that erodes the loyalty of the average member. Well, we believe in free enterprise. We believe in "pay for performance." So maybe five is too limited for entrepreneurial people. But is there a limit? Should there be? How about the CEO making ten times the average employee's pay? Or fifty times? A hundred? Counld anyone be loyal and committed to the American CEO (a hired gun, not the founder) who paid himself 625 times the average pay in his company? Of course not. Can anyone be committed to an executive team taking millions in bonuses while the workers are asked to take a cut? Of course not. If you're an average worker, how does it make you feel to know that the average CEO's pay has rocketed from 34 times yours to 150 times in just the last fifteen years?

Compounding the problem of these grotesque spreads in pay is the issue of consequences at the top—otherwise known as "pay for performance." One would think that pay for performance should mean more pay if performance is good, and less pay if performance is bad. But like generals who don't fight, too many executives appear to want everyone on pay for performance but themselves. The news from the United States in particular is not encouraging. The most recent analysis of CEO pay at America's biggest companies reveals a pay plan that most of us would die for. The comparison shows varying levels of company growth and decline in earnings per share (EPS)—and the average growth in CEO compensation at each level.

Here is a pay-for-performance plan that says if company earnings go up 10 percent, you get a 28 percent raise. And if earnings drop 30 percent, you still get a 6 percent raise. In fact, you can drive your company's earnings straight into the ground, a whopping

COMPANY EPS	CEO COMPENSATION
+10%	+ 28.0%
(20%)	+ 7.6%
(30%)	+ 6.1%
(71%)	0.0%

70 percent drop, and still feel no pain. There appear to be no negative consequences for this privileged crowd.

Of course, integrity at the top means a lot more than just not stealing from the company through your pay packet. It also means little things like not breaking the law. Or insisting that customers get value for their money. Or making sure that employee safety is really a top priority. Or old-fashioned items like being honest, keeping your word, and not asking people to make sacrifices you're not willing to make. But don't get the wrong idea. Shaky integrity at the top is not a cultural distinction of Americans. Ask the German executives who just can't resist selling contraband chemicals and missile components to every two-bit dictator in the world. Or the Pakistanis behind BCCI, the bank swindle of the millennium that has left depositors high and dry all across the world. Or even ask the Japanese.

Hirotsugu Iikubo is an old friend and a successful Japanese entrepreneur who has taken to writing books about Japanese management practices. Around the turn of the century, his grandfather was the first Japanese to be ordained a Methodist minister, and Iikubo inherited a fire and brimstone sense of corporate ethics, which spills over into his writings. During a wide-ranging discussion on Japanese enterprise, he offered this surprising view: "The most significant change seen among Japanese companies is exemplified by this scandal [the Sumitomo Bank scandal involving manipulation of share prices]. This is a question of ethics or codes of conduct of large Japanese companies. My belief is if we had what we call *Zaibatsu* groups—the Mitsubishi family, the Mitsui family, the Sumitomo family, those are the founding families of major Japanese enterprise up until the end of the war—if the Zaibatsu were in command of the Japanese companies, this type of scandal would never have happened. Now the big change is, the CEOs of many, or at least some, Japanese companies, have as their top objective a good performance record during their time—and other things become secondary. So I think if the Sumitomo family had the authority, the Sumitomo bank scandal wouldn't have happened because within the family rulings, one should not make money by sacrificing others, ever. This was more important than any short-term period of performance. Since the war, when the families were more or less purged and the professional managers began to take over we're seeing more and more of this." Iikubo went on to explain that he wasn't judging the personal morals or ethics of founders of companies versus professional managers. His only point was that even in Japan, different objectives produce very different behavior.

Ross Perot, that Texas-sized entrepreneur of entrepreneurs, is always good for a final word on integrity at the top. Remember, he's the guy who likes to hire commandos to rescue his people and who set his salary at $68,000 in 1965 and never raised it again. For such acts, Perot had and still has the most fanatically loyal employees of any CEO I've ever come across. The reason is fairly straightforward. He practices what the good book preaches. Says he: "If I set the curriculum at the Harvard Business School, God forbid, the first and most important course would be human nature. . . . Suppose somebody says, 'Look Ross, I'm very busy. What's the most important thing you can tell me about leadership?' I'd say, 'Just treat people the way you'd want to be treated.' Then he'd say, 'That's the golden rule.' And I'll say, 'That's right.' " Oh, so simple to say and so hard to do for those overpaid folks at the top. But of course they can't treat others as they treat themselves —it would bankrupt the company in a quarter!

Judging personal integrity is risky business and not really the point. But the necessity for honorable leadership won't go away. At minimum, if high-flying managers really want to get everyone on board the good ship enterprise, they, themselves, have to be along for the ride. Leading a bureaucracy back to enterprise is not the time or place to rise above the fray. Certain entrepreneurial behaviors have to be set at the top, not because they're moral rules, but because no one else will buy in if they're absent. Exhibiting complete integrity and accountability—being prepared to take the consequences of the company's performance right on the chin—is the entrepreneurial behavior to start with. Plato had his version of integrity at the top and Anita Roddick has hers. Iikubo-san has his for Japan, and Ross Perot's is pure Texas. And you have to have yours, if you hope to have anyone following as you charge across the Rubicon of enterprise.

4. Keeping It Simple—
The 80/20 Chinese Solution

> Chinese companies won't take on an MBA syndrome just because they're mixing a little bit of a management ingredient into this huge vat of Chinese entrepreneurship.
> —Victor Fung, founder,
> Prudential Asia

Making things, selling things, and servicing things: how complicated can business be? Well, that depends on whom you ask. Like brain surgeons working on an in-grown hair, some people are deep into management overkill. For them, enterprise is an esoteric science, much too complex for the man in the street. Others—Soichiro Honda and William Lever come to mind—make it look as simple as doing what comes naturally. And keeping it that way is the only genius required. Like life in general, then, doing business can be a whole series of choices about keeping things in perspective—about getting things in the right balance. Like products and customers. Or debits and credits. Or how much managing and how much entrepreneuring.

This is the quarrel with general management theory and practice. Running a business isn't *that* complicated. It certainly doesn't require any esoteric skills. To be sure, there can be complicated problems, but they mostly relate to inventing and developing complicated products. They have little to do with the "management" of business. None of this would matter except for the matter of balance. Every hour and every dollar devoted to big company managing and its bureaucratic trimmings is an hour and a dollar taken away from working on the fundamentals of enterprise. And this balance is frighteningly out of balance in most bigger companies.

All management practice is not "bad." Some of it is solid common sense. But a good case can be made that large segments of the professional management universe, both inside the company and with the army of experts outside, are just off pushing their own agenda for their own benefit. When the only job of some managers is to manage managers who manage other managers, we have to wonder. When planning systems and organization studies are re-done year after year, what's going on? When the United States turns out seventy-five thousand MBAs a year and still loses ground to "MBAless" Germany and Japan, what's the point? And when hundreds of managers lose thousands of man-days in seminars on "how to better manage your time," it's time to start asking some tough questions. The toughest may be how much managing is enough? Or perhaps even more to the point, how much devotion to day-in and day-out basics is enough? What should the balance be?

For a change, let's not ask the management experts this management question. Let's turn to some folks at the extreme, people who are in no danger of losing their entrepreneurial spirit to what they call the "MBA syndrome." The Chinese are commonly accorded top rung when it comes to a proclivity for entrepreneuring. Chinese companies in fact have had a near 100 percent dependency on entrepreneurship. And it has worked pretty well. If you have any doubts, check the numbers in Hong Kong, Singapore, and Taiwan—and the bristling southern rim of mainland China. Victor Fung in Hong Kong comes from a long line of these very successful entrepreneurs. But he also has impeccable credentials from MIT and the Harvard Business School—as both student and professor. In short, Fung knows both sides of this game. After teaching business at Harvard, Victor returned home in 1976 to run the family business, Li and Fung. It's the largest Chinese trading company in Hong Kong and was started by his grandfather eighty-five years ago—who reputedly cornered the firecracker market by being the first to package them in paper instead of mud.

After six years at the helm, Victor struck out on his own. In 1986 he founded Prudential Asia, a new-age, highly entrepreneurial merchant bank catering to the fast-growing, midsized company market throughout Southeast Asia. The majority of these up-and-coming tigers are Chinese-owned, part of the "pervasive Chinese network" Victor knows so well. He controls 40 percent of the venture, while his 60 percent "sugar daddy" is the $200 billion Prudential Insurance Company of America. I met Victor in the Young President's Organization, a worldwide group of irredeemable workaholics. True to form, I found him working away on a Saturday afternoon in his Hong Kong office. I was hoping he would take time out to explain how the red-hot entrepreneur of Hong Kong was getting along with the cool management guru of Harvard.

Victor Fung never disappoints. Here's the Chinese solution to "how much is enough" and a few other gems thrown in at no extra cost: "The Chinese network in Southeast Asia is pervasive. Chinese often account for a couple percent of the population in some countries, but they could account for the majority of the wealth. They control the real economic interests. What is going to be interesting in the 1990s is seeing how the Japanese and the Chinese influences mingle. They will both compete and cooperate, and I think all over Southeast Asia you will see that anomaly. But going back to Chinese entrepreneurship, I think the Chinese up to now have been very famous for building businesses, but not large organizations. There is a saying in Chinese that it is very hard for businesses to survive past the third generation. There is another saying that if you pit one Chinese against one Japanese, you pick the Chinese any day because the guy has initiative, he's driving, and smart in many ways. But if you take ten Chinese against ten Japanese, you will have to pick the Japanese all the time. The Chinese can't get organized. They all want to be the boss. So that spirit of entrepreneurship, that spirit of wanting to be the boss, is both a strength and a weakness in the Chinese organization.

"Of course, creating a Chinese IBM is not the goal. In the twenty-first century we probably won't see a Chinese IBM. But we will see a hundred medium-sized IBMs. This gets you into the question of what is an optimal size for a company. My own feeling, at least for this part of the world, is that if you are in the $250 million range, that's a very good and comfortable size. You've got critical mass. But you are not so big that the boss cannot say hello to the people. At most you have several thousand people at that size. You are still in touch. Beyond that you have to split it off like an amoeba. And that may be the 'Chinese syndrome' for the future.

"Now the other thing that I think is interesting in the Chinese makeup is that it is very difficult for the Chinese to distinguish between ownership and management. To you Westerners, it is a very simple concept. You have professional managers and you have shareholders. They could be one and the same or they could be a completely separate group. The Chinese don't have that concept. If you own, you obviously are going to manage things, and nobody gets to manage unless they are an owner. It explains a lot of what goes on in Chinese organizations."

So where does this leave Chinese companies as they roar into a sure-to-be different twenty-first century? "This is very interesting. It used to be that Chinese companies ran out of management when they ran out of relatives. When all the brothers and cousins are in major positions, that's it. You can't expand anymore. The interesting thing over the past twenty years in the Chinese world— the network in Hong Kong, Southeast Asia, and indeed China itself—is that you are beginning to get what I would call the 'MBA sons' coming back. There is some move toward professional management. You are beginning to see change from within the family

because the son, the MBA son, has now gotten these strange West-
ern ideas about structure and organization. There's another impetus
I believe. It's easy for Chinese to try to control everything when
they are dealing within a country that they know, whether it's
China, Hong Kong, or even Malaysia. When you move beyond
your national boundary, you become a multinational. You begin
to realize that sending your cousin to Vancouver works only up to
a point. At some point you've got to use local nationals. So almost
by necessity, Chinese companies are becoming less family-based,
less culture-based, as they grow."

Is Victor ready to call in a team of management consultants to
save the poor Chinese entrepreneur? Well, hardly. Victor Fung
may have Harvard-ese in his head, but he's got Chinese in his blood:
"But of course it's all relative. Frankly, Chinese companies won't
take on an MBA syndrome just because they're mixing a little bit
of a management ingredient into this huge vat of Chinese entrepreneurship. All of this is a leveling experience. We don't want to
and aren't going to run our companies like an MBA organization—
with all organization and no spirit. We want to keep 80 percent of
the spirit and put in maybe 20 percent organization ideas. In American companies, sometimes you see only 1 percent spirit and 99
percent organization. You lose it completely. Obviously we don't
want that. But I think for us, this will be a very helpful ingredient.
Especially if it's just the right mix. The 80/20 mix."

Who knows if 80/20 is the right combination? On its face, it
does look like a better bet than 1/99. Most of us would even settle
for a 50/50 split down the middle, which would be a revolutionary
change in most large organizations. But looking for the perfect
percentage isn't the issue. What's really important has to be keeping
your eye on the basics—the simple substance of enterprise—and
then using a management idea here or there that can help you do
it better. It's being able to separate the important from the merely
clever.

Not that Asians are the only ones that keep it simple, but
Soichiro Honda was a man who could really separate the rice from

the bran. From the personal recollections of Atsushi Kimura, we get the picture of a man hard to fool. Kimura should know. He spent a lot of years around Mr. Honda. For the first fifteen years of his career, in typical Honda fashion, he did everything from production to sales to personnel. In the late seventies he became VP of personnel for Honda USA and eventually wound up as director and general manager of Honda R&D (Mr. Honda's first love) back in Japan. Just three months after the great founder's death, I met Kimura in Tokyo where he's now running the Honda foundation for auto safety.

"He was the son of a village blacksmith," said Kimura slowly, making sure I got the right picture of the man he idolized. "Yes, a poor person. So he understood the meaning of human suffering. He only graduated from primary school. He didn't go to any university. But he understood what was most important in people—and how to keep good human relations. He learned how to repair cars from being a blacksmith. Well, at that time not so many cars. Mostly motorcycles and bicycles and a few fire engines. He always looked straight at the problem, touched the problem, and figured out what caused it so that it could be repaired. He could think with his hands. He learned by working. This was important even after he became president of Honda. He didn't like sitting behind the desk at Honda headquarters. He preferred to look around, in R&D or in the plants. Sometimes these university- or college-graduated engineers would give him a concept presentation. He could get very upset. He would say, 'Why don't you give me a real example? Something I can see and understand. How can I believe what you say?' Then after a week or so, the engineers would make a prototype of the product or the part and present it again to Mr. Honda. Then he got very interested and would say, 'Okay, now I understand it.'

"The same with the MBAs. I don't know why, but sometimes we hired MBA people. Mr. Honda never thought of these people as the enemy, but he always looked for their real capability and intelligence. He wanted to know the core of their philosophy—whether it was marketing or technology or whatever they were talking about. He always asked, 'Is this person just window dressing or is there a truth and substance in him?' He never trusted just words and charts. He needed to understand what was behind them. That was his way."

Perhaps Mr. Honda's way is the best way. Look for the "truth and substance" of what management theory may have to offer. And chuck out the window dressing. Then get on with the simple things, those basics of enterprise that you really have to do well. Perhaps this is the way to strike the best balance. Just stop doing all those things, so flawlessly presented, that look too good to be true. The odds are you'll be right.

That's about what Jack Welch did and he was right. GE turns one hundred this year, fit as a fiddle, because Welch started asking tough questions ten years ago. As *Fortune* puts it: "In the nineties, Welch believes, a corporate Gulliver is doomed without the Lilliputian virtues he calls 'speed, simplicity, and self-confidence.' To get them, the scrappy CEO has mounted a radical assault on the canons of modern management—which GE largely wrote." Long carrying the now dubious honor of being called "the Harvard of corporate America," GE single-handedly invented or popularized much of what passes as modern management technique. From strategic planning to hierarchical management to systematic market research, GE was the think tank of how to keep it complicated! GE got it so complicated that by the seventies it was looking like the GM of the nineties. Into this bloated yet micromanaged bureaucracy stepped Jack Welch. It takes a big man to turn back the clock, but that's exactly what he did. From *Fortune* again: "Those ideas formed the core curriculum at Crotonville, GE's Management Development Institute in Ossining, New York. What's happening at GE now . . . is an explicit rejection of many of the old principles. In the past decade, Welch, now fifty-six, has tried to infuse the company with a sense of entrepreneurship, and in doing so has become one of the country's most admired CEOs." To get "most admired," the least you'd better do is start asking the tough questions. How much is enough? How complicated can it be? And how can we make it simpler? If you're stuck in the bureaucracy and surrounded by a bunch of corporate brain surgeons, even just asking the questions could be a leap forward.

Last but by far the most important step in transforming bureaucracy to enterprise is starting over with the entrepreneurial basics. It's the central message of this book, and nobody ever said it better than Walt Disney.

5. Starting Over with the Spirit of Enterprise

> The inclination of my life—has been to do things and make things which will give pleasure to people in new and amazing ways. By doing that I please and satisfy myself.
>
> —WALT DISNEY, founder,
> The Walt Disney Company

Sound too simple? More magic than science? Not to Walt Disney. His common-sense description of how he built the world's greatest entertainment company is in fact an exquisite prescription for enterprise. Behind this bit of Disney "management wisdom" lie the four uncompromising practices that underpin the success of all entrepreneurs and their high-growth companies. This is where you ought to be spending 80 percent of your time.

"The inclination of my life"—it's philosophical yet practical. It's value-driven. It determines what you do and how you do it. Entrepreneurs are driven by a **sense of mission**.

"do things and make things which will give pleasure to people"—making products to please customers. A unified picture of what you're up to. The soul of business: **Customer/Product Vision.**

"in new and amazing ways"—new, creative, innovative ways to please customers. An entrepreneurial necessity driven by a sense of urgency. It's called **High-speed Innovation.**

"I please and satisfy myself"—motivated and inspired by the consequences of their own actions. Entrepreneurs are **Self-inspired** to do what they do.

If you're searching for the spirit of enterprise, search no further. These are the four fundamental practices of entrepreneurs: the zero-based basics that fuel product innovation, customer satisfaction, and worker commitment and shareholder return. They're not magic, and they're not science. They're just old-fashioned common sense.

The rational response to starting over with zero-based enterprise goes something like this: "Where's the research? What's the plan? And why change now?" Behind such caution is almost always an overpowering commitment to business as usual. You've just spent three lifetimes getting re-organized, "empowering" your people, and getting the best strategy money can buy. Why "dismantle" all this for the spirit of enterprise, for Walt Disney's common sense? The fact is, business as usual has never been a good idea. And in today's environment, *management as usual* will get you a one-way ticket to the junk heap—along with the 84 percent of big companies that bite the dust.

For the first time in history, the entire, global economic pie is up for grabs. There is an explosion of new markets. Millions of new competitors are entering the battle each year. No market is safe. No product is protected. For commerce and industry, the "new world order" is already here. A sea change of winners and losers is taking place now. The evidence is everywhere. Size and weight will no longer get you into the winner's circle. Fast-moving, customer-driven entrepreneurship will. For big business everywhere, it's time to learn some very old lessons—very fast!

Of course, you can always hope for the best. Build more bureaucracy and batten more hatches. Maybe "bigger is better" will do better next time. Or you can cut your losses and start over today. Dismantle the bureaucracy, blow the hatches, and break it all up—in a hundred little entrepreneurial pieces. If you're really searching for the spirit of enterprise, you'll know what to do. After all, it's just common sense.

EPILOGUE

The Enterprise of Nations

Enterprising Nations and Enterprising Companies

The spirit of enterprise doesn't live in a vacuum. It's greatly influenced by the sweeps of history—and the larger political and cultural forces they bring. For better or worse, all companies ultimately reflect these forces. Enterprise is a collage of historical context, very dependent on the quality of the political leadership and the creativity and energy of the people. Because it's an enterprising nation that produces enterprising companies, our search concludes with a look at the national environment. History has given us two memorable lessons about the enterprise of nations and their companies.

First, the great twentieth-century experiment of mass producing the spirit of enterprise was a giant flop—for both countries and companies. From the Kremlin in Red Square to the General Motors Building on Michigan Avenue, top-heavy bureaucratic control is bad for "business." A younger Mikhail Gorbachev, as minister of agriculture, discovered that the 4 percent of Soviet farmland under independent family cultivation produced a whopping 30 percent of the country's food. Even a dyed-in-the-wool communist like Gorbachev had to admit, "There must be a lesson there somewhere." About the same time, GM Chairman Bob Stempel, who runs a company with a bigger GNP than most countries, discovered he had the highest-paid workers and the lowest employee morale of any car company in the world. In both the Kremlin and the General Motors Building, something had gone very wrong. Neither big government nor big business could deliver the enterprise of the people.

Second, the history of prosperity shows a continual coming and going of winners and losers. The nineteenth century belonged to the Europeans, spearheaded by the Victorian Liberals of Great Britain. The twentieth-century winner is clearly North America, with the United States emerging as the richest nation in the history of the world. The twenty-first century is up for grabs, but the smart money and all the trends are on the side of Asia, led by Japan and over a billion hard-working Chinese. Individual countries experience enormous ups and downs. In the *Rich Get Poor* category is the dizzying decline of Great Britain, the world's wealthiest and most powerful country at the end of the nineteenth century. For a *Poor Get Rich* version, you can't top the economic miracle of Taiwan. Poorer than Albania as recently as 1950, the Republic of China today has the greatest foreign reserves of any country in the world. And the United States, clearly at a crossroads, is facing a serious decline in its share of the world's prosperity. Countries, like companies, are victims of their own hard-to-change life cycles.

The point to ponder is what really causes the rise and fall of a people's prosperity? We know that no nation has ever stayed rich forever—not the great dynasties of China, the Romans, the Ottomans, nor the British. But why? Do the winners just indulge themselves and wait to be knocked off by more enterprising upstarts? Is there anything we can really do to change the course of history?

Consider this premise. It really doesn't have to be this way.

There's no law of nature or principle of economics that says prosperous nations must lose their spirit of enterprise and decline. After all, how hard can it be for people to leave their country in a little better shape than they found it? The simple secret is, the underlying principles that propel growth and decline in business are very much at work in the rise and fall of economic states: pursuing a worthy mission, producing goods and services a little better than your neighbor, being a bit innovative, and motivating yourself to do a fair day's work. These are the behaviors that produce prosperity in companies—and nations too. If they're alive in the national leadership and in the people, you're on your way. If they go, decline and fall can't be far behind. Don't just take my word for it. Ask the Brits.

The Rich Get Poor— the Battle Britain Lost

For an example of growth and decline, Great Britain's story is hard to beat. Brilliant histories, as only the British can write them, have attempted to explain the decline of the British Empire. A simpler answer may suffice. Britain simply turned its back on the spirit of enterprise that made it the wealthiest nation in the world for more than a hundred years.

With the unification of 1801 officially creating the United Kingdom, the British embarked on one of the great economic surges in history. By midcentury, the British engine of prosperity was under full steam, propelled by two resolute national forces. First was the rise of the hard-working and hard-praying entrepreneurs of Victorian Liberalism. This golden era of enterprise was led by devout Quakers and Congregationalists like Titus Salt, Jeremiah Colman, George Cadbury, and William Lever, all passionate believers in self-help, global free trade, and minimal government interference. The essential second force was of course the great populist and Liberal Party leader W. E. Gladstone. As chancellor of the exchequer (and soon-to-be prime minister), Gladstone laid the foundation of the world's greatest free-market economic system. In place of high duties and regulation, Gladstone demanded and got from British industry radical improvements in the quality of life for the working class. Behind this one-two punch of inspired entrepreneurship, fostered by enlightened government policy, the British sailed into the twentieth century with the largest navy, the largest economy, and by far the deepest pockets of any country on earth.

What happened? Well, a lot of people say it's tough to go through two world wars and a depression, and watch all your colonies turn into countries, without going broke. But if Germany and Japan have taught us anything, it's that national setbacks can be turned around in a hurry by hungry and hard-working people. No, what happened to Great Britain is that the nation's spirit of enterprise just died a slow death. Long before the decline was so painfully obvious, the emphasis of the nation was shifting from growing to reaping, from enterprising to managing. It happens with any nation that has been too comfortable too long. The UK's competitive spirit was slowly giving way to self-satisfaction and dividing the spoils of other people's work.

Self-satisfied people make easy prey for hungier competitors. While Britons were looking inward, and sorting out their good fortune, the Germans and Americans were setting their sights on the world. The poor-cousin Germans were hungry and their industrial enterprisers were on the march. The country bumpkins across the Atlantic were very hungry and were bursting with a rough-and-ready spirit of entrepreneurship. What happened next was a high-noon, industrial shoot-out in which Britian lost its nineteenth-century lead in industry after industry—from heavy equipment and light machinery to chemicals and pharmaceuticals. It was a clean sweep by the Germans and Americans.

Britain became its own worst enemy as future product and

market possibilities were increasingly cut off at the knees by vested interests. Gottlieb Daimler and Karl Benz produced the world's first commerical cars in Germany in 1886 even though English inventors like Herbert Stuart and Edward Butler were decades ahead of them. But the powerful British horse and buggy cartel lobbied to keep speed limits at only four miles an hour until 1986—effectively stalling the start-up of an automotive industry. By that time Britain was permanently behind the Germans. In 1895, Lord Kelvin, who was president of the Royal Society, rocked would-be British aviation pioneers by declaring that further research on "flying" should be abandoned. His visionary reason: "Heavier-than-air flying machines are impossible." With such inspiration from above, is it any wonder that would-be British entrepreneurs started scratching their heads and leaving in droves? There was no Gladstone in sight, and the Cadburys and Levers of the future were booking passage for Australia, Canada, and the United States.

In 1946, a depression and two world wars later, the UK fell in line with most of the world and took a sharp left turn. This was the death knell to Britain's fading spirit of enterprise. Business became evil and government became the dispenser of all good. Enterpreneurs were painted as the enemies of social progress. While the Germans and Japanese were digging themselves out of the rubble, Westminster was burying the nation's enterprise under an avalanche of expensive good intentions. Law after law was passed to socialize this and regulate that. Huge companies were taken over in this government-knows-best environment.

All the characteristics of national enterprise were dying. There was no remaining sense of mission, no high national purpose. Visions of new product and market opportunities, such as computers, were blurred and confused. British innovations almost never made it to market. When they did, they were so poorly made that they didn't work anyway. And employees seemed primarily self-inspired to bring their companies to their knees. By the 1970s, Great Britain was leading the world in workdays lost to strikes. To make matters worse, Britain's best and brightest shunned business careers for the more respected profession of government bureaucrat. British industry, the *envy* of the nineteenth century, had become the *laughingstock* of the twentieth. The economy was in shambles and getting worse. A truly humbling moment came when this great empire had to go hat in hand, like a third-world banana republic, to the IMF to beg for loans. By the late seventies, memories of the empire could no longer cover the terrible reality: Great Britain, that once-mighty powerhouse of enterprise and prosperity, was in a free-fall toward national poverty.

Margaret Thatcher's "enterprise burst" in the 1980s intervened to at least break the fall. Thatcher's clarion call to reverse the cycle of decline was blunt: "Capitalism made us prosperous at home and allowed us to feed the poor abroad. Socialism proved the road to poverty and serfdom." The "Iron Lady" and her government set the country on a decade-long effort to re-create an "enterprise culture" throughout the British Isles. Whether the legacy of Margaret Thatcher will be a long-term rebound or simply a last hurrah remains to be seen. If nothing else, she gave the people of that island kingdom an eleventh-hour choice—a choice to create an economic miracle, as another island people, halfway around the world, are doing today.

The Poor Get Rich— Taiwan's Economic Miracle

While the British were going broke, a band of displaced Chinese were accumulating so much money that today they have trouble re-investing it all. Economists call this extremely rare ailment "Dutch Disease." Today it's the biggest, maybe the only, economic problem facing the Republic of China on Taiwan. Welcome to the place that provides living proof of how commonsense policies and hard-working people can change a very poor country into a very rich country in fewer than two generations—a place where the spirit of enterprise created a national economic miracle.

Outsiders have to remember that the mainland Nationalists had been ravaged by war with Japan since 1931 and were then driven out of their homeland in a bloody civil war with Mao's communist hordes. They ended up on a mountainous island, one-tenth the size of California, with few assets and virtually no natural resources. How, then, did this small group of people, beaten and broke in the 1950s, accumulate a $76 billion surplus in foreign reserves by the 1990s—more than Japan, or Germany, or the United States— more than any country in the world? Well, it turns out that the causes of Taiwan's skyrocketing prosperity since 1950 are the same old things. This is a story of unadulterated, uncomplicated, all-out enterprise—egged on at every step by the government. The one absolutely clear fact about this tiny speck of land in the South China Sea is that it didn't get rich by browbeating its entrepreneurs.

The man to ask is the Honorable K. T. Li. The venerable, eighty-two-year-old Cambridge-educated physicist is widely recognized as the principal architect of "Taiwan's economic miracle." Born on the mainland, he arrived on the island along with everyone else after the communist victory. He has served as minister of economic affairs, minister of finance, and minister of state. Today he carries the title "senior advisor to the president—Republic of China." Talking to him is like taking a cram course in the history of the twentieth century. He has seen it all. Naturally, the question that everyone wants to ask Minister Li is how did it happen? So I asked him for the single most important lesson in creating national prosperity. His surprising answer: "It's population control. More important than any economic theory. When you have such a large number of young born, you have to create jobs for them. So you have to be practical. People growth and economic growth have to be together. I think this is the most important thing. Now it is definitely against the Chinese philosophy. Confucius says that if you do not have descendants, you are a failure. Well, we did it without laws. We talked quietly to the people. They know that at the third or fourth child the situation becomes bad. Their house is bad. Not enough food. Look around. Whether it's Catholic, Muslim, Buddhist, where you find poor countries, you find too many people. No work, no opportunity, no hope."

I had expected more of an economist's answer, but of course the architect of Taiwan's economic miracle never studied economics, a fact he seems quite proud of: "Of course, the finance minister has many economists as advisors. They all tried to agitate me in one direction or another, and I took it with due respect. But in the end, it only requires someone with common sense to make the judgments." Fair enough. But was there an economic policy at work, or did this $76 billion get here by accident? Is it a fluke that Taiwan has maintained about 9 percent GNP growth for four straight decades? At this point, Minister Li reached back into some painful history: "Yes, we had an idea of what to do. And we had a clear idea of what not to do. We reasoned that runaway inflation and rural poverty were the main reasons for the rise of communism on the mainland. These we were determined to avoid. Also, we determined that everything we did should foster private initiative, be highly pragmatic, and be implemented in some logical order. This last point—the right policy at the right time—is very important to development. You'll see why.

"The first thing we knew was that the largest part of the labor force was in agriculture. Increasing the earnings of the farmers would help keep the economy stable—that's very important. We had to introduce land reform to make the farmer more prosperous. Many countries did land reform. If you do land reform and forget about the farmer, there are many new problems. We wanted to make sure that if farmers worked harder they made more money. So land was sold at only two and a half times the fixed value of the yield. As yield went up, it became easier and easier for the farmer to pay off the land. This we wanted. We wanted owner farmers, not tenant farmers with great, rich landlords. Another thing about agriculture is that countries have to be able to feed themselves. Especially poor countries. They go broke if they have to import food. So everything we did in the early days was to help the farmers prosper. If they increased output, they prospered. Farmers will do that if you let them. It worked very, very well. We are now of course big exporters of food like rice and sugar.

"Next, we were still very poor and we decided that our industry had to concentrate on producing those things our own people really needed. *Import substitution*, it was called. It wasn't a long-term policy, but it created jobs for people and reduced the cost of imports. At that time we inherited from the Japanese occupiers a lot of state-owned enterprises. We decided to break these up and sell them as smaller businesses to our people. All these could be handled by the private sector better, so we sold them at very reasonable prices. A lot of the former landlords became investors for the first time in small enterprises. We wanted to create entrepreneurs. Y. C. Wang, the "plastics king" of the world, started this way. The government sold the plants, helped find the private investors, did everything we could to create domestic business. Many countries do import substitution, but that's all they do. We quickly moved on to export.

"Because this is a small island, I knew we could not depend on just substituting imports. We would saturate ourselves with no more growth possibilities. So how could we overcome this problem? We had to create an economy for exports. No one believed we could compete at the international standard. Doing this required investment. We encouraged everyone to save. No tax at all if they saved their money for two years. We knew this required foreign companies to invest in Taiwan for the export business. We knew companies hate red tape. We decided to eliminate all the red tape. We set up the world's first export zone, in Kaoshiung in 1966. We put one government office in the zone, and the companies there never had to go to any government agency except that one office right there. For smaller companies, we started the idea of individual bonded warehouses for export. We put one customs employee in each warehouse to make it efficient for that one company. We did everything we could think of to encourage exporting.

"In all these phases we wanted the individuals—the farmers, the domestic businessmen, the exporters—to become prosperous. We thought that was the way to avoid what had happened on the mainland. I should add that fighting inflation all the way was also a big part of the policy. We never took the easy way on money. We even had to sell our gold, but we never printed money we didn't have. So I think we have learned a lot about poverty and inflation, the two lessons we brought from the mainland."

Sounds pretty straightforward, doesn't it? Watch the birth rate, make everyone prosperous, and don't go broke in the process. But there's a much deeper message in K. T. Li's words. It's about the underlying roles of a nation's government and its people in fostering the spirit of enterprise. I asked Dr. Chi Hsieh, the country's top academic economist, to summarize these key points of Taiwanese policy. His polite but blunt answer says it comes down to more a matter of will than brains: "Government, knowing what to do and having the will to do it are separate universes. Taiwan was certainly going against the tide in the world. The government worked hard to prevent any expansion of the public sector. They privatized most of the public enterprises. They encouraged the private entrepreneur to a great extent. And the government picked a very tough way to deal with inflation. Most countries take the easy way, printing the money and behaving like really big government is really good government. Taiwan in the fifties was very, very conservative financially. Even though the popular thing was to spend, the government did not spend. They had strong will. No one believed they could stick with it. Maybe K. T. Li believed, but most didn't. But today, they still stick to this policy.

"Of course, this all requires hard work by the people. But I believe this is also economic, not just a cultural thing. It's a famous debate in the textbooks. Any country has to decide where to keep its best people. In some countries, especially the socialistic countries, the best people will go to the government. That is where they can do the most good, become famous, and so on. In Taiwan, all the opportunity was in the private sector. So the young people who want to achieve, the entrepreneurs, will not join the government. They will go to the private sector. This is just common sense. The really important point for all countries is to find a way to let the people taste the development. Participate in it. That means that, if they do certain things, they and their families will be better off. Government's job is to stand by and watch and try to create a lot of these kinds of opportunities for the people. It's all common sense."

Echoes of Victorian Liberalism? Indeed, it's a classic case of a country on the rise: historical crisis as the starting point; government policy favoring and fostering entrepreneurs as the best way to expand the national pie; and talented, hard-working people responding to the opportunity. If nothing else, Taiwan has a government and a people fairly obsessed with creating prosperity. You could call it their national sense of mission. Of course, Taiwan has had its share of critics over the tradeoffs made on the road to prosperity.* But with an amazing seventy times increase in per capita GNP over forty years and one of the most equal distributions of income in the industrialized world, the Taiwanese seem content to keep doing what they're doing.

---

* Making tradeoffs is nothing new in Taiwan. The original, fundamental tradeoff made by Chiang Kai-shek and his defeated government was economic freedom for political freedom. Thanks in large part to economic "detente" with the People's Republic of China, that original tradeoff is rapidly becoming a relic of Taiwan's past. Another has been inattention to infrastructure. But the government recently announced the largest single public works program ever undertaken by a country: a whopping $300 billion across 779 separate projects to improve services throughout the country. Few countries in the world could afford this, but today Taiwan can. Maybe these are just more examples of K. T. Li's "right policy at the right time"!

Unleashing the American Spirit of Enterprise

The battle that Britain lost and the miracle of Taiwan show once again that it's not natural resources or external conditions that determine economic winners and losers. It has always been and continues to be the quality and depth of the nation's spirit of enterprise.

America's engine of prosperity, viewed on a global scale, probably peaked in the mid-1970s. All kinds of theories, many diametrically opposed, are offered up to explain what's wrong. In fact, the reasons for America's relative decline have a familiar ring: that same old inward-looking complacency; the muddying of the sense of mission; a slide in national competitiveness; the loss of urgency; and too many people waiting for someone else to do the work. It has that definite feel of a people beginning to see prosperity as more of a right than a reward—and of a country with a faltering spirit of enterprise.

As Ross Perot says, "America's number one problem is we're goin' broke, folks." Perot's no economist, but he can add and it just doesn't add up. We're pushing a $4 trillion national debt and a $400 billion annual deficit, and no one at the helm seems to care. *None* of America's future challenges will be conquered at this rate.

Across America there are a lot of entrepreneurial bright spots, to be sure, but there are also some very alarming trends in the competitiveness of the work force. America is producing armies of young people who can sort of read and write—and nothing else. They don't know how to grind a valve, wire a circuit board, or even put up a wall that won't fall down. By the millions, they are heading straight for the black hole of unskilled labor. While four hundred thousand skilled-worker visas were granted in 1991 to fill good-paying American jobs, our own unskilled children competed with migrant labor or worse—a tragedy for them and a suicidal competitive position for America.

And finally, serious action to solve these solvable problems has been replaced by a great national upsurge in hand-wringing. America too often is sounding like a nation of finger-pointers. The rich blame the poor. The poor blame the rich. Management and workers blame each other, and everyone blames the Japanese. With our economic well-being slipping through our fingers, such talk isn't just cheap, it's absolutely worthless—and self-fulfilling.

The more "enterprising" strategy for America is to stop blaming and start concentrating on what we do best. The two uncontested facts of America's greatness have been its grand experiment in democratic freedom and its bountiful supply of the spirit of enterprise. These have always been our national treasures. The evidence is telling us that a full-blown revival of that spirit of enterprise is urgently needed. Re-instilling the spirit in the whole country may sound complicated, but the fundamental questions to ask aren't. You'll recognize them all:

▪ A National Sense of Mission

What is America's mission in the twenty-first century? Is everyone committed? How in the world are we going to pay for it? If you don't know the answers, join the rest of us. We do know that Thomas Watson's three famous beliefs, which guided IBM so well for seventy-five years, would never have gotten off the ground if the company had been broke or if every little department went off and made up its own list of beliefs. That would put any company's goals on hold—as it's clearly doing today for America's national sense of mission.

▪ America's Customer/Product Competitiveness

Is America headed in the right direction to have the smartest and hardest-working labor force in the world over the next several generations? When Walt Disney said, "The inclination of my life has been to do things and make things . . ." he wasn't daydreaming about managing a big studio. He was talking about his own day-in and day-out *performance* and *commitment* to be the best in the world at his craft. He was talking about working smarter and harder than any competitor—exactly the same qualities that determine the competitive positions of entire countries!

▪ The Urgent Necessity to Act

Can America be the first rich country in history to conquer complacency? Do we have a national sense of urgency about solving old problems and exploring new frontiers? That's what it's going to take. Enterprising countries, like companies, are fast-moving and innovative—always. You can see it in entrepreneurial industries like Biotech, where Chiron's Ed Penhoet says it's the horse-race environment that's produced all their amazing advances.

▪ A Nation of Self-inspired People

America has always been brimming over with self-inspired people. The question today is, what are we inspired about? How serious are we really about leaving the country in better shape than we found it? Economists say our children will be the first generation in American history to be less prosperous than their parents. This isn't what American heros like John Johnson had in mind as they struggled to build a better future. Back in 1946, Johnson's grandmother hocked her furniture to loan him four hundred dollars to start a magazine in Chicago. Against great odds he created *Jet* and then *Ebony* and built the largest black-owned company in America. John Johnson did his part in making things better for his people and his country. How about us?

Making things better was also what Arch Sproul had in mind when, at age fifty-two, he unleashed his entrepreneurial spirit on the world. Sproul embodies the best of the American spirit of enterprise. He also inspires an additional and final lesson for ensuring our prosperity in the global economic war we face: attack with our greatest strength and aim the American entrepreneurial spirit dead center at worldwide competition.

Taking the American Entrepreneurial Spirit Global

> I got it because I was there and said I could do it.
> —Arch Sproul, founder,
> Virginia International Company

"Certainly we've got problems in this country. We've got unemployment. We've got homelessness. I don't know how to overcome them. But I really think if we had more of a worldwide outlook, if we were really more interested in international trade, it would help the United States. I think that's the spirit America should have. We haven't had to do that up to now because we were so huge and had such an enormous economy, there was no real incentive to get out in the world to find out what was going on. But I think that the time has now come. Those days are over forever."

This is seventy-seven-years-young Arch Sproul, a son of the Great Depression, who had his first overseas experience on the beaches of Normandy. On D Day, June 6, 1944, Captain Sproul led an assault company on Omaha Beach. His reward for this international adventure was the Distinguished Service Cross, the Bronze Star, and three Purple Hearts. It also opened his eyes to a very big world full of opportunity. After the war, Sproul went home with his new English bride and did his duty as good husband, good father, and good local insurance man. But he never forgot that big world outside. In his fifties, when many are setting their sights on retirement, Sproul set his sights on international enterprise. From making furniture in Manila, to mining diamonds in the Congo, to searching for King Solomon's mine in Egypt, Sproul went on a worldwide treasure hunt for opportunity. It all resulted in some minor successes, some moderate failures, and the discovery of the mother lode of natural gas in the jungles of Indonesia. His is a story of unbridled, international entrepreneurship—an American doing what Americans do best.

"I was fifty-two years old when I went to Indonesia for the first time. I went entirely on my own. Three of us put one thousand dollars in a pot and I went. I always say the two things that got me into Indonesia were the Portuguese diamond mines in the Congo and looking for King Solomon's mine in Egypt. Through the people in these places, I met this Indonesian who fired my enthusiasm about the opportunities in his country. That first trip was purely a look-see. I had heard about large nickle deposits, but that didn't work out. I said, well, I'm not going to just come up a water hole, so I bullied my way into the office of the advisor to President Suharto. No appointment or introduction or anything like that. Well, we got to talking about things in Indonesia and that's where I learned about the natural gas possibilities. To make a long story short, they gave me an exploration concession. I'd never explored for oil or gas in my life. I know it doesn't make any sense, but I really think I got it because I was there and said I could do it.

"It was slim pickings for some time. I remember going to the bank when Margaret's mother died. I needed to borrow some money in order to take my wife back to England for the funeral. The little company I formed held the Indonesian concession and I tried to use it as collateral. The local banker said, 'That stock isn't worth the paper it's written on!' I don't think he even knew where Indonesia was. He'd never been outside the United States in his life. Most of my friends were saying, 'What the devil is Arch Sproul doing running around the world? He doesn't know what he's doing.' Fortunately, it turned out that I did know what I was doing.

"Well, I learned the gas exploration business right there in the jungle. But of course I needed help to do it. The first thing I did was ask Roy Huffington* to join me. Roy was a young Harvard geologist working in Houston and an adventurer like me. Well, we went to Indonesia and we found a huge field of natural gas in the jungle. It was 11 trillion cubic feet of gas, which is more than Prudhoe Bay in Alaska. And it was in a very small field, only twenty-five miles long by about ten miles wide. A huge, rich deposit. Practically every well hit oil and gas. We had very few dry holes. Today it's the largest LNG plant in the world."

Arch Sproul has some very definite ideas about how to find opportunities and what to do with them after you find them: "Anyone can go to any of our big companies like IBM and be transferred to a foreign country, which is a good experience. But I wasn't employed by any corporation when I went to Indonesia. I was flying by the seat of my pants—and I made it okay. Nobody was paying anything. No salary, no pension, nothing. If you're interested in adventure, I think the opportunities are just as great now as they ever were. They're probably even greater because the world is much smaller, transportation is much simpler, and there's no part of the world that you couldn't be in in a very short time. Yes, the opportunities are great. If I were a young man, I would definitely be over there trying to do something. And I think you've got to have an attitude of not just what can I take out of a place but what can I give to them that will help them. I think all my overseas partners knew I was not grabbing or an ugly American coming in and taking everything away from them. The Indonesians are wonderful people, and we always had fair deals with them in the gas business. It did help them, and of course it was good for us too."

Sproul's no fan of the current state of America's preparedness to face an increasingly global economic battle—right down to our retarded knowledge of geography: "I'm afraid too many of our schools and our colleges are insular. They've no horizon outside of

---

* Huffington of course became a legendary figure in the oil and gas business in his own right, forming the very successful Roy A. Huffington, Inc.—all spun off his and Sproul's early adventures.

this country. Yet the horizon is great outside the country. I think our schools should be spending more time educating our young men and young women in international relations and international business. In the business schools we should definitely have more emphasis on trade and international entrepreneurship. I think it's terribly important for the future. It's not a question of whether you can or can't teach it. You've got to fire young people's enthusiasm. Somehow you've got to ignite a spark in their minds and their attitudes that this sounds great—I'd love to take a chance on it. Why, we've got very few people around, and I mean very few, who even have any idea of geography. Everybody said to me, 'Oh, you're going to Indonesia. Where's that?' And I'd have to say it's in Asia—exactly halfway around the world.

"People ask where's the opportunity today? Well, I think it's there, period. You have to go find it. I used to go around the world four or five times every year. And I would stop in places like Egypt or Turkey. I got to know some people in Istanbul and got into this King Solomon mine venture. I didn't make any money on it, but I learned a lot and had a lot of fun. Today the Far East has tremendous opportunities. After communism there are also tremendous opportunities in Eastern Europe—in Hungary, in Czechoslovakia. There are tremendous opportunities everywhere, even inside the country—like up in Alaska. I've always been fascinated by Alaska and the possibilities up there. There are probably more opportunities today than we ever had before. Those opportunities are out there today. Right now. I know they're there. If I were younger, I'd be out there right now!"

What in the world would happen if 250 million Americans shared Arch Sproul's view of the worldwide possibilities? And where would America be in the twenty-first century if, like Sproul, we actually got off our duffs and made those possibilities come true? One thing's for sure. We wouldn't be sitting around wringing our hands and looking for someone to blame. Well, it can happen. It had better happen! Spoul's message is the "Go everywhere" version of Horace Greeley's "Go west, young man" 150 years ago. Greeley was right and so is Sproul. From here on in, America doesn't need just entrepreneurs. Those days *are* over forever. We need international entrepreneurs: twenty-first century enterprisers who are willing and able to compete in every nook and cranny of the globe. The time *has* come to unleash the American entrepreneurial spirit on the world!

America is at a crossroads. Our share of the world economic pie is shrinking. Our standard of living is at great risk. It doesn't have to be. The challenge of our time is to forget about managing America's decline—and get busy creating America's future prosperity. We the people are the only ones that can do it. Think about it, but not too long. The enterprise of the nation and the well-being of our children hang in the balance.

INDEX